Jossey-Bass Teacher

Jossey-Bass Teacher provides K–12 teachers with essential knowledge and tools to create a positive and lifelong impact on student learning. Trusted and experienced educational mentors offer practical classroom-tested and theory-based teaching resources for improving teaching practice in a broad range of grade levels and subject areas. From one educator to another, we want to be your first source to make every day your best day in teaching. *Jossey-Bass Teacher* resources serve two types of informational needs—essential knowledge and essential tools.

Essential knowledge resources provide the foundation, strategies, and methods from which teachers may design curriculum and instruction to challenge and excite their students. Connecting theory to practice, essential knowledge books rely on a solid research base and time-tested methods, offering the best ideas and guidance from many of the most experienced and well-respected experts in the field.

Essential tools save teachers time and effort by offering proven, ready-to-use materials for in-class use. Our publications include activities, assessments, exercises, instruments, games, ready reference, and more. They enhance an entire course of study, a weekly lesson, or a daily plan. These essential tools provide insightful, practical, and comprehensive materials on topics that matter most to K–12 teachers.

MORE PRAISE FOR *READING LEARNING CENTERS FOR PRIMARY GRADES*

"Dr. Wait's new edition offers creative yet practical ways for busy teachers to enhance student learning. In addition to the step-by-step directions, detailed diagrams, and rich resource lists, the book offers teaching strategies that are grounded in learning theory. Every primary teacher will find ideas to use tomorrow!"

—Patricia Tolbert, dean, Academic Services, Baylor University

"What an incredible resource for faculty everywhere who will better understand the importance of integrating curriculum with this powerful resource at their fingertips. This book contains a wealth of information designed to excite and ignite imaginations within an academic setting."

—The Reverend Jean Dodd, head of school,
San Jose Episcopal, Jacksonville, FL

"Busy and harried teachers will be thrilled to discover Dr. Shirleen Wait's rich and expanded resource for creating classroom learning centers. *Reading Learning Centers for Primary Grades,* an updated and detailed edition of her popular book, allows teachers to set up a wide variety of centers easily and to spend their time implementing the engaging, enriching, and fun academic activities instead of worrying how and what to plan. This renowned educator has provided teachers with a wide range of tips, hints, suggestions, and materials to use and modify year after year. These learning centers and activities meet NCLB standards and address the needs and learning styles of all children in the class. Dr. Wait has outdone herself!"

—Betty Menacher, national consultant manager,
Pearson Learning Group

"Dr. Wait has just the right background to produce a book like this—one that will help teachers, home-schooling parents, and learning center leaders integrate technology into teaching successfully. She's spent years creatively integrating technology in education in a wide variety of environments. It's not always easy to do this, and Dr. Wait's book will jump-start the process for everyone."

—Steve De Pangher, principal, De Pangher Consulting

Reading Learning — Centers — for Primary Grades

Monthly Theme Units, Activities, and Games

Second Edition

SHIRLEEN S. WAIT, Ph.D.

JOSSEY-BASS
A Wiley Imprint
www.josseybass.com

Published by Jossey-Bass
A Wiley Imprint
989 Market Street, San Francisco, CA 94103-1741   www.josseybass.com

ISBN-13: 978–0–7879–7579–1
ISBN-10: 0–7879–7579–6

Printed in the United States of America
SECOND EDITION
PB Printing 10 9 8 7 6 5 4 3 2 1

ABOUT THIS BOOK

If you are a primary teacher, a reading specialist, or a beginning teacher who wants to "center" your reading instruction, this book is for you. *Reading Learning Centers for Primary Grades* will help you design robust, engaging centers that reflect a variety of learning styles and developmental levels. If you are already using centers successfully, this book will give you ideas to enrich them further. You might even surprise your class by creating a completely new center, such as the thematic Word Play Center.

Learning centers are child-centered. They meet the needs of young learners because learning center work is real and hands-on, not vicarious. At the centers, children are actively involved in purposeful, meaningful activities that help them explore language, make decisions, solve problems, and discover meaning. Children become independent learners because many activities include answer keys. The center approach is also an efficient way to integrate different literacy elements—listening, speaking, reading, and writing. In her book *The Beginning Reading Handbook: Strategies for Success,* Gail Heald-Taylor (2001) states that organizing the classroom into centers not only provides more space for movement but also satisfies young learners' needs to socialize, talk, move about, listen to stories, read, and write.

Children need meaningful daily practice as they learn. Learning centers allow them to explore and practice strategies in small groups. Games at the Word Play Center can be played again and again, providing multiple opportunities to reinforce new vocabulary and skills. And because multiple copies of the games can be created, you can send them home with students for further practice.

Because the emphasis at the centers is on learning, not teaching, centers work well with many teaching approaches—whole language, basal reader, phonics, strategy-based instruction, a balanced approach, or a combination of approaches. And the open, inviting room arrangement provides for any type of grouping you wish to use—collaborative groups, literature groups, interest groups, needs groups, cooperative learning groups, mixed-ability groups, or partner groups.

Reading Learning Centers for Primary Grades is divided into seven sections:

- Section One, "Managing Learning Centers," tells how to organize your classroom to accommodate centers, set up a schedule for easy management, provide materials, keep track of work, and evaluate work done at the centers.

- Section Two, "Organizing Learning Centers," describes materials for center activities and shows how to make simple storage containers.

- Section Three, "The Learning Centers," describes seven learning centers—Teacher, Library, Listening, Computer, Art, Writing, and Word Play—and tells how they serve students of differing abilities and learning styles.

- Section Four, "Learning Center Thematic Units," presents twelve thematic units for the classroom and activities for the Word Play Center. Each includes directions for setting up two areas—dramatic play and thematic games. Each also suggests thematic activities and children's books and provides reproducible board, card, sorting, and matching games.

- Section Five, "Learning Center Skill Games," includes forty hands-on board, card, sorting, and matching games for abbreviations, antonyms, compound words, consonant blends, consonant digraphs, contractions, figurative language, homophones, syllables, and synonyms. Blank cards are provided so you can add your own words or produce your own games.

- The appendix, "Correlation with Standards," shows how the activities described here correlate with state standards.

- "Additional Resources," at the back of the book, gives the information you will need to find the reference materials mentioned in this book.

Reading Learning Centers for Primary Grades will help ensure your students look forward to reading and doing these exciting activities. The learning centers will certainly enliven your classroom!

Shirleen S. Wait

To my husband, Pete, who has loved me all the way through two editions of this book!

—S.S.W.

ABOUT THE AUTHOR

Shirleen S. Wait received a doctorate in reading education from Florida State University. She has taught in elementary schools as both classroom teacher and reading specialist. She studied the developmental education concept in the United Kingdom and has used learning centers for reading instruction since 1967.

Shirleen was the reading specialist for Project CHILD (Changing How Instruction for Learning is Delivered), originally a Florida initiative. The CHILD instructional system uses a learning center approach and Dr. Wait developed the entire K–5 reading curriculum, which includes hundreds of learning center activities. As national curriculum specialist for a major software publisher, she developed a two-hundred-page thematic curriculum guide for using computers in the classroom in a learning-centered structure. She now acts as consultant and curriculum developer for Atlantic Beach Connections LLC, a company that she owns and operates.

Shirleen holds memberships in Phi Delta Kappa Honorary Fraternity, Phi Kappa Phi Honor Society, and Delta Kappa Gamma Society International, and is a member of *Who's Who in American Education.*

ABOUT THE ILLUSTRATOR

Jan Schumacher was the artist for both this volume and the first edition of the book. She studied fine arts and graphic design at the University of Iowa and has spent much of her career in support of educators. She lives and works in Austin, Texas, where she continues to work for education and public outreach. Her work has included illustration, graphic design, animation, and project management for a wide variety of learning materials at pre-K through the college level. She has been a member of production teams for Disney Interactive; Holt, Rinehart and Winston; Simon & Schuster; and Scott Foresman Science, among others.

Jan believes that education is our best tool for worldwide growth and change. A digital portfolio of her work can be seen at www.janschumacher.com.

ABOUT THE CONTENT DEVELOPERS

FIRST EDITION

Cindy Koch was the content developer for the first edition of this book. She created the bulletin boards, game cards, sorting games, and matching games for the following themes: School Days, Pumpkin Patch, Native American Tepee, Winter Wonderland, Spaceship, Springtime, Restaurant, and Valentine's Day and Dental Health Month. All of Cindy's work is included in this edition.

SECOND EDITION

Jeanette Anderson, who developed the Black History Month Word Play Center, has a B.A. in psychology from the University of West Florida as well as an M.A. in education. She coordinated the organizational efforts of parents, community, and church leaders to frame, develop, and facilitate several charter schools in the Tampa Bay area. She is currently the principal of the Anderson Elementary Academy, an urban neighborhood school, which she cofounded with her sister, Dr. Loretta Anderson. Jeanette has a sincere, down-to-earth teaching style and a special talent for creating an environment that motivates and ignites learning. She has years of experience working with multicultural and urban students and is skilled in problem-focused interventions and engagement of resistant and difficult students.

Bob Ashmead served as consultant for the black heritage stamps and furnished the stamps used in the Black History Month theme. He has collected stamps since age five, and attends stamp shows in the United States and abroad. His interest in world geography and travel comes from stamps—he wished to see and explore the faraway places that many stamps depict. A lifelong educator, Bob has a B.A. in education from the University of Florida and an M.A. in teaching from Jacksonville University. He has held positions as teacher and headmaster on the mission field—Nigeria and Papua New Guinea—and as a high school social sciences teacher stateside.

Lisa Corso, who developed many of the learning center activities, has twenty years' experience as an educator in both public and private school settings. Currently, she teaches kindergarten in a private school, where she was instrumental in establishing and running the school's educational tutorial center. She has also taught reading comprehension and test-taking skills to elementary students. Lisa received her B.S. degree from Seton Hall University and holds an M.A. degree in learning disabilities. She and her family currently reside in Jacksonville, Florida.

Joan Dismore, a librarian and storyteller, developed Joan's Choices, the read-aloud selection list in the recommended books section of the Teacher Center unit. For nineteen years, she conducted story hour for pre-K through grade three and library skills classes for grades four through six. She served as program chair and president for her local library association and is currently volunteering at a children's clinic, where she has organized a family resource center. At the clinic she reads stories to children in waiting rooms. Because of this work, Joan was chosen as Jacksonville, Florida's, 2004 Volunteer of the Year.

Teresa Harrison, who developed the Cinco de Mayo Word Play Center, is a native Spanish speaker who has worked for nine years as a bilingual kindergarten teacher. Married with two children, ages nine and two, Teresa currently teaches at the Anderson Elementary Academy in Tampa, Florida. She says: "I believe that music and games are effective methods of teaching children of all ages."

Joan Jecko holds two master's degrees—an M.S. in computer applications from NOVA University, and an M.A. in teaching from Jacksonville University. In 1995, Joan founded the Learning Place, an afterschool inner-city tutorial program in Jacksonville. In the year 2000, she developed a Latin enrichment program for San Jose Episcopal Day School, also in Jacksonville. The curriculum was published by a grant from the Florida Council of Independent Schools. Joan developed the Roman Holiday Word Play Center.

The Pan Family pooled their collective experiences to develop the Lunar New Year Word Play Center. Linda Pan Fox (Singapore) and P. Ann Pan (California) combined their resources and also tapped the experience of their mother, Regina Hsu Pan (native of Shanghai, now living in Virginia), and their sister-in-law, Chinghua Fox (native of Taiwan, now living in California). Regina Hsu Pan was educated in Chinese schools and was the calligraphy artist for the game cards; P. Ann Pan furnished her original drawings and directions for making firecrackers.

CONTENTS

I. Managing Learning Centers I

2.   Organizing Learning Centers   21

3.   The Learning Centers   29

4. Learning Center Thematic Units 95

Contents   **XV**

5.   Learning Center Skill Games   281

Appendix: Correlation with Standards   371

Additional Resources   379

EXPLAINING LEARNING CENTERS TO PARENTS

If learning centers are new to parents, you must explain how centers provide valuable learning experiences for children. Included in this section is a letter to parents that explains the rationale for a learning center approach. The letter invites parents to an open house where you can talk about the purpose of each learning center. This is an opportunity for parents *and* their children to work as partners doing simple learning center activities.

When talking to parents about learning centers, make the following points:

- Every child has a favorite way to learn. Learning centers include many kinds of activities.

- At the centers, children look, listen, move, touch, and create as they learn. This fosters a positive atmosphere for all types of learners.

- Each center has a purpose for developing part of the literacy process: listening, speaking, reading, and writing. After a strategy has been introduced, it can be practiced using all the senses.

- The center activities are at different learning levels; children can work according to their need and their level.

- The teacher has more time for direct instruction with individuals or small groups because the other children are occupied with independent work.

- Work at the centers provides social interaction. Children work together as partners or in small groups to practice what they are learning.

- Because activities at the centers are engaging, time on task is increased.

- Behavior problems are reduced because children move around. The decision making required helps them become independent learners.

- Children do not have to finish their work to go to a learning center because the activities at the centers *are* their work.

- Dramatic play allows children to use language that is not part of their daily conversation but will be a part of many of the books they read. When they encounter the words in reading, they will have had first-hand experience using them in their role-play.

A LETTER TO PARENTS ABOUT READING LEARNING CENTERS

Dear _____,

    I hope that by now your child has told you about the learning centers in our classroom. Reading is very important and one of my goals is to encourage good reading habits. I try to make our classroom an exciting place where your child can participate in many kinds of learning activities.

    In our classroom, the children regularly work with me. They also work at learning centers with stimulating activities designed to develop language skills. These activities include reading, listening, speaking, creating, and writing. Children read books, work on projects, listen to story tapes, write and illustrate stories or books, play real and imaginary roles, follow recipes, and play reading games. They work at the centers with a partner or with other students. I encourage them to discuss their work and help each other. Because our activities include preparing food using easy recipes, let me know if your child has any food allergies.

    I invite you to come to an Open House to see the learning centers and participate in a center activity with your child. Or make an appointment to visit our classroom to see how the learning centers work. I'll be happy to talk to you about your child's progress.

Sincerely,

_____

Teacher

....

OPEN HOUSE

WHERE: _____

WHEN: _____

I/WE CAN COME TO THE OPEN HOUSE (CIRCLE ONE): YES   NO

NAME(S): _____

1 MANAGING LEARNING CENTERS

CREATING AREAS

A learning center is a designated area that holds purposeful activities, a variety of materials, and activity directions. Learning centers can work in any classroom because they require no special furniture or arrangement. Some teachers prefer an informal atmosphere with no assigned seats—students work at the centers in chairs or on the floor and keep personal items and school supplies in a box or tote tray. When they finish at one center, they move to another.

Learning centers are also effective in classrooms where each student has an assigned table or desk. A center might be a table or a cart where activities, directions, and materials are provided. Students work at the center or at their own seats.

Centers don't require expensive dividers or furniture. A cart or bookshelf makes a great Library Center. Put a carpet remnant and cushions on the floor near the books. Children can read on the floor area or at their own desks. Design the learning centers the way you want them—on bookshelves or tables, in baskets, on the floor, or under tables. Get your creative juices flowing. The children will love it!

HOW TO BEGIN USING LEARNING CENTERS

Each learning center has a different focus and allows children to participate in a different way. Seven learning centers are described in this volume: Teacher Center, Library Center, Listening Center, Computer Center, Art Center, Writing Center, and Word Play Center. Even if you've never used learning centers you can begin with some that are easily created with materials found in classrooms—the Teacher Center, Library Center, Writing Center, and Listening Center, for example. When these centers are working well, you can add others until you are providing a balance of activities.

ACQUIRING LOW-COST FURNITURE

Make your centers attractive (and comfortable) with low-cost or free furniture. My favorite Library Center featured furniture rescued from a church trash pile. All it required was a home-repair job and a good scrubbing. Parents made cushions from inexpensive fabric and added a bright carpet remnant. The children were thrilled. Here are some sources for low-cost furniture:

- Ask parents, colleagues, friends.
- Search attics, garage sales, flea markets, rummage sales.
- Check with electric and telephone companies and electrical suppliers (empty wire spools make great low tables).
- Create grant proposals.
- Host creative fundraising events, such as car washes or spaghetti suppers.

ARRANGING THE ROOM

Here are some practical considerations:

- Organize the room into an active half and a quiet half. Put the Listening, Library, and Writing Centers in the quiet half and the Teacher, Art, Computer, and Word Play Centers in the noisy half.
- Place the Teacher Center where you can see the entire room. Even when you are working at the Teacher Center, you will be able to observe students as they work at the other centers.
- Make sure the Reading and Writing Centers have adequate lighting.
- If you have a sink in your room, place the Art Center near it.
- Place the Listening and Computer Centers near electrical outlets.
- Locate at least one center on the floor. Children like working at floor centers and this saves furniture for other purposes.
- Organize desks in clusters, rather than rows, to create more floor space that can be used for learning centers.

See the illustration of two possible floor plans.

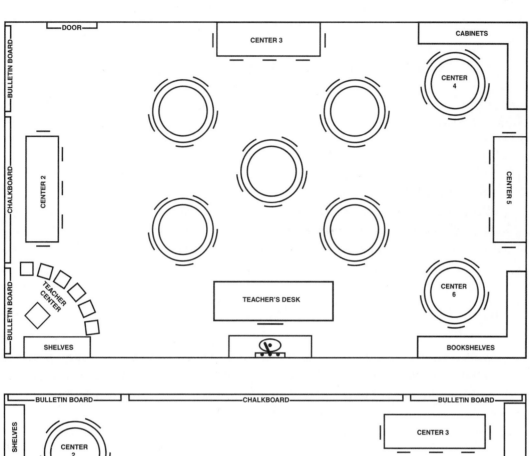

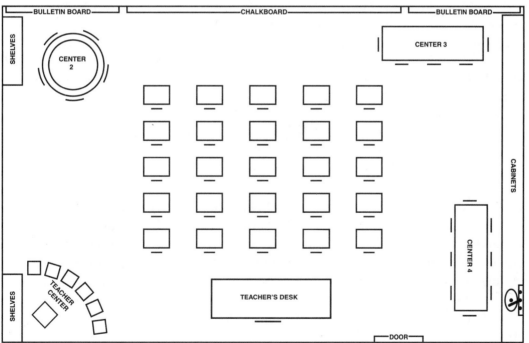

STRUCTURE AND PLANNING

Learning centers require structure. This section describes a three-stage plan for implementing learning centers. First, here are five considerations:

1. Which centers do you wish to use? It's usually a good idea to start with four centers—when these four are working well, add more until you have the total number of centers that you want.

2. What behaviors do you expect from children while they work at the centers? Are they allowed to talk quietly about their work? Will they work as partners? What happens when a child misbehaves?

3. What traffic patterns will help children move easily from one center to another?

4. Who will answer questions about work at the centers? Should a child interrupt the teacher or ask another child?

5. What do children do if they finish their work at a center? Do they move to another center? Are there books or reading games for them to work with when they finish their center assignment? Who is going to clean up? Where will the supplies be placed?

If this is your first experience with learning centers, implement your plan in three stages. As you learn to manage one stage, move on to the next.

STAGE 1

Center Visitation

For learning centers to meet the needs of all children, you must schedule *every child* to visit each center. (Special-needs children learn best when actively involved in their work, and hands-on center work is great for them.) Stage 1 introduces four learning centers. During Stage 1, divide the children into four teams—assign each team to a learning center for twenty minutes. At the end of the twenty minutes, move each team to a new center so that in one hour and twenty minutes every team will have visited all four centers. Twenty minutes is an approximate time—shorten or lengthen the time if you wish. It may be best to begin with ten minutes and work up to twenty.

Sample Schedule

8:40–9:00	Opening and housekeeping details
9:00–9:20	First center assignment
9:20–9:40	Second center assignment
9:40–10:00	Break and snack
10:00–10:20	Third center assignment
10:20–10:40	Fourth center assignment

Implementing Stage 1

1. Set up four learning centers—the Teacher Center and three other centers.

2. Divide the class into four groups—literature groups, interest groups, special-needs groups, basal reader groups, mixed ability groups, and so on. You can call them teams.

3. Make an assignment board so that you can assign teams without an announcement. (See the illustration on page 6.) On posterboard or a chalkboard, tape four envelope pockets, one for each center. Write the name of each team on an index card. The index cards fit into the pockets, indicating the assignments. Use the assignment board to assign the first centers and have a preassigned rotation routine—clockwise, for example.

Ten-Day Training Program*

Students can work independently or with partners at the centers. A ten-day training period helps children learn important procedures so that work at the centers will go smoothly. Ten days may seem like a long time to spend on training, but you will find that the time is well spent.

Instead of working with one team yourself, spend the first week circulating and helping at all the centers. Observe groups working, praise good behavior, and stop unwanted behavior.

Day 1. Conduct a class meeting, announce team assignments, and explain behavior expectations and traffic patterns. Have each team practice walking from one center to another. Then let the children help develop a set of class rules for working at the centers. Write them on a chart for display.

---

*Note: Ten-day training program adapted from Project CHILD (Changing How Instruction for Learning is Delivered). Courtesy of the Institute for School Innovation (www.ifsi.org), Sarah Butzin, Ph.D., executive director.

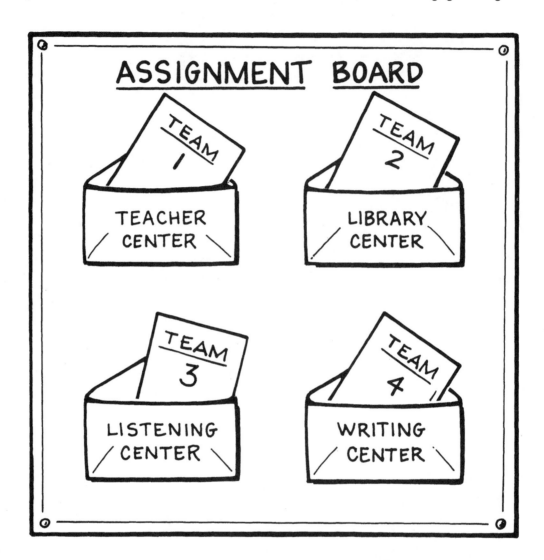

Day 2. Explain the assignment board and introduce each center. Explain the purpose of each center and show examples of the kind of work that will be done there. Explain where to get materials, find the task assignment, and put finished and unfinished work. Have children role-play getting materials and putting finished and unfinished work away. Have them practice walking to and from the centers once again.

   Role-play using a soft voice (whisper). Many children can be reading aloud and playing games at the same time without disturbing each other if the voice level is low. Have a hand signal to use in case the noise level gets too high.

Days 3 to 5. Each day, review the rules and expectations. Use the assignment board to assign the teams to four centers. At each center (including the Teacher Center), provide an independent activity that the children can complete in twenty minutes. If twenty minutes seems too long, change the schedule to accommodate a shorter time. As children work, you should circulate, observe, answer questions, and praise good behavior. When center time is over, have a class meeting. Discuss what went well and what needs improvement. Be consistent in enforcing your expectations. It's easier to learn good habits than to unlearn bad ones!

Days 6 to 7. Continue to review the class rules and use the assignment board. If the centers are functioning well, continue to circulate as you did the previous three days. If the centers are running smoothly, sit with the children at the Teacher Center while they complete an independent activity. Continue to observe the behavior at the other centers to see if teams can work independently.

Days 8 to 10. Continue to use the daily assignment board. By now, children should be on task at the learning centers. If they are, begin group instruction at the Teacher Center. If the centers are not functioning well, continue observing for a few more days. Stay at Stage 1 until you are comfortable with it and ready to add more centers. This could be several days, weeks, or months.

STAGE 2

Center Visitation

Stage 2 expands the number of centers to five or six. During Stage 2, assign each team to a learning center for twenty minutes (or whatever time period worked well in Stage 1). Children still spend an hour and twenty minutes visiting four centers, but they do not visit every center every day.

Sample Schedule

Day 1   Children visit centers 1, 2, 3, and 4. (Close 5 and 6.)
Day 2   Children visit centers 1, 2, 5, and 6. (Close 3 and 4.)
Day 3   Children visit centers 3, 4, 5, and 6. (Close 1 and 2.)

When you close the Teacher Center, work with children at other centers, such as the Writing Center or the Word Play Center. You may wish to work with special-needs children every day at the Teacher Center. After they work with you, have them visit three other centers that are open that day.

Implementing Stage 2

1. Create one or two new centers in addition to your four existing centers.

2. For each new center, tape an additional envelope pocket to the assignment board.

3. Periodically, provide "Free Choice Day." During one or two twenty-minute sessions, open all the centers and let children decide which ones to visit. Don't require that teams stay together at the centers. If a center is full, children can take an activity from the center to work with at their desks.

STAGE 3

Center Visitation

Stage 3 allows students greater choice of centers and incorporates a management chart instead of an assignment board. The management chart is used two ways:

- As a wall chart for children to check off the centers they visit
- As a teacher chart to check off the work the children complete at the centers

Groups (teams) of students meet with the teacher in the Teacher Center. When children are not in the Teacher Center, they choose which other centers to visit. Teams are not required to stay together at the centers. This allows children to work with all the students in the room, and special-needs children are not "locked" into an inflexible group. For this reason, Stage 3 should be your goal even if it takes a while to reach it.

At first, require children to stay at each center for the full twenty-minute session. Then let them choose another center. Provide books or games (see Section Five of this volume) for those who finish center tasks early. Later, try letting children change centers when they finish their assignment, rather than waiting the full twenty minutes. Every child should make a daily visit to the Library Center *or* the Writing Center—if these centers are full, books or writing activities can be taken to a table or desk.

If a center is full, children can work at their seats or on the floor near the center. You may have to limit the number of children who can work at a particular center (the Listening or Art Center, for example) to the number of chairs at the center. If this is the case, put a number card on the wall that tells how many can work at the center.

Learning Center
Management Chart

Learning Center

Student

Note: Management chart courtesy of Ardyth Ann Stanley.

Allow one hour and twenty minutes for students to visit centers. Tell children that they are responsible for visiting every center. Teach them how to keep track of center visits on the management chart. If more than four centers are open, allow them two days for visiting every center and completing their work assignments.

A few children will probably need more structure than this. They cannot handle free choice of centers on a daily basis. Continue to assign them to centers as you did in Stages 1 and 2, but let them help you plan their schedule. Give them "Free Choice Friday." If they respond well, add other Free Choice days, one at a time, until they are responsible for their own schedule all or most of the time.

Implementing Stage 3

1. Photocopy the management chart shown on page 9, fill in the students' names, and write the names of the centers in the spaces across the top. Hang the chart at eye level. You may want to make a larger version of the chart on posterboard.

2. Post the time that each team is to meet with you at the Teacher Center.

3. Have children check the chart to indicate which centers they visited.

PROVIDING MATERIALS

The success of a learning center classroom largely depends on the teacher providing sufficient center materials and directions to keep children motivated and on task. In Stages 1 and 2, provide separate assignments for each team that extend the learning that takes place at the Teacher Center and fits with the team's ability level—there should be different expectations for different ability levels. For instance, if you have created a Writing Center, have every child writing, even though some are better at writing than others. Be sure that each assignment can be completed in the twenty-minute time period in which children will be at each center. And since some children will work faster than others, provide activities from this book for the children who have finished their assignment. Use games shown in Sections Three and Four even if you have not yet set up a Word Play Center.

Help children to be self-sufficient at the centers by providing activities that vary in difficulty level so that each child can work at an appropriate level. Where possible, make the activities self-checking. Provide an assignment card with clear directions, answer keys, and samples of finished products (that is, work samples, assignments). Finished products should be basic so that children create their own work rather than copying the finished product. Provide common materials—paper, pencils, and so on—so children don't have to bring anything to the center with them.

KEEPING TRACK OF WORK

Keeping track of each student's work may seem like an impossible task, but it is not. Hands-on activities at the centers cut down on paperwork. At each center where assignments are products, provide containers—boxes, folders, or baskets—for finished and unfinished work.

Photocopy the management chart once again and fill in the students' names. In the space across the top, write the names of products you are checking. Each day, inspect the centers and check off successful completion of each child's work. Another idea is to have a place in your grade book for center work. As it is finished each day, put a check or grade to let you know it is completed. Toward the end of the week you can see at a glance who needs to complete work or go to a center not yet visited. This is especially important when students are choosing centers rather than being assigned to centers. Some centers, like the Library Center, can be "anytime" centers. Students can go there when they finish their work at the other centers.

Provide each child with a portfolio for keeping finished work and writing samples. Provide each team with a box for storing portfolios. Keep the boxes of portfolios in a place that is available to you and the children. Allow time each week to distribute finished work for children to file in their portfolios.

EVALUATING LEARNING AT THE CENTERS

It is important to give children feedback frequently. Use multiple forms of assessment, because there are many ways to make children aware of their progress (Owocki, 2001). The following methods work well in a learning center environment.

Observation

Teacher observation is a powerful evaluation tool. The Teacher Center is a natural place to observe individual children daily. Even if you are observing groups, you will be able to assess individual reading behaviors. Observing children as they work helps you know what each child is doing, determine which children need help, plan what each child needs next, and note progress over time. Observation allows you to immediately create send-home activities for extra practice. Here are some suggestions to get you started in observation.

Teacher Center Observation. If you hold regular reading conferences with children, you will be observing all of their reading behaviors. These are some behaviors to look for as children work with you in small groups:

- *Emergent readers:* Observe children as they recognize letters, blend phonemes, produce rhyming words, isolate consonants, and identify or blend onsets/rimes. (*Onset* is the consonant at the beginning of a syllable; *rime* is the rest of the syllable. Onset /b/ plus the rime /ake/ blends to make the word *bake.*) Comprehension is very important, even for early readers—in retelling or dramatic play they should be able to retell or reenact the story, showing that they understand the meaning.

- *Developing readers:* Observe to see if they know regular letter-sound correspondences and use them to figure out words. See if they can use onsets and rimes to create new words with blends and digraphs. (*Blends* are two consonants together; each consonant keeps its sound: /br/. *Digraphs* are two letters that make a different sound from the individual letter sounds: /sh/.) At this stage they should recognize 125 to 150 high-frequency words as they read and should be somewhat fluent in materials on their reading level. They should be able to summarize text, compare books by the same author, and talk about books that relate to the current theme.

- *Independent readers:* See if they can easily read short, regularly spelled words and if they can figure out longer words by using spelling patterns. Independent readers should be reading fluently, more focused on meaning than vocabulary, and more guided by print than by illustrations.

Plan to observe children frequently as they work at the other centers. While you observe, children at the Teacher Center can finish an assignment or take a few minutes to read independently or with a partner. Every two weeks, plan a special observation day. To do this, close the Teacher Center and use the time to observe and take notes as children work at the open centers.

Library Center Observation. These are some behaviors to look for:

- Emergent readers should hold books and turn pages correctly, read (or pretend-read) daily, choose reading in their free time, and choose a variety of genres—literature, fiction, nonfiction, and informational text. They should be able to point to words as they read, and say some of the words they point to. They should also be able to use illustrations to make predictions.

- Developing readers should read daily. They are able to read books with more complex themes and story structures, handle more sentences per page, figure out some unfamiliar words, and self-correct when they mispronounce or misread a word. They can understand causes and effects, themes, and the intent of the author.

- Independent readers should read chapter books—perhaps a chapter a day. They eagerly participate in "Author Studies," which compare several books by the same author. They successfully read a variety of genres—literature, trade books, nonfiction, poetry, and plays. They read easily and fluently.

Listening Center Observation. Children should be intent on material they are listening to. They should choose a variety of listening activities and be able to retell or discuss a book after they have listened to it.

Computer Center Observation. Children at all reading stages can be taught to log on and off independently and work with software at their level. If children are working as partners, observe to see how they work together. If one child is figuring out all the answers or dominating in some way, make an adjustment. You may have to change the partnership or allow only half the computer time for each one so each can work alone. Some computer programs provide scores. Have children record them on index cards and keep them in their portfolios. (See the section on hard copies.)

Art Center Observation. Most art projects should be connected to the reading, writing, listening, and thematic instruction going on in the classroom. Children at all reading levels can create artwork showing that they have comprehended material that they have read or listened to. Art is especially important for emergent readers and writers because they are not able to write a lot of text. But their artwork can tell a story, describe characters, and show what they know about a topic even before they become fluent writers.

Writing Center Observation. These are some behaviors to look for:

- Emergent writers are eager to write and communicate meaning. Some beginners are still using scribbles, strings of letters, and drawings as they write. But as children progress, they begin to use words from classroom charts, labels, or the Word Wall (see Section Three for more on this) to create simple stories, labels, signs, and greeting cards. They should be able to write responses to something that they read, even if they are still in the scribble stage. They will read (or pretend-read) their own writing and the writing of others in the class (Schickendanz, 1999).

- Developing writers' skills are often linked with their reading skills—the better readers are the more accomplished writers. At this stage, children can write for meaning and can improve their writing through feedback from you or their peers. They should be spelling words correctly from the Word Wall and making reasonable attempts to spell words that they have not previously used (Hall, 1981). The writing workshop, in which children write every day, is especially helpful; for more on writing workshops see the Writing Center described in Section Three.

- Independent writers have the skills, patience, and maturity to go through several writing stages. They should be able to publish books using process writing, also described in paragraphs on the Writing Center in Section Three.

Word Play Center Observation.   Children at the Word Play Center should be occupied with two types of activities, *dramatic play* and *games*.

- Dramatic play includes talk—talk while constructing the plot and planning what the characters will say, and talk during the actual role-play (waitress, astronaut). Both types of verbal exchanges are important in language development. Expect to observe that the children will spend much of their time in planning what they will do. Sometimes planning will take more time than actually playing the characters. This is characteristic of this type of learning experience.

- Manipulatives and games include word scrambles, crossword puzzles, magnetic letters, and reproducible games from this book. Look to see how children are using the manipulatives and note which children need help. And look to see how children use answer keys. Do they check their work with the key, or do they need an answer key to assist them as they play the game?

Reading Conferences

Meet individually with children so that you can listen to them read aloud. Keep a record of each conference—note rate of reading, fluency, problem-solving strategies, and comprehension. Offer support, recommend strategies to try, and suggest books they might enjoy. Check their reading log and encourage them to choose materials from the different genres. If they are fluent enough to keep a response log, check what they have written. Offer support and suggestions where needed.

Writing Samples

Meet weekly with each child to go over work in each one's writing portfolio. Journals are another good tool for documenting growth over time. Let children publish (see Section Three) and share some of their finished products. Praise their achievements and help them decide where they need more work.

Running Records

Running records assess word-recognition accuracy. As a child reads aloud, the teacher uses a recording tool (such as a photocopy of what the child is reading) to record deviations from the written text—self-corrections, mispronunciations, teacher intervention, and so on. Running records help the teacher see what types of mistakes are made and provide information about decoding strategies, reading rate, and fluency. For more information, see Sharon Taberski's *On Solid Ground: Strategies for Teaching Reading K–3* (2000).

Retelling

Retelling can be used as a stand-alone evaluation or part of the reading conference. The child reads or listens to a story (or other text) and retells it to the teacher. Retellings provide a valid assessment of a child's understanding of the text. They assess comprehension, familiarity with story structure, and the ability to recall and summarize information. Keep notes on each child to document growth over time.

Self-Checking

Self-checking helps children take responsibility and become independent learners. Provide ways for children to check their work at the learning centers. Provide only one activity per day that you must check.

The reproducible games in this book include answer keys. Don't require children to learn words *before* they can play a game. Allow them to learn *as* they play. As they learn, they will use the answer keys less and less often. Note this in your observations.

Hard Copies

At the centers, children produce a variety of work samples—writing samples, artistic creations, scripts, word lists, reading logs, journals, and so on. All are evidence of learning. Make a folder for each child and keep samples of work that document progress.

LEARNING CENTERS AND SPECIAL-NEEDS CHILDREN

In her book *Strategies for Developing Emergent Literacy,* Wilma Miller (2000) presents a detailed discussion on special-needs children, including ESL, LEP, LD, ADD, AD/HD, EMH, severely mentally disabled, and children with hearing impairments. She concludes that "well-organized and well-equipped learning centers make it possible for children with special needs to learn a great deal on their own through playful interaction with materials while teachers provide attention to individuals or small groups" (p. 284). A Web site that links to resources for parents and teachers about the Individuals with Disabilities Education Act (IDEA) is http://ed.gov/offices/OSERS/IDEA/the_law.html.

Section Three of this volume provides detailed descriptions of each learning center and all the activities mentioned here. The following paragraphs outline briefly how each center's activities are helpful to children with special needs.

The Teacher Center

Special-needs children can fit into all activities that occur at the Teacher Center. Here are some approaches to use at the Teacher Center and how each can help children with special needs.

- *Reading aloud, big books, shared-book experiences, and predictable books.* Children with poor vocabulary skills can learn from listening to someone read and reread books containing new words that are introduced and illustrated; ESL students greatly benefit from shared-book experiences (Robinson, Ross, and Neal, 2000).

- *Choral reading.* Research has shown that choral reading, using big books, and using books with repetitive language improve comprehension and word identification in LEP children (Miller, 2000).

- *Language experience approach (LEA).* Miller states that "LEA is probably the most single useful approach for teaching all types of children with special needs" (Miller, 2000, p. 284). Language experience is also appropriate for children who are culturally or linguistically different from mainstream reading materials because LEA matches both the experiences and language patterns of the learners (Hall, 1981).

- *Songs and chants.* Songs and chants can be hands-on and include many learning styles. If you make singing a reading activity, special-needs children can quickly learn to chime in and read aloud with you and take turns pointing to the words. Special-needs children benefit by getting some body action into group reading activities, so hand motions and simple instruments make this activity especially appealing.

- *Storytelling.* All children love to tell and listen to stories. Storytelling develops oral language, vocabulary, and comprehension.

- *Book talks.* All children can talk about books they are reading because the learning center approach allows children to work with partners and to read at their own levels.

- *Individual and small-group instruction.* The Teacher Center is a natural place to work with special-needs children using scaffolding strategies that provide ongoing support. Anne Soderman, Kara Gregory, and Louise O'Neill (1999) give a detailed description of this strategy in *Scaffolding Emergent Literacy: A Child-Centered Approach for Preschool Through Grade 5.* (See Additional Resources at the back of the book.)

- *Reciprocal teaching.* Research shows that reciprocal teaching has positive effects on high-risk children; participants functioned well during these lessons and their listening comprehension improved (Burns, Griffin, and Snow, 1999).

- *Individual conferences.* Reading conferences can be adjusted to fit the needs of special-needs children.

- *Children's presentations.* Special-needs children should participate in presentations such as puppet shows, art shows, and the Author's Chair, all conducted at the Teacher Center.

- *New activity instruction.* Even more so than children without special needs, special-needs children always need an introduction to learning center activities because they will be working independently at the centers.

- *Games.* All children learn quickly through games because they are engaging and multisensory, and children play them again and again. This volume includes reproducible games at different levels. You can use the games as they are or adjust them to fit the level of a child in need.

- *Pocket charts and flannel boards.* Pocket chart and flannel board activities allow children to touch and move as they learn. These work at any reading level and are especially effective with special-needs learners.

The Library Center

The Library Center should be equipped with multilevel and multiethnic reading materials so that children can select those that suit their interest and their reading level. It is a good idea to allow children to borrow books to read with someone at home. Intervention programs that involve parents or caretakers have had positive effects on reading achievement both in kindergarten and in later grades (Robinson, Ross, and Neal, 2000).

The Listening Center

Digital books, videotapes, and other media approaches are especially useful because they are multisensory—more than one sense is used while learning. They also allow for repetition.

The Computer Center

Computers are helpful to special-needs children because they are highly motivating. Computer-based learning is multisensory—children look, listen, speak, touch, and move as they learn. (See "Recommended Software" in the Computer Center, Section Three.)

The Art Center

Special-needs children gain a sense of achievement through art. They can illustrate their writing, draw a story, make characters, decorate books, make book jackets, and so on. The Art Center also encourages children to express their cultural heritage through art.

The Writing Center

At the Writing Center, children write at their own level. Writing reinforces reading because a good writing program increases the amount of time that children spend with text. In fact, some programs for struggling readers have used writing as an aid to reading (Clay, 1975). Special-needs children may be at the very early stages of writing (scribbling, writing strings of letters, and so on). Let them begin where they are and they will soon see themselves as writers. This is important because, like the other language processes (reading, listening, and speaking), writing is learned through practice.

The Word Play Center

The Word Play Center is a learner-centered environment that stimulates children's imaginations. Special-needs children can work at their own levels and yet share multisensory, thematic activities through social interaction and creative play. The themes represent real-life experiences that expand vocabulary and provide opportunities for learning language using problem solving, listening, speaking, art, music, and cooking. In addition, dramatic play at the center increases vocabulary and comprehension for all children, including those with special needs. ESL students in particular develop content knowledge through play.

To find more resources for children with disabilities, visit these Web sites (Burns, Griffin, and Snow, 1999):

- Special Education Resources on the Internet (SERI): http://www.seriweb.com
- National Information Center for Children and Youth with Disabilities Resources: http://www.nichcy.org/#about
- Parents Helping Parents Resources: http://www.php.com
- Family Village Resources: http://www.familyvillage.wisc.edu
- Office of Special Education Programs Resources: http://www.ed.gov/offices/OSERS/OSEP/index.html

2 ORGANIZING LEARNING CENTERS

FINDING MATERIALS

Commercial Materials

Interesting learning centers require a variety of materials. There are many free or inexpensive commercial learning center materials, but sometimes you have to use your imagination to adapt them. Here are a few tips:

- Begin to look at everything—egg cartons, fabric, cereal boxes, and so on—with this idea in mind: How can I use this in a learning center activity?

- Keep an eye out for clearance tables. Frequently, excellent educational games have been reduced to a fraction of their original cost. Before you buy, check to see that all the game pieces are intact. And make sure that players must read or use a reading skill to play the game.

- Out-of-date basal readers make great storybooks. Cut out individual stories, staple the pages together, and let the children create covers. Or cut out the illustrations and use them with a flannel board.

Teacher-Made Materials

Creating learning center materials is time-consuming. It is wise to enlist the help of colleagues, parent volunteers, paraprofessionals, and students to create original, made-to-order materials. Save yourself time by putting the children to work, too. They can cut and color the reproducibles in this volume after you have photocopied them. If you laminate the finished pieces, they will be durable.

Ongoing Materials

Since finding good activities is an ongoing pursuit, it is important to have board games, card games, puzzles, and matching activities that can be used over and over. This book is filled with games and activities that children enjoy playing repeatedly. You might wish to add interesting puzzles, flash cards, software, slates, commercial games, and a flannel board with story pictures.

STORING CENTER MATERIALS

Since learning center materials include games and manipulatives, it is essential to have good storage. There are several options for storing current center materials and those not currently being used.

- The board games included in this book should be made on file folders, by copying the game-board halves and gluing them inside a file folder (see Section Five). Label each folder with the name of the game board and store it in a file cabinet, a large cardboard box, or a shopping bag.

- Keep game cards in containers that are easy to store—small boxes, labeled envelopes, or self-sealed plastic bags (see the following).

- If your room lacks storage space, keep commercial games and puzzles at the centers to be used as ongoing activities.

- Don't store sorting containers. Instead, use the same containers over and over. The label can be easily changed if you attach it to the container with tape, a clothespin, or a large paper clip.

- Whenever possible, use shopping bags, plastic self-sealing bags, and envelopes as storage containers. They are easily folded and stored.

- Store all the activities for individual themes together so you can gather everything you need at one time. Empty photocopy-paper boxes are great for this.

MAKING STORAGE CONTAINERS

You will want attractive containers in which to store the center activities. As already noted, many free or low-cost items can be used as storage containers, among them: shopping bags, super-sized beverage cups, envelopes, plastic bags, floral baskets, stationery boxes, coffee cans, cookie tins, ice cream and popcorn tubs, and fruit crates. Here are a few ways to use them:

- Use mailing envelopes (brown or white, various sizes), plastic bags, and empty stationery boxes to hold card games, matching games, and other games.
- Use cylinder containers to hold sorting games.
- Use shopping bags to hold board games.
- Use envelopes or small boxes to hold various other games.
- Use baskets to hold the envelopes and boxes.

Envelopes and Plastic Bags

Large mailing envelopes are inexpensive, easy to decorate, and capacious enough to hold sorting, card, and matching games. Self-sealing plastic bags serve the same purpose and last longer than envelopes. However, bags sometimes cost more than envelopes and cannot be decorated with crayons or markers.

To make envelope containers, you will need:

- Mailing envelopes (with eyelet and clasp)
- Masking tape
- Hole punch
- Crayons or colored markers

1. Cover the gummed edge of the envelope flap with masking tape. The tape will cover the hole that's in the gummed edge; reopen the hole with a hole punch. This way, you prevent the envelope from sealing but allow the brad to slip through.

2. With a colored marking pen, write the name of the game on the front of the envelope.

3. Have children decorate the envelope with crayons or markers.

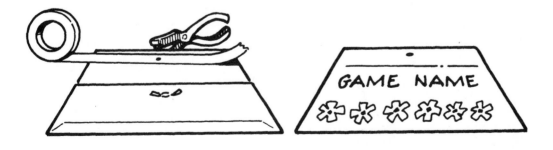

To make plastic bag containers, you will need:

- Gummed labels (mailing labels or name tags) and a marker
- Self-sealing bags in assorted sizes
- Decorative stickers

1. Write the name of the game on the label and attach it to the bag.
2. Decorate each bag with a sticker.

Stationery Boxes

Store games in small, sturdy boxes, such as stationery boxes. If the box is pretty, it needs no decoration. All you need to do is to label it.

For each box to be decorated, you will need:

- Old greeting cards, wallpaper, or self-stick vinyl
- Scissors
- Glue
- Label and marker

1. Have children cut designs from old greeting cards and glue them to the box top or cover the box with decorative wallpaper or self-stick vinyl.
2. With a colored marker, write the name of the game on the label. Attach the label to the box.
3. Glue the answer key inside the box lid.

Cylinder Containers

Use cylinder containers—coffee cans, large-sized drinking cups, oatmeal boxes, and theater popcorn tubs—to hold sorting games. Cylinders are easily decorated with paint, stickers, and colored masking tape.

For each container, you will need:

- Can, large-sized cup, oatmeal box, or popcorn tub
- Spray paint or small can of enamel and paint brush
- Colored masking tape in a contrasting color
- Decorations such as stickers (optional)
- Label (an index card or the sorting game pattern)

1. Clean each container.
2. Following the directions on the paint can, apply two coats of enamel to the outside of each container. Allow time for the paint to dry.
3. Bind the open rim of the container with colored masking tape. This adds a colorful border and prevents cut fingers (coffee cans) and frayed openings (oatmeal boxes).
4. If you wish, decorate the painted container with stickers.
5. Attach a label to each container with a clothespin, tape, or a large paper clip.

Shopping Bags

Shopping bags are good for storing board games because they are large but save space when they are hung on cup hooks at the learning centers.

You will need:

- Old magazines and greeting cards
- Scissors and glue or rubber cement
- One or more paper shopping bags or gift-sized shopping bags
- A strip of oak tag or an index card (for a label)
- Cup hook

1. Have children cut pictures from magazines or greeting cards. The pictures can represent one of the themes described in this volume, such as Winter Wonderland.
2. Have the children glue the pictures onto the shopping bag to create a scene.
3. Describe the contents of the bag on the label: "Board Games," for example.
4. Glue the label to the front of the bag.
5. Hang the bag on a cup hook at the learning center.

Baskets

Baskets are great for storing games that are in small boxes or plastic bags. They usually need little or no decoration.

For each basket, you will need:

- Index card (label) and marker
- Hole punch
- Ribbon

1. Write the contents of the basket on the index card.
2. Punch a hole in the card and tie it to the basket handle with a colorful ribbon.

3 THE LEARNING CENTERS

This section explains the purpose of each learning center and provides complete instructions and diagrams for setting up the centers.

THE TEACHER CENTER

The Teacher Center is easy to create because most classrooms already have an area for reading instruction. By adding a few materials, you can make this space into a comfortable, attractive meeting place for the whole class *and*

for small groups—literature groups, skill or strategy groups, cooperative or collaborative groups, and special-needs groups. The center arrangement should fit your teaching style; children can sit on chairs or on the floor and you can sit or stand as you work with them. Suggestions for setting up a Teacher Center are included in this chapter.

No strategy or method described in this section is as important as you are. The teacher is the most important element in the instructional process! *Starting Out Right: A Guide to Promoting Children's Reading Success* (Burns, Griffin, and Snow, 1999), summarizes these practices of excellent teachers:

- Create a literate environment in which the children have access to a variety of reading and writing materials.

- Present intentional instruction for reading and writing, using trade books and other literature and providing practice using games and activities separate from connected text.

- Carefully choose instructional-level text from a variety of materials, with a reliance on literature, big books, and linking reading and writing activities.

- Create multiple opportunities for sustained reading practice in a variety of formats, such as choral, individual, and partner reading.

- Adjust the intensity of instruction to meet the needs of individual students.

- Encourage children to consciously monitor their understanding; competently manage activities, behavior, and classroom resources. [p. 112]

How to Use the Teacher Center

The Teacher Center is the appropriate home for the following activities.

Read-Aloud Sessions. Reading aloud to children (with interactive discussion) is an important Teacher Center activity. Emergent and developing readers need to be read to every day to see how books work and to hear how a good reader handles text. Reading aloud introduces them to a variety of genres and makes them aware of titles, authors, illustrators, and publishers. As you read you have the opportunity to model specific strategies—how to determine word meanings, to think and comprehend, to analyze story structure, and to retell or summarize what's been read. Read-aloud sessions are also a good way to introduce themes, content areas, and poetry.

Listening to stories increases vocabulary and the ability to listen. Research shows that children who entered school as readers were most likely read to at home—another good reason to make reading aloud a daily activity.

And when disabled readers hear someone read aloud, they receive the same benefits that successful readers do.

Often, books read aloud, even books above the children's reading levels, are the most popular books in the classroom. So after a read-aloud session, display the book at the Library Center, where children can read it on their own. For further information on reading aloud to children, see *Read-Aloud Handbook* (2003) by Jim Trelease.

Big Books. Big books are large-sized books created for choral and group reading. They are designed so that several children (or the whole class) can see the words and read along with the teacher. The book can rest on a stand, an easel, or in the teacher's lap. Children can take turns pointing to the words as the class reads the book together.

Children love to "read" big books over and over, and repeated readings give them the practice they need to gain independence. After children are familiar with the story, move the book to the Library Center so individuals or small groups can continue to read it.

Big books are sold by publishers and retail stores, but it is easy and fun to make your own. Use chart paper and colored markers for printing stories, rhymes, songs, or anything you wish. Let children illustrate the pages and fasten them together with rings, staples, or yarn.

Shared-Book Experiences. In a shared-book experience, the teacher uses a big book as a group reading experience with the intention of developing language and reading skills (Holdaway, 1979). For instance, after the story is familiar to the group, the teacher uses it to demonstrate how to decode new words using letter sounds and patterns, illustrations, or context clues. For more information on shared reading, see Soderman, Gregory, and O'Neill (1999).

Predictable Books. Group reading of predictable books is fun *and* worthwhile. Children in the early stages of reading, as well as those who are struggling with reading, can very quickly join this activity and "read along." If the book is easy, emergent readers can "retell" it. So after you use these books several times in the Teacher Center, put them, too, in the Library Center for further practice.

Choral Reading: Songs and Chants. Skill in oral reading can develop through choral reading, and choral reading can be hands-on and include many learning styles. Children love to sing songs, and singing can become a reading activity when the teacher creates song charts containing all the words of a song and then points to the words as the group sings. This activity also works well with rhymes, jump rope chants, school cheers, raps, and poems (see next paragraph). Children quickly learn to chime in and read aloud with the teacher and can take turns pointing to the words. This activity is especially fun if the song is accompanied by hand motions. Adding simple instruments is another idea. For example, team a Native American chant with instruments made from oatmeal boxes and pencils, or have children create "instant instruments" by tapping pencils or fingers, shaking keys or change purses, or clapping their hands. It's fun and helpful to get some body action into group reading activities.

Choral Reading: Poetry. Choral reading is a wonderful way for children to learn poetry. Like songs and chants, poetry lends itself to sound effects—clicking pencils, rhythm instruments, or tapping feet. Children love to dramatize by playing the parts as the poem is read. Keep a list of good poems readily available, because it's great to present a poem (new or familiar) every day. Poetry doesn't have to be restricted to the Teacher Center—poems may be recited while students line up, as they change groups, and so on. One good idea is to have a week dedicated to the work of one poet, somewhat like an author study (Cullinan, 1987). When children become familiar with poetry, they can write their own poems at the Writing Center and record them to store at the Listening Center.

Storytelling. Children love to tell and listen to stories. Storytelling translates their experiences into words and develops their oral language, listening skills, and confidence (Owocki, 2001; Whitehead, 1999). So why not make familiar show-and-tell sessions into storytelling opportunities? To begin, have each child show an object (from home) and tell a story about it. When the process is familiar, let them tell stories they create at the Writing Center. You might even build in a practice session—at home or with a partner—before they tell their story to the group. Some groups may enjoy putting on a dramatic play about the story after it is told.

Book Talks. Book talks are given in a group setting by a child who has finished reading a book, either independently or with a partner. The child introduces the book, retells some of the events (except for the ending), and talks about the characters, a favorite part of the book, and something learned. Often after a presentation the book becomes popular because book talks help "sell" the book to other children.

Language Experience Approach (LEA). LEA is highly effective with emergent, early, and struggling readers because it's personal and uses the child's own experiences, ideas, and language. LEA shows the relationship between talking and writing and stresses reading from left to right, letter sounds, and sight words. Roach Van Allen, professor emeritus at the University of Arizona, began researching this process in the 1960s. He approached it from a child's point of view (Allen, 1976):

What I think about I can say.
What I can say I can write (or someone else can write).
What I can write (or someone else has written for me) I can read.

LEA can be used to create or retell stories (in children's own words), report on a field trip, write words for a song, or write group letters and thank-you notes. In fact, children can dictate anything they can talk about—labels, vocabulary cards, sentence strips, or greeting cards. These creations should be read again and again or recorded and placed in the Listening Center. Before you know it, children will be reading them independently (Allen and Allen, 1982).

Effective with both individuals and groups, LEA integrates listening, speaking, reading, and writing. If you are using LEA for the first time, begin with a motivating activity—a field trip, art experience, or cooking project. Then have a conversation or discussion to help organize ideas and provide motivation.

- *LEA group dictation.* During group dictation the teacher uses a large chart and marker, and as the children dictate, the teacher records their exact words in large print. When the dictation is finished, the teacher and children read what has been written together.

- *LEA one-on-one dictation.* Individual dictation gives a single child total participation in LEA. Using a paper or notebook, the teacher records what the child dictates and together they read back what was written. The child can illustrate each creation, bind several into a book for the Library Center, and record the book for the Listening Center.

Phonological Processing and Phonemic Awareness Activities. *Phono-logical processing* is the ability to hear and comprehend language sounds. It involves noticing, thinking about, and manipulating individual sounds in words. The term *phonemic awareness*—an understanding of spoken language—is often used interchangeably with the term *phonological awareness*. The fact is that phonemic awareness is a subcategory of phonological awareness (Soderman, Gregory, and O'Neill, 1999). Phonemic awareness is understanding the smallest units of sound in words (phonemes) and phonological awareness includes larger sound units (syllables, onsets, and rimes) (International Reading Association, 1998).

The Teacher Center is a great place in which to present activities that develop phonological processing and phonemic awareness; doing so should be part of every program for emergent and early readers and writers. Like other literacy behaviors, these develop over time and with practice. Fortunately, children usually enjoy practice activities that are in game form. Small groups work well for many activities. These will get you started:

- *Rhyming:* Have children recognize pairs of rhyming words; fill in rhyming words while listening to nursery rhymes; create rhymes with real and nonsense words; fill in rhyming words as you read nursery rhymes.

- *Beginning and ending sounds:* Have children listen for words that begin or end with the same sound; line up to the sound of their first or last name.

- *Count phonemes:* Ask, "How many phonemes in /b/a/t/?" Sound this out for them. (*Answer:* Three phonemes.)

- *Clap syllables in words:* Have children clap hands, snap fingers, or use simple instruments (such as tapping pencils) to count syllables in words (or jump to count the syllables).

- *Segment and blend:* Play these games: segment sentences into words (count words in a sentence); isolate initial consonants in single-syllable words (/t/ is the first sound in *tall*); blend separate sounds that you say (/b/a/t/ is *bat*); listen to separately spoken phonemes (mmm-ahhh-mmm) and blend them (*mom*).

- *Substitute phonemes/change words:* Play games to change words. For example, change *rake* to *cake, make, bake, Jake*.

- *Word families:* Let children dictate charts of rhyming words and word families for the Word Wall (see page 78).

- *Matching sounds:* Children point to classroom pictures that show the images represented by words with the same beginning (or ending) sound as their first or last names.

- *Blend onsets and rimes:* Onsets are speech sounds before a vowel (/b/s/p/) and rimes are the vowel and what follows (-ake). Words that begin with vowels only have a rime. Words are formed by combining onsets and rimes (*bake, cake, lake*). An easy game is this: "Tell all the words that we can form using -*ake*."

- *Alliteration:* Play a game where children think of words that begin with the same phoneme. Then create a sentence or phrase with those words. For example, "Terry took two turtles to town."

Individual and Small-Group Instruction. The Teacher Center is a natural place to work with children individually and in small groups—phonemic awareness groups, alphabet or word study groups, literature groups, guided reading groups, interest groups, special-needs groups, basal reader groups, or groups formed to provide short-term support to children having difficulty. (Note that children who are struggling need a very small group and a lot of scaffolding.) Groups should be flexible; struggling readers in particular need to be with other children. It's best not to lock children into a specific group over a long period of time. Include one-on-one and small-group instruction as often as possible.

Guided Reading. In guided reading a small group of children with similar reading ability read multiple copies of the same text. The book should be at the group's instructional level, not at an independent level. The teacher provides assistance when needed. If the session is used to help with predetermined skills or strategies, the teacher models how the strategy is used before the reading begins. Children can read silently, but early readers may prefer to read out loud quietly. When discussing the story the teacher leads children to predict, compare characters, recall events, and summarize the text.

Reciprocal Teaching. This method teaches four comprehension strategies: predicting, questioning, summarizing, and clarifying. During the session, the teacher shows children how to comprehend the text as they take turns asking and answering questions. *Starting Out Right,* edited by Susan Burns, Peg Griffin, and Catherine Snow (1999), states that the content used in reciprocal teaching is centered on themes that, over time, build children's knowledge of a topic. When you choose a theme from this book for your classroom setup, you can use the same theme for your reciprocal teaching content.

Short Lessons. Reading processes are learned over time and need to be discussed often. On a regular basis, conduct short lessons that model or support reading and writing—phonological processing activities, sequencing activities, shared-book experiences, semantic mapping (word webs), KWL (What I Know, What I Want to Learn, What I Have Learned), and retelling the contents of a trade book.

Children's Presentations. The Teacher Center can become a forum where students share work from the other centers with their team or with the entire class. An "Author's Chair" for sharing writing, a stage for a puppet show, or a "gallery" for shows from the Art Center should be permanent features of the Teacher Center. Ideas for presentations include these:

- *Puppet show:* Children use puppets to read character parts or retell a story.
- *Reader's Theater:* Children act out a story (Owocki, 2001).
- *Book talk:* The child introduces the book, describes a favorite character or event, explains what was learned, and compares the book with other books.
- *Displays:* Children who create products at the learning centers—writing, tape recordings, art, music—make a presentation to classmates.

- *Author's Chair:* This is a special chair for young writers who have published a book (or other text), have practiced it, and are ready to read it to the class or a small group. On some occasions, you may wish to invite other classes in to hear authors' presentations. ("Published" works are stories that the child writes, illustrates, and assembles. See additional information about publishing in the Writing Center section.)

New Activity Instruction. Most new activities and games need an introduction so that children are clear about the teacher's expectations as they begin their independent work at the centers. At the Teacher Center, introduce each new game or activity to the entire class or to small groups. Go over new vocabulary or strategies and establish clear expectations and guidelines for completing the game or activity.

Games. Children learn quickly through games, so take time to play hands-on games at the Teacher Center. Use the reproducible games in this book, commercial games, or games you create especially for each group. Well-designed games teach decision making and critical thinking skills as well as reading skills. Before you place games at the centers, first demonstrate how they are played at the Teacher Center.

Pocket Charts and Flannel Boards. Pocket charts, available at most schools, are holders for word cards and sentence strips. Flannel boards have many uses and are easy to make (see the directions on page 37).

Use your pocket chart to practice sentences from big books and dictation charts; practice new words; fill in blanks to complete sentences; and match compound words.

Use your flannel board to tell stories; sequence pictures; and match sentences to pictures; and match compound words.

Individual Conferences. Finally, the Teacher Center is a comfortable place for meeting with individual children. Holding a regular conference with each child—two or three times a week—provides the opportunity to:

- Hear the child read aloud or discuss a writing sample.
- Note progress and give individual attention or support.
- Observe strategies used and teach new strategies.
- Check comprehension by asking the child to summarize, retell, or discuss the main points of a text.
- Discover the child's genre preferences and encourage variety in choices.
- Recommend books you think the child would enjoy.

For more information on reading conferences, see Bergeron and Bradbury-Wolff (2003), Schwartz (1988), and Taberski (2000).

Basic Equipment

Here's what you will need to set up the Teacher Center:

- Student seating, either in chairs or on the floor
- A teacher chair or place to stand
- Storage shelf for materials
- Instructional materials
- Pocket chart, sentence strips, and vocabulary cards (make special cards from seasonal games by copying key words from game cards onto index cards)
- Chart and stand with markers
- Easel or stand for big books, flannel board, and a pocket chart (a chalk rail works well)
- Flannel board with story pictures
- Rhythm instruments
- Games taken from this book or from other sources
- A poster or sign that reads: "Teacher Center"

Arrange the Teacher Center in an area with good lighting. Position your place in the center so you will be able to see all other centers while you are there. Place the chart stand and easel nearby. Place the storage shelf nearby to hold books and boxes of story pictures, rhythm instruments, and so on. Stand big books, flannel board, and extra charts nearby. Describe the contents of each box on a label: "Rhythm Instruments," "Story Pictures," "Pocket Chart Cards." Attach a label to each box and store the boxes on the shelf. Hang the sign or poster.

Making a Flannel Board

You'll need the following materials:

- Solid-color flannel four inches longer and wider than plywood
- One piece three-eighths-inch-thick plywood that's two feet by four feet
- A staple gun and staples

Lay the flannel flat on the floor. Lay the plywood flat on the material so that two inches of material shows all around the plywood. Fold excess flannel over the edge of the plywood. Pull the flannel taut, turn under the raw edges, miter the corners, and staple it to the plywood.

Many items adhere easily to a flannel board, including felt shapes, magazine pages, greeting cards, and pages from old basal readers backed with flannel.

Recommended Books: Joan's Choices

The following lists of read-alouds and storytelling books were developed by Joan Dismore, a veteran teacher, librarian, and storyteller (see "About the Content Developers"). Joan says: "The stories I've listed are ones I use over and over—they've proved to be well received and enjoyed. Many times I read or tell the story using puppets or appropriate stuffed animals." This list is by no means complete; you may wish to include many other books in your Teacher Center. However, Joan finds that children ask for the stories shown here year after year. Award-winning books are noted.

Kindergarten

All the Beatrix Potter books

All the Eric Carle books

All the Ezra Jack Keats books

All the *Froggy* books by Jonathan London, illustrated by Frank Remkiewicz

All the Leo Lionni books

All of Eric Hill's *Spot* books

Baby Crow by John A. Rowe

The Gingerbread Man (any version)

Goodnight Moon by Margaret Wise Brown

I Like It When by Mary Murphy

Mama, Do You Love Me? by Barbara M. Joosse, illustrated by Barbara Lavallee

Mary Had a Little Lamb by Iza Trapani

Mr. Gumpy's Outing by John Burningham

Mr. Willowby's Christmas Tree by Robert E. Barry, illustrated by Robert Barry

Noah's Arc by Lucy Cousins

The Real Mother Goose, illustrated by Blanche Fisher Wright

"Stand Back," Said the Elephant, "I'm Going to Sneeze" by Patricia Thomas, illustrated by Wallis Tripp

Time for Bed by Mem Fox, illustrated by Jane Dyer

The Tiny Star by Arthur Ginolfi, illustrated by Pat Schories

What Did They See? by John Schindel, illustrated by Doug Cushman

What Do You Say, Dear? by Sesyle Joslin, illustrated by Maurice Sendak

When We Were Very Young by A. A. Milne

Grade One

Aesop's fables for children (any version)

The Ant and the Elephant by Bill Peet, and all his other books

The Bremen Town Musicians by the Brothers Grimm

The *Frog and Toad* books by Arnold Lobel

If You Give a Mouse a Cookie by Laura Joffe Numeroff, illustrated by Felicia Bond

King Bounce the 1st by Helme Heine

Little Toot by Hardie Gramatky

Mike Mulligan and His Steam Shovel by Virginia Lee Burton

Now We Are Six by A. A. Milne

Olivia (and all the Olivia books) by Ian Falconer

The Polar Express by Chris Van Allsburg (Caldecott Medal)

The Princess and the Pea by Hans Christian Andersen, illustrated by Dorothee
    Duntze

Red Fox and His Canoe by Nathaniel Benchley

Stellaluna by Jannell Cannon

Stories That Never Grow Old: A Collection of Stories and Verses for Children by
    Watty Piper, illustrated by Lois Leski

The Story of Babar by Jean de Brunhoff

Tuesday by David Wiesner (Caldecott Honor Book)

Where the Wild Things Are by Maurice Sendak (Caldecott Medal)

Why the Sun Was Late by Benjamin Elkin

Grade Two

Beauty and the Beast as told by Marianna Mayer, illustrated by Mercer Mayer

Big Fraid, Little Fraid by Ellis Credle

Bunny and the Beast by Molly Coxe, illustrated by Pamela Silin-Palmer

Did You Carry the Flag Today, Charley? by Rebecca Caudill

The Fisherman Under the Sea by Miyoko Matsutani

The Grey Lady and Strawberry Snatcher by Molly Bang (Caldecott Honor Book)

Just So Stories by Rudyard Kipling

Peter Pan by J. M. Barrie, illustrated by Trina Schart Hyman

Rabbit Hill by Robert Lawson (Newbery Award)

Raggedy Ann and Raggedy Andy Stories by Johnny Gruelle

Saint George and the Dragon by Margaret Hodges, illustrated by Trina Schart
    Hyman

Sleeping Ugly by Jane Yolen, illustrated by Diane Stanley

Stone Soup (any version)

Tikki Tikki Tembo (any version)

Tom Tit Tot, a variation of Rumpelstiltskin (any version)

The Velveteen Rabbit by Margery Williams

Whitebird Folktales (see the Tomie de Paola version)

The Wind in the Willows by Kenneth Grahame

Winnie-the-Pooh by A. A. Milne

Activities

You can organize many activities at the Teacher Center; here are a few suggestions.

Classroom Labels. Create classroom labels as a whole-class activity using thick (wide) black markers and index cards or sentence strips. Let the children help choose items to be labeled—clock, sink, calendar, and so on—and let them dictate what goes on each label. Make each label large enough to be seen from all areas of the classroom. As you write ask the children how they think the word begins and ends, but when you write the label use standard spelling. Have the children read the word with you as you tape the labels under the appropriate objects. Make labels over time rather than all at once, and review them often. Use labels as a reading activity. Using a yardstick or pointer children work as partners, reading labels around the room.

Pocket Chart Activity. Teach a rhyme, chant, or song to the class or a small group. Use hand motions or rhythm instruments, if appropriate. After the children know the words, let them watch you write each line on a sentence strip, using a wide marker. Sing or chant each line—one at a time—and place it in the pocket chart. Then sing or chant the whole song together. After children learn to read the sentence strips, they can match them with identical sentence strips, match word cards to sentence strips, or create an illustrated rhyme booklet.

Story Extensions for Big Books and Read-Alouds. Read *Mrs. Wishy Washy* by Joy Cowley.

- Children act out the story at the Teacher Center (or the Word Play Center).

- With your help, children construct a "favorite character" class graph. Write the names (and use picture illustrations) of the characters along the bottom of a large piece of rolled bulletin-board paper. Children write their names above their favorite character. Post and discuss the results.

Read aloud several books by the same author.

- Construct a "favorite book" class graph. Write the names of the books along the top of a large piece of rolled bulletin-board paper. Children write their names under their favorite book. Post and discuss the results.
- At the Art Center children draw a picture about their favorite part of their favorite book.

Here are some additional read-aloud, shared book, and predictable book story extension ideas. Have the children:

- Dramatize the story.
- Reread or pretend-read the story.
- Draw a picture about the story.
- Write (or tell) another story with the same characters.
- Write (or tell) another story with a different plot.
- Write (or tell) another story with a different ending.
- Retell the story.
- Borrow the book to read, pretend-read, or have family members read to them at home.

KWL. Brainstorming before reading for information or taking field trips helps young readers organize both their thoughts and the reading purpose. KWL is a group activity for doing this. Use a wide marker to draw the following chart on a whiteboard or piece of chart paper. Record what children say in the first two categories. At the end of the discussion read the chart together. After the children have completed the reading or field trip, have another group discussion and fill in the third column. Compare what they have learned with what they wanted to learn. How are the lists alike and different? Ask what children can do to learn the things they still want to learn.

What I Know	What I Want to Learn	What I Have Learned

Name Games. Take a photo of every child in the class. Attach each photo to an index card and print a corresponding index card with the child's name. Display the pictures and name cards together at the Teacher Center. Read the names daily until the children are familiar with them. Then do the following:

- Play a group game where children match names with photos.
- Put the cards and photos in the Word Play Center to use as a matching activity.
- Make a class album with the children's photos and names for the Library Center.
- Put cards with the first name of each child into a bag. Every morning, select one and hold it up for the class to see. The child who belongs to the name stands up. The teacher then hides the name so the child can spell the name from memory. The teacher also writes the name on a large piece of graph paper, one letter per box. Each day, select another name and repeat the procedure. As the names are written on the graph paper, the class compares and contrasts the names' similarities and differences—number of letters, length, number of words in the names (such as Mary versus Mary Ann).

Fill in the Blank. This activity works well in a small group and can be done with big books, dictation charts, and pocket charts.

Select a big book that children are familiar with and use large sticky notes to cover some of the words. Don't cover the same word twice. Make a word card for each covered word.

Give each child in the group two or three word cards. As the group reads the book, the child who has the word that fits holds it up. Uncover the word to see if it is a match. When most children are able to do this activity, put it at the Library Center or the Word Play Center.

Author Study.   Here are several author study activities:

- Over several days, conduct read-aloud sessions with a selection of books by the same author. During interactive discussion make comparisons of how the books are alike or different and record ideas on a whiteboard or chart. Discuss the author's style. Each day reread the chart and record new information on it.
- Locate videotapes and audiotapes of the author's stories or make audiotapes of the books you are reading. Keep these in the Listening Center.
- Keep books by the author in the Library Center.
- At the Computer Center, have children visit the author's Web site.
- Have children create a story in the author's style at the Writing Center and illustrate it at the Art Center.

For a detailed discussion of author studies and a comprehensive list of appropriate selections listed by author, see *The Beginning Reading Handbook: Strategies for Success* by Gail Heald-Taylor (2001).

Thematic Activities

Thematic activities relate to a theme your class has chosen to explore. Activities appropriate for all kinds of themes include these:

- Play pocket-chart games using vocabulary that is theme-related (write sentences or key words from the game cards in Section Four on sentence strips).
- Demonstrate hands-on games made from reproducibles for the theme (see Section Four).
- Tell flannel-board stories that relate to the theme.
- Read literature and trade books that relate to the theme.
- Create and read theme-related big books.
- Sing related songs with the help of song charts.
- Write language experience (LEA) stories that are related to the theme.
- Have the children dictate theme-related greeting cards.

The following specific theme units are described in detail in Section Four. Here are some theme-based activities that are appropriate for the Teacher Center.

- *School Days:* Create an alma mater and a school cheer for a song chart.
- *Pumpkin Patch:* Play musical instruments (such as maracas) made from gourds.
- *Native American Tepee:* Create Native American music for a song chart; decorate coffee cans to use as drums.
- *Winter Wonderland:* Demonstrate winter sports equipment, such as ice skates or skis.
- *Black History Month:* Books are listed in the Black History Month theme in Section Four. Read as many as possible with the class.
- *Spaceship:* Create a spaceship choral reading for a song chart. Learn to read the names of galaxies, planets, and star formations.

- *Springtime:* As a group, write a story about planting seeds. Act out a spring story from literature, a trade book, or a basal reader.

- *Cinco de Mayo:* Learn some of the Spanish words that are featured in the Cinco de Mayo theme in Section Four.

- *Lunar New Year:* Let the children create a lion dance on the playground and then dictate a story chart about it.

- *Restaurant:* Sing restaurant commercials using song charts; use kitchen items such as spoons for musical instruments.

- *Roman Holiday:* Play "Simon Says" using the Latin names for the body parts (see Section Four).

- *Valentine's Day and Dental Health Month:* Create a dental health song and a valentine poem for song charts.

THE LIBRARY CENTER

A class library provides daily access to a variety of books and other interesting reading materials. Children who read a lot show high levels of achievement in vocabulary and comprehension, and daily independent reading is a must if children are to develop good reading habits. You'll be delighted at the number of children who will read when they can choose their own books and read them as part of their daily work. Easy-to-read books—a simple story, limited text, illustrations that match the text, and natural syntactic language—give emergent and beginning readers an opportunity for daily practice that helps them become fluent readers. So provide plenty of books that children can read independently. In addition, provide books that will challenge your children—books they can tackle with less accuracy and fluency. Books that are a bit more difficult tend to stretch young readers. The Library Center can also be used for group activities—peer reading, cross-age reading, shared reading, and cooperative reading activities.

Encourage children to keep a record of the books they read at the center. Make a booklet for each child by stapling together several sheets of lined paper. Make a cover out of construction paper that is titled BOOKS I HAVE

READ. Students use the booklet as a reading log in which to note the title, author, and date they finish a book; fluent readers can write their personal response to the book (for more details, see "Activities" on page 52).

You might want to consider a system, perhaps color coding, for organizing books at readability levels. Rotate books on a regular basis and expand materials to fit themes, author studies, and other current happenings in the room. Children will want to borrow books, so keep a sheet of paper and pencil handy so they can write down their name and the name of the book they borrow.

Basic Equipment

Here's what you will need to set up a Library Center:

- *Student seating.* Get a table and chairs, a couch, a comfortable chair, an area rug, cushions, carpet squares, or beanbag chairs.
- *Bookshelves or book carts.* If you don't have a shelf that displays books with the covers facing out, stand a few books up so their covers show. Some teachers place books in square plastic baskets with the covers facing out. It's a good idea to place a label on each basket to denote contents. For example: "Animals A–Z." Note that the younger the children are, the more open the bookshelves should be.
- *Wall space.* Display charts and big books introduced at the Teacher Center.

Print materials you will need for the Library Center include these:

- Books from a variety of genres on the reading levels of individual children in the class—excellent literature, interesting and popular trade books, big books, joke and cartoon books, biographies, poetry, predictable books, alphabet books, wordless books (for which children create their own stories), songs, and books written by the students
- Informational books and materials, factual books, including catalogues, telephone books, cookbooks, children's magazines and newspapers, atlases, maps, globes, and other reference materials
- Environmental printed material, such as—posters, traffic signs, road signs, rest room signs, labels, calendars, menus, coupons, food containers, and so on
- Materials that reflect various racial and ethnic groups and variety of cultures, especially those represented in the local area (and classroom)
- Charts dictated by students
- Books and other reading materials related to the current theme

- Interesting, easy, and predictable books and materials for "practice reading" to build fluency
- Interesting books and materials for children with reading disabilities
- Rebuses (stories with pictures in place of difficult words)
- Flannel board for story retellings, sequencing activities, and poetry presentations
- Puppets or stuffed animals related to available literature (Soderman, Gregory, and O'Neill, 1999)
- Labels for shelves ("Cookbooks," "Animal Stories," and so on)
- A sign-up sheet and pencil for those who wish to borrow books
- A poster or sign that reads: "Library Center"
- A poster or sign that reads: "Don't Be a Litterbug! Put Your Books Away."

Once you have obtained the necessary items, arrange the Library Center in a well-lit area near your bookcase or bookshelves. Organize the reading materials on the shelves. Attach the labels to the shelves. Put the sign-up sheet and pencil on top of the bookcase or bookshelves. Post the signs.

Acquiring Materials

There are several ways to acquire materials for the Library Center:

- Borrow books from the school's media center.
- Join a children's book club; some offer free books when students order books.
- Search flea markets, garage sales, and secondhand bookstores where children's books are plentiful and inexpensive.
- Cut separate stories out of outdated basal readers. Staple each story and create a cover for it using wallpaper scraps.
- Move charts and big books from the Teacher Center to the Library Center for independent reading.
- Create smaller versions of songs, rhymes, chants, and big books used at the Teacher Center. Children like to read these over and over, and they provide good practice and build fluency.
- Student-created books can be photocopied and bound so the original creation can be sent home. Children love to display their own writing for others to read.
- Make cartoon books by cutting cartoons from newspapers and magazines and gluing them to notebooks.

Recommended Books

The following is a list of children's Notable Books, Caldecott Medal and Honor Books, and Coretta Scott King Author or Illustrator Award and Honor Books that were chosen by the American Library Association from 2002 to 2004. For other American Library Association (ALA) book, recording, video, and software recommendations, see http://www.ala.org.

Emergent and Early Readers

Agee, Jon. (2002). *Milo's Hat.* When Milo the Magician needs a new trick for his failing show, he turns to a bear (ALA Notable).

Alarcón, Francisco X. (2002). *Iguanas in the Snow.* Illustrated by Maya Christina Gonzalez. This collection of seventeen poems printed in English and Spanish features Latino children in a San Francisco multicultural setting (Pura Belpré Author Award Honor Book).

Barton, Byron. (2002). *My Car.* Sam loves his car and the bus that he drives at work (ALA Notable).

Booth, Philip. (2002). *Crossing.* Illustrated by Bagram Ibatoulline. A poem about a freight train, set in the 1950s (ALA Notable).

Carle, Eric. (2003). *"Slowly, Slowly, Slowly," said the Sloth.* The sloth appears lazy to other animals in the rain forest. The message: accept yourself (ALA Notable).

Cobb, Vicki. (2004). *I Face the Wind.* Illustrated by Julia Gorton. This science book for the very young includes observations and experiments about the wind (Sibert Honor Book).

Crews, Donald. (2002). *Inside Freight Train.* The contents of a freight train are shown in this easy-to-read book (ALA Notable).

Davies, Nicola. (2004). *Surprising Sharks.* Illustrated by James Croft. This is a wonderfully illustrated book about some amazing creatures (ALA Notable).

Dillon, Leo, and Dillon, Diane. (2003). *Rap a Tap Tap: Here's Bojangles—Think of That!* This book is a glimpse into the life of Mr. Bojangles Robinson. The book features a wonderful refrain and beautiful paintings (Coretta Scott King Illustrator Award).

DiTerlizzi, Tony. (2003). *The Spider and the Fly.* A new rendition of an 1829 tale by Mary Howitt; it features a villain, a damsel in distress, and many interesting pictures (Caldecott Honor Book).

Dunrea, Olivier. (2003). *Gossie & Gertie.* This funny story is about the friendship between two goslings (ALA Notable).

Ehlert, Lois. (2002). *Waiting for Wings.* Caterpillars change into butterflies and explore garden flowers (ALA Notable).

Falconer, Ian. (2002). *Olivia Saves the Circus.* Olivia fills in as a circus lion tamer, a juggler, and a tightrope walker (ALA Notable).

Falwell, Cathryn. (2002). *Turtle Splash: Countdown at the Pond*. The turtles are counted from ten to one as they leave their log for the bottom of the pond (ALA Notable).

Fleming, Candace. (2003). *Muncha! Muncha! Muncha!* Illustrated by G. Brian Karas. Three bunnies outsmart Mr. McGreely and eat the vegetables from his garden. A funny, predictable read-aloud (ALA Notable).

Fleming, Denise. (2003). *Alphabet Under Construction*. A delightful mouse constructs the alphabet using various methods. This is a colorful picture book (ALA Notable).

Floca, Brian. (2004). *The Racecar Alphabet*. Examples of cars produced from 1901 to 2001 make this an exciting alphabet book (ALA Notable).

French, Jackie. (2004). *Diary of a Wombat*. Illustrated by Bruce Whatley. This delightful tale about Australia's most endangered mammal includes a wombat's diary entries and her training of human neighbors (ALA Notable).

Graham, Bob. (2002). *"Let's Get a Pup," Said Kate*. After Kate's parents help her select a dog from the pound, they continue to think of the one they left behind (ALA Notable).

Henkes, Kevin. (2002). *Sheila Rae's Peppermint Stick*. Sheila Rae teases her sister Louise with candy, until an accident inspires them to share (ALA Notable).

Hoberman, Mary Ann. (2002). *You Read to Me, I'll Read to You: Very Short Stories to Read Together*. Illustrated by Michael Emberley. This is a good read-aloud book of poems (ALA Notable).

Inkpen, Mick. (2002). *Kipper's A to Z: An Alphabet Adventure*. Kipper and Arnold stroll through the alphabet (ALA Notable).

James, Simon. (2004). *Little One Step*. Three lost ducklings tell the youngest one to take one step until they find their mother (ALA Notable).

Jenkins, Emily. (2002). *Five Creatures*. Illustrated by Tomek Bogacki. A young girl explores the likenesses and differences between family members (ALA Notable).

Johansen, Hanna. (2003). *Henrietta and the Golden Eggs*. Illustrated by Käthi Bhend. Translated by John Barrett. The story is an allegory about a hen who pursues better living conditions on a poultry farm (Batchelder Honor Book).

Little, Jean. (2002). *Emma's Yucky Brother*. Illustrated by Jennifer Plecas. Emma experiences joy and dismay when the family adopts a four-year-old boy (ALA Notable).

Livingston, Star. (2002). *Harley*. Illustrated by Molly Bang. Harley the llama wants to be a pack animal, but becomes a great sheepherder (ALA Notable).

Long, Melinda. (2004). *How I Became a Pirate*. Illustrated by David Shannon. This read-aloud features Jeremy's good news and bad news about being a pirate—he doesn't take baths or eat vegetables but no one tucks him in at night or reads him a story (ALA Notable).

McCarty, Peter. (2003). *Hondo & Fabian.* This story shows how a dog and cat, who are friends, spend their day—the dog at the beach and the cat at home (Caldecott Honor Book).

McMullan, Kate. (2003). *I Stink!* Illustrated by Jim McMullan. A garbage truck with personality talks with readers as it makes its rounds (ALA Notable).

Morales, Yuyi. (2004). *Just a Minute: A Trickster Tale and Counting Book.* This Mexican counting book features Grandma Beetle and Señor Calavera; appropriate for the Cinco de Mayo theme (Pura Belpré Illustrator Medal Book).

Paige, Robin, and Jenkins, Steve. (2004). *What Do You Do with a Tail Like This?* Illustrated by Steve Jenkins. This is a delightful science lesson on the body parts of thirty animals (Caldecott Honor Book).

Paye, Won-Ldy, and Lippert, Margaret H. Head. (2003). *Head, Body, Legs: A Story from Liberia.* Illustrated by Julie Paschkis. This wonderful creation story is from the Dan people of Africa (ALA Notable).

Recorvits, Helen. (2004). *My Name Is Yoon.* Illustrated by Gabi Swiatkowska. Yoon, a Korean girl, loses her shyness and becomes a happy schoolgirl in America (ALA Notable; Ezra Jack Keats New Illustrator Award).

Rohmann, Eric. (2003). *My Friend Rabbit.* Mouse and Rabbit share a new toy airplane with disastrous and hilarious results (Caldecott Medal).

Sayre, April Pulley, and Sayre, Jeff. (2004). *One Is a Snail, Ten Is a Crab: A Counting by Feet Book.* Illustrated by Randy Cecil. The book presents counting, adding, and multiplying using the feet of animals as they play on the beach (ALA Notable).

Shannon, David. (2003). *Duck on a Bike.* This is a delightful barnyard tale of a duck who has a wild bike ride. Predictable text makes it an easy read and fun for a read-aloud session (ALA Notable).

Simont, Marc. (2002). *The Stray Dog.* A surprise encounter turns into a family love affair in this delightful story (Caldecott Honor Book).

Sis, Peter. (2003). *Madlenka's Dog.* Madlenka takes a walk with her newly imagined dog (ALA Notable).

Steen, Sandra, and Steen, Susan. (2002). *Car Wash.* Illustrated by G. Brian Karas. A ride in a car wash turns into an undersea adventure, complete with sea creatures (ALA Notable).

Stevens, Janet, and Crummel, Susan Stevens. (2002). *And the Dish Ran Away with the Spoon.* Illustrated by Janet Stevens. This is a new twist on an old nursery rhyme (ALA Notable).

Thomas, Shelley Moore. (2003). *Get Well, Good Knight.* Illustrated by Jennifer Plecas. A good knight cares for three sick dragons. This is an easy reader with lots of repetition (ALA Notable).

Willems, Mo. (2004). *Don't Let the Pigeon Drive the Bus.* A pigeon uses conniving arguments to get behind the wheel of a bus (Caldecott Honor Book).

Wilson, Karma. (2003). *Bear Snores On*. Illustrated by Jane Chapman. Bear sleeps as the forest animals throw a party in his lair (ALA Notable).

Winter, Jonah. (2003). *Frida*. Illustrated by Ana Juan. Frida overcomes suffering to become a wonderful Mexican artist; appropriate for the Cinco de Mayo theme (ALA Notable).

Developing and Fluent Readers

Chodos-Irvine, Margaret. (2004). *Ella Sarah Gets Dressed*. Sarah Ella is a bold and confident girl who wants to make a fashion statement (Caldecott Honor Book).

Fraustino, Lisa Rowe. (2002). *The Hickory Chair*. Illustrated by Benny Andrews. Louis, a young blind boy, finds all the notes his grandmother left for her loved ones, except him (ALA Notable).

Gerstein, Mordicai. (2003). *What Charlie Heard*. This biography of composer Charles Ives shows how he took everyday sounds and made a new kind of music (ALA Notable).

Gerstein, Mordicai. (2004). *The Man Who Walked Between the Towers*. This true story recounts the daring feat of the spirited young Frenchman who walked a tightrope between the World Trade Center twin towers in 1974 (2004 Caldecott Medal).

Look, Lenore. (2002). *Henry's First-Moon Birthday*. Jenny helps her baby brother celebrate his first-month party; appropriate for the Lunar New Year theme (ALA Notable).

Lowry, Lois. (2003). *Gooney Bird Greene*. Illustrated by Middy Thomas. This "storyteller" book features Gooney Bird Green, a second grader, who tells unbelievable stories (ALA Notable).

Lunge-Larsen, Lise. (2002). *The Race of the Birkebeiners*. Illustrated by Mary Azarian. This is a true story of brave skiers who risked their lives to save Norway's baby prince in the year 1206 (ALA Notable).

McKissack, Patricia C. (2002). *Goin' Someplace Special*. Illustrated by Jerry Pinkney. In the 1950s, Tricia Ann rides segregated buses to the public library where "All are welcome"; appropriate for the Black History Month theme (Coretta Scott King Illustrator Award).

Mills, Claudia. (2002). *Gus and Grandpa at Basketball*. Illustrated by Catherine Stock. With Grandpa's help, Gus scores in a basketball game (ALA Notable).

Mollel, Tololwa M. (1999). *My Rows and Piles of Coins*. Illustrated by E. B. Lewis. Saruni is saving his money to buy a bicycle in order to help his mother deliver her goods to market. The story setting is Tanzania (Coretta Scott King Illustrator Award).

Montes, Marisa. (2002). *Juan Bobo Goes to Work*. Illustrated by Joe Cepeda. This is a retelling of a traditional Puerto Rican folktale—the funny story of Juan Bobo at work (Pura Belpré Illustrator Award Honor Book).

Nolan, Jerdine. (2003). *Thunder Rose*. Illustrated by Kadir Nelson. This is a tall tale about an unusual little girl who performs amazing feats (Coretta Scott King Illustrator Award).

Palatini, Margie. (2002). *The Web Files*. Illustrated by Richard Egielski. A barnyard crime is solved by a duck and his partner—shades of TV's *Dragnet* (ALA Notable).

Pinkney, Jerry. (2003). *Noah's Ark*. This retelling of the well-known flood story features beautiful pencil and watercolor illustrations (Calecott Honor Book).

Rappaport, Doreen. (2002). *Martin's Big Words: The Life of Dr. Martin Luther King, Jr.* Illustrated by Bryan Collier. This is a picture-book biography of the great civil rights leader (Calecott Honor Book).

Ryan, Pam Muñoz. (2002). *Mice and Beans*. Illustrated by Joe Cepeda. Rosa Maria prepares for her granddaughter's birthday. The book includes some Spanish words and is appropriate for the Cinco de Mayo theme (ALA Notable).

Schroeder, Alan. (Reprint Edition, 2000). *Minty: A Story of Young Harriet Tubman*. Illustrated by Jerry Pinkney. The story of Harriet Tubman's childhood, written for young readers, tells how Minty (her childhood name) dreamed of escaping her life of slavery on a plantation; appropriate for the Black History Month theme (Coretta Scott King Honor Book).

Siegelson, Kim L. (1999). *In the Time of Drums*. Illustrated by Brian Pinkney. In this retelling of a Gullah legend, a boy and his grandmother who are plantation slaves on one of Georgia's coastal islands long to be back in Africa; appropriate for the Black History Month theme (Coretta Scott King Illustrator Award).

Willey, Margaret. (2002). *Clever Beatrice*. Illustrated by Heather Solomon. This French-Canadian tale features a poor girl who outwits a giant (ALA Notable).

Woodson, Jacqueline. (2002). *The Other Side*. Illustrated by E. B. Lewis. Two girls challenge the notion that sides must be drawn between black and white (ALA Notable).

Activities

The following activities are appropriate for the Library Center.

Books I Have Read. Photocopy the following information onto plain paper and staple together several sheets for each child. Finish the reading log by attaching a plain-paper or construction-paper cover with staples, rings, or yarn. Have children decorate their covers and write their names on the front.

For beginning readers, use this format:

BOOKS I HAVE READ

Title: _____

Date read: _____

One teacher who uses reading logs with beginning readers suggests that teachers draw three faces in the reading log—a smiley face, a frowning face, and a straight face. After the child reads the book, she circles the one that expresses how she felt about it. Construct a class graph of the results.

For independent readers, use this format:

BOOKS I HAVE READ

Title: _____

Author: _____

Date finished: _____

What I think about the book: _____

_____

Book Talks. The child chooses a book, reads it, and prepares to talk about it to the whole class or a small group. Here is what the child should discuss:

- Title, author, illustrator, publisher
- The character or characters (explaining why he is talking about this particular one or ones)
- What he enjoyed about the book and what he didn't enjoy
- Why he would choose to read another book by this author

Overhead Projector Activity. Use blank transparencies to create overheads of stories and songs from charts from the Teacher Center. Pairs of children can practice reading them using the overhead projector.

Thematic Activities

For any theme, have books that match the theme available at the center. Some activities are as follows:

- Let beginning readers read independently; they benefit from reading to themselves out loud so they can hear what they read (Bergeron and Bradbury-Wolff, 2003).
- Pair children who are on the same reading level or on different levels (so they can help each other) for partner reading (Bergeron and Bradbury-Wolff, 2002).
- Allow children to check out thematic books to share with someone at home.

- Allow them to choose a thematic book to share with a friend.
- Let them choose a thematic book for a book talk or a book discussion at the Teacher Center.
- Have them read a thematic big book or a story chart from the Teacher Center; this activity is fun to do with a reading buddy or in a small group.
- Have them read thematic poetry, comics, environmental print.
- Have children conduct research that fits the theme.

Here are some Teacher Center activities for the themes detailed in Section Four:

- *School Days:* Read newspaper and magazine ads featuring back-to-school clothing and school supplies.
- *Pumpkin Patch:* Read fall seed catalogues and pumpkin recipe cookbooks assembled by classmates.
- *Native American Tepee:* Display totem poles created by the children for everyone to read. (See Section Four for directions.)
- *Winter Wonderland:* Read weather reports.
- *Spaceship:* Read reference materials appropriate for children that contain articles on space, planets, the stars; read science books with chapters on space.
- *Springtime:* Read spring seed catalogues.
- *Cinco de Mayo:* Read Spanish words that are featured in the Cinco de Mayo thematic unit in Section Four.
- *Lunar New Year:* Children read books about the Lunar New Year.
- *Restaurant:* Read food and nutrition books, cookbooks, menus, and magazines that feature food.
- *Roman Holiday:* Partners use a pointer to read Latin-English bulletin boards.
- *Valentine's Day and Dental Health Month:* Read valentine messages and dental health brochures.

THE LISTENING CENTER

Listening to someone read is a great way for children to develop vocabulary and concepts. In a listening center children experience regular auditory activities, which can increase their ability to listen effectively. Emergent readers gain information and learn to recall characters, events, main ideas, and details. Listening also builds background knowledge, increases vocabulary, and is a good way to introduce fine literature.

The center is easy to create because tape recorders, CD players, and headphones are available in most schools. With a multiple headphone jack, several children can listen to a story using one tape recorder. Be sure to place the Listening Center near an electrical outlet. The children can sit at a table or on floor cushions or an area rug. If your classroom lacks space for a Listening Center, tuck it into a corner of your Library Center and post two sets of signs—one set for the Library Center and one for the "listening corner" of the library.

Basic Equipment

Here is what you will need for the Listening Center:

- A table and student seating—chairs, stools, cushions, beanbag chairs, or simply an area rug or carpet squares
- An electrical outlet
- A tape recorder or several of them, a CD player or several of them (with multiple headphone jacks and headphones), a VCR or DVD player (optional)
- Red and green stickers to mark tape recorder buttons
- Books with matching audiotapes or CDs, both commercial sets and sets created by the teacher and students
- Recorded student-created books
- Videocassettes and VCR (and DVDs and player, optional)
- Teacher- and student-recorded language experience stories
- Plastic self-sealing bags and labels
- A clothesline, clothespins, and two large screw eyes
- A poster or sign that reads: "Listening Center"
- A poster or sign that reads: "Rewind your tape and put it away."
- Large index cards or pieces of paper on which to write assignments

Arrange the student seating near an electrical outlet. To help children remember which buttons to push to turn on the tape player, stick a green circle on the "forward" button and a red sticker on the "reverse" button. Plug the headphone jack and headphones into the tape player and set it on the table or other stable, accessible place. Make a clothesline—install the screw eyes, several feet apart, into a wooden molding or windowsill near the center. Thread the clothesline through both screw eyes and tie a knot around each screw eye. Label each bag with the name of a story. Place each matching set— book and tape or CD—into an individual plastic bag. Seal the bags and hang them on the clothesline with clothespins. Post signs and student assignments.

Acquiring Materials

You can acquire audio materials for the Listening Center as follows:

- Purchase books with matching tapes from catalogues or bookstores.
- Purchase tapes of favorite songs (with words), or record the class singing and choral reading sessions. Make books to match the recordings.

- Have children record books that they have written, or record a book together with a child by reading along with her. While recording, discuss the story and praise the student. Use a clothesline (see the following activities) to store each book and tape for all students to enjoy.

- Make tapes of big books and charts created at the Teacher Center. Also make small versions of those big books and song charts. Provide a matching tape for each.

- Borrow books with matching audiotapes from your school media center.

- Create audiotapes of favorite books or stories from basal readers.

Recommended Audiobooks

Here is a small sampling of the many wonderful books that include accompanying CDs or audiotapes.

Audiobooks

Burton, Virginia Lee. (1943). *Katy and the Big Snow*. Katy, a tractor, pushes a bulldozer in the summer and a snowplow in the winter so that townspeople can do their jobs.

Burton, Virginia Lee. (1939). *Mike Mulligan and His Steam Shovel*. Mike Mulligan proves that his outdated steam shovel is still useful.

Fleming, Candace. (2003). *Muncha! Muncha! Muncha!* Illustrated by G. Brian Karas. Three bunnies outsmart Mr. McGreely and eat the vegetables from his garden. A funny predictable read-aloud (ALA Notable).

Freeman, Don. (1968). *Corduroy*. A stuffed bear waiting hopefully in a toy department finds a home with a little girl.

Gerstein, Mordicai. (2003). *What Charlie Heard*. This biography of composer Charles Ives shows how he took everyday sounds and made a new kind of music (ALA Notable).

Keats, Ezra Jack. (1962). *The Snowy Day*. The story of a boy who wakes up to discover that snow has fallen during the night (Caldecott Medal).

Lobel, Arthur. (2003). *Frog and Toad Audio Collection*. Four easy-to-read stories for young children—includes *Frog and Toad All Year*, *Frog and Toad Are Friends*, *Days with Frog and Toad*, and *Frog and Toad Together*.

Lobel, Arthur. (2003). *Mouse Soup*. A mouse devises a clever and entertaining way to distract Weasel from making mouse soup.

McCloskey, Robert. (1949). *Blueberries for Sal*. This is the story of a little girl and a baby bear who hunt for blueberries with their mothers (Caldecott Honor Book).

McCloskey, Robert. (1941). *Make Way for Ducklings*. Mr. and Mrs. Mallard try to find the perfect spot for their ducklings (Caldecott Medal).

Piper, Watty. (1978). *The Little Engine That Could*. Little Blue Engine tries to pull a stranded train full of toys and good food over the mountain.

Simont, Marc. (2002). *The Stray Dog*. A surprise encounter turns into a family love affair in this delightful story (Caldecott Honor Book).

Sendak, Maurice. (1964). *Where the Wild Things Are*. Max puts on his wolf suit and imagines a land filled with lovable monsters (Caldecott Medal).

Thomas, Shelley Moore. (2003). *Get Well, Good Knight*. Illustrated by Jennifer Plecas. A good knight cares for three sick dragons. This is an easy reader with lots of repetition (ALA Notable).

Rosen, Michael. (2004). *We're Going on a Bear Hunt: Listen and Join In!* Illustrated by Helen Oxenbury. The book is the old camp chant: We can't go over it. / We can't go under it. / Oh, no! / We've got to go through it!

Slobodkina, Esphyr. (1938). *Caps for Sale*. This is an easy-to-read story about a peddler and a band of mischievous monkeys.

Activities

Here are some enjoyable Listening Center activities.

1-2-3 Listening. You will need self-sealing bags, an audiotaped story, and index cards with a word or sentence written on them describing each important story event. Decorate the self-sealing bags. In each bag put an audiotaped story and cards. The child listens to the story and arranges the cards (events) in proper sequence.

Record and Listen. Children need a tape recorder, a blank tape, and a book that they can read (or "pretend-read"). They record themselves reading the book, and then play back the tape and listen.

Compare-Contrast. Children need a book, a matching video, and a VCR. After viewing the video of a book, children compare and contrast the video and the book. They can do this individually or in a group.

Character Study. Children choose a story they wish to listen to. Provide the following directions to children who can read; explain the directions to emergent readers.

1. Listen to the story. Decide which character you want to draw.

2. Visit the Art Center and draw a picture of the character. (Or make a puppet, paint, finger paint, and so on.)

Thematic Activities

Activities appropriate for all kinds of themes include these:

- Children listen to a recorded book while reading the book.
- While listening, children imagine a story setting; later, they reproduce it at the Art Center.
- Children listen to a story and retell it at the Teacher Center.
- Children use wordless books to tell and record a story for others to hear.
- Children record their own writing to share with others at the Listening Center.

Here are some specific-theme activities:

- *School Days:* Listen to tapes of the alma mater and school songs.
- *Pumpkin Patch:* Record favorite stories about the fall season.
- *Native American Tepee:* Children record their own tapes to go with the totem pole stories they've created.
- *Winter Wonderland:* Listen to songs and stories about winter.
- *Spaceship:* Listen to tapes and read-alouds, and watch videos about outer space.
- *Springtime:* Listen to springtime songs and poems.
- *Cinco de Mayo:* Children record and listen to Spanish words that are featured in the Cinco de Mayo theme in Section Four.
- *Lunar New Year:* Record the class as they conduct a noisy lion dance or dragon parade. Keep the recording at the Listening Center.
- *Restaurant:* Record and listen to restaurant commercials. Have students record themselves reading menus of their favorite foods.
- *Roman Holiday:* Record the class as they play "Simon Says" using the Latin names for the body parts. Keep the recording at the Listening Center.
- *Valentine's Day and Dental Health Month:* Record valentine messages and the dental health song written at the Teacher Center.

THE COMPUTER CENTER

If you really want to turn children on to learning, create a Computer Center. The computer is a powerful learning tool because it provides self-paced, active, hands-on learning. Children are highly motivated by computer graphics, sound effects, and formats, and they use multiple senses—thinking, reading, listening, writing, and touching—as they learn. "Talking books" now feature on-screen book pages that allow children to select words, phrases, or entire pages for the computer to read aloud. Storybook software features both electronic and hard copies of the story. To gain fluency, children can read the story online, then practice-read it with the printed material. Modern word-processing software encourages writing because, for some, using the keyboard to write and edit is easier than using paper and pencil. Even kindergarten children can learn sufficient keyboarding skills to publish their own writing.

If you decide to create a Computer Center, you'll need to find good software. Build a collection of computer activities for literature, phonics and word analysis, vocabulary, comprehension, and word processing. Software that produces stationery and greeting cards is also quite useful.

Children will be able to use the computer more often if they work with partners or in small groups. Post a list of partners and set a timer. When one pair finishes, they quietly signal the next pair on the list. Students waiting to use the computer can read, work with puzzles or games, or work at another center.

If your school has a computer lab, use it as an off-site Computer Center. Arrange to rotate small groups of students on a regular basis for computer reading activities. Work with the person in charge to choose a balance of activities that include phonics and word analysis, vocabulary, and comprehension.

Basic Equipment

You will need this equipment to set up the center:

- Student seating—chairs for each computer
- An electrical outlet
- One or more computers with power strips
- Tables to hold computers
- Earphones
- A printer or printers

You will also need these materials:

- Software and software storage boxes
- A timer
- Printer paper
- A poster or sign that reads: "Computer Center"
- A chart to list names of partners
- A poster or sign with student directions: "When you finish, signal the next person" (or next set of partners)
- An assignment poster

Place the table near the electrical outlet. Arrange the computers, software storage boxes, timers, earphones, and printers on the tables. Provide chairs for each computer. Load paper into the printer following the instructions provided. Post signs, partner lists, and assignments.

Acquiring Materials

Here are some good ideas to get you started:

- Borrow software from the school media center.
- Check the school district's technology department to see if free or low-cost software is available. Some school districts have purchased software site licenses; find out if your district provides this resource.

- Use software available with basal readers.
- See the following descriptions for a limited list of software to get you started.

Recommended Software

Although software companies and products change, these programs and Web sites were current at the time of this book's publication.

Stories and Books

The Internet Public Library Youth Division features many educational activities to see and do, including online stories and books. For more information, visit http://ipl.org/youth.

Living Books offers online access to a wealth of educational books and activities. Inexpensive one-year memberships are available. Story titles include *Just Grandma and Me* and *Arthur's Teacher Troubles.* As a story is presented, each word is voiced and highlighted. Some books are interactive puzzles. Visit Living Books at http://Livingbooks.com.

The online version of *The Cat in the Hat* provides simple games and activities. Users arrange a puzzle, shoot baskets, create funny faces on a framed picture, and draw on a mini-whiteboard. They join Thing One and Thing Two playmates in chase and counting games. Each activity increases familiarity with the computer, and some also strengthen spatial and causal relationships. *The Cat in the Hat* includes the complete illustrated print version of the book, so users can practice their reading skills offline. ALA Notable Software; available at http://www.broderbund.com.

How the Leopard Got His Spots is a narrated and illustrated version of Rudyard Kipling's classic story. Appropriate for ages six and up. ALA Notable Software; available at http://www.microsoft.com.

Edmark's Stories & More features award-winning children's books with engaging multistep activities that teach comprehension, interpretation, evaluation, and literature appreciation. Each title is sold separately. Contact http://www.riverdeep.net/edmark.

Antelope Publishers features browser-readable children's books on CD-ROM; visit http//www.antelope-ebooks.com/JUVENILE/.

WiggleWorks books and software provide instruction in five key areas of No Child Left Behind and Reading First: phonemic awareness, phonics, fluency, vocabulary, and comprehension. WiggleWorks helps teachers scaffold instruction and move students toward reading independence. Visit http://www.scholastic.com/wiggleworks.

Skills

Reader Rabbit is available from the Learning Company. Numerous Reader Rabbit products address literacy skills—the alphabet, phonics, structural analysis, and so on. The products are sold in stores and on a number of Internet sites. Contact the Learning Company at (800) 852-2255.

Dr. Seuss Kindergarten is produced by Broderbund Software for children ages four to six. Follow Gerald McGrew as he collects different animals for his zoo through 250 activities that teach phonics, measurement, and other math and language skills. Children can listen to over fifty Dr. Seuss characters such as Sneeches and Barbaloots, who talk to them in rhyme as the activities are introduced. Graphically interesting games make for an enjoyable and educational experience. Visit http://www.broderbund.com.

Dr. Seuss Preschool, also from Broderbund, is also for ages four to six. Horton, Yertle, and other Dr. Seuss characters lead children through interactive games that teach letter recognition, counting, and other essential prereading skills. Smooth integration of animation and sound makes for a seamless presentation that only enhances the concepts presented. This engaging software will delight and educate children. Visit http://www.broderbund.com.

Word Processing

Kidspiration 2, created by Inspiration Software Inc., is for K–5 learners. It provides an easy way to apply the proven principles of visual learning. Students build graphic organizers by combining pictures, text, and spoken words to represent thoughts and information. It also includes seventy-five ready-made activities, a Venn diagram option, and a one-click transfer to word processors. Contact Inspiration Software at webmaster@inspiration.com or (800) 877-4292.

PixWriter, by Slater Software Inc., is a program for beginning writers. When the child selects a button, the word and picture appear, and the computer speaks. The program features over three thousand color pictures and has the ability to import photos and other clip art. Contact Slater Software at (877) 306-6968.

Keyboarding

Type to Learn Jr. was created by Sunburst Communications for grades one to three. Children progress from keyboarding awareness to beginning typing. It has three activity areas that teach using the keyboard keys to complete the text displayed, typing numbers, and typing short sentences with punctuation. Students also learn how to type Internet and e-mail addresses. Contact Sunburst Communications at http://www.Sunburst.com.

UltraKey, by Bytes of Learning, Inc., is a typing program for all ages. UltraKey is clear and straightforward, directly instructs students in the art of typing, provides them with regular and meaningful feedback, and lets teachers adjust the program to suit students' needs. It features multimedia and voice-accompanied instruction, coupled with a friendly and comprehensive learning management system. Contact Bytes of Learning at http://www.bytesoflearning.com.

In *Garfield's Typing Pal,* Garfield the Cat teaches the basics of typing. Exercises increase in difficulty as children become more skilled at keyboarding. Games such as *Cookie Catch* and *Cosmik Ball* improve skills and encourage children to continue playing. ALA Notable Software for grades two and up; available at http://www.demarque.com.

Art

In *Disney Magic Artist Deluxe,* the computer screen becomes the canvas. With icons of many artists' tools and a palette of thousands of colors, this program provides hours of drawing fun. ALA Notable Software; available at http://disneyinteractive.com.

Software for Special-Needs Students

The Don Johnston Company is a leader in products for students with reading and writing difficulties. Literacy options for primary ages include the UKanDu Interactive Reading Series, UKanDu Little Books, UKanDu Switches, Too!, and Write:Outloud, a talking word processor for ages six and up, which helps children self-correct as they write. Visit http://www.donjohnston.com.

Teachers' Institute for Special Education custom-designs unique keyboarding software and typing books for the physically handicapped, learning disabled, dyslexic, and bilingual student. In its Keyboarding for Individual Achievement series, each software program and typing book is a complete course. Visit http://www.special-education-soft.com.

Words Their Way, an Alpha-Smart product, features word study for phonics, vocabulary, and spelling instruction. Visit http://alphasmart.com.

Thematic Activities

Activities appropriate for all kinds of themes include these:

- Use word-processing software to write thematic stories or reports.
- Use stationery and greeting card software to create theme-related items.

Use the computer to accomplish the following specific-theme activities:

- *School Days:* Write back-to-school stories.
- *Pumpkin Patch:* Create colorful greeting cards.
- *Native American Tepee:* Write totem pole stories. (See Section Four.)
- *Winter Wonderland:* Create winter greeting cards.
- *Black History Month:* Write a story about a favorite African-American "hero" or "shero."

- *Spaceship:* Write outer-space stories.
- *Springtime:* Create Earth Day posters.
- *Cinco de Mayo:* Write with some Spanish words that are featured in the Cinco de Mayo theme of Section Four.
- *Lunar New Year:* Use greeting card software to create Lunar New Year good-luck messages.
- *Restaurant:* Create menus using the word processor.
- *Roman Holiday:* Write the Latin words for the body parts, days of the week, and so on.
- *Valentine's Day and Dental Health Month:* Use greeting card software to make valentines. Create a paragraph telling three reasons for eating healthy snacks.

THE ART CENTER

At the Art Center, children respond to reading by creating visual expressions of their ideas and feelings about what they have read. Making art requires visualizing, thinking, and planning and allows children to experiment as they learn. Art can tie directly into what the children are reading and learning, but children can also engage in art simply for the purpose of enjoying, creating, and learning new art techniques.

Art should be part of any primary language program—it can be the initial component in oral language expression. In *Language Experience Activities* (1982), authors Roach Van Allen and Claryce Allen say: "Ideas that are difficult if not impossible for many children to grasp from reading are available in the paintings, sculpture, and crafts of artists. These ideas, once spoken, are basic to the further development of writing and reading" (pp. 196–197). The authors explain that the Art Center is a place for:

- Self-expression through multiple media
- Communicating in realistic and abstract forms
- Illustrating poems, stories, and books
- Viewing and reviewing communication processes used by many artists

Basic Equipment

You will need the following:

- Student seating
- Storage shelves
- A poster or sign that reads: "Art Center"
- A list of students; students check off their names after they have used the easel
- A poster or sign with student directions: "When you finish, put your materials away."
- Student assignments (to be posted near the center)

You will also need:

- Art supplies—many materials for exploration and expression: paper of all sizes and types, crayons, markers, colored chalk, paints, brushes, finger paint, scissors, glue, paste, hole punch, magazine or catalogue pictures, wallpaper scraps, and so on
- Clay and playdough compound for modeling
- Blocks and construction materials
- Pieces of lace, yarn, felt, buttons, cloth, and glitter for decorating
- Easel (optional)
- Newspapers or plastic sheets (for covering tables or floor)
- Cans or jars for mixing paint or soaking brushes
- Small jars or muffin pans at easel for holding paint; larger containers of water for washing brushes while painting
- Painting smock (an adult shirt turned backwards, for example)

If your room has a sink, arrange the Art Center near it. Place the easel near the student work area; hang the smock on it. While one child uses the easel, a small group can work at a table or on the floor near it. Put half-filled paint jars in the easel holders and provide a brush for each color of paint. Fill and store labeled boxes on the shelves. You may wish to keep art materials in your storage closet and bring out only those materials needed for an activity. Post signs, assignments, and check-off sheet.

Making Modeling Compound*

This playdough will stay soft for several weeks. You need:

Food coloring

One cup water

One cup salt

Two cups flour

Two tablespoons alum

Two tablespoons salad oil

Add color to water. Then mix all ingredients together until smooth.

Activities

Here are a few Art Center activities.

Illustrations for Books and Poetry. Illustrations for publishing manuscripts can be as creative as you wish—sponge paintings, string paintings, crayon rubbings, and so on. For example:

Read *The Cherry Tree* by Daisaku Ikeda.

- Children use chalk or crayons to create a background—sky and grass.
- Then they paint on a tree trunk, or cut one out of a pattern or design, and glue it onto the page.
- They create blossoms by dipping fingers into paint and "dabbing" it onto the branches. This is pretty, fun, and creative!

Read *Caps for Sale* by Esphyr Slobodkina.

- Children draw trees and cut out a traced or a hand-drawn monkey.
- They select a picture from an assortment of magazine pictures.
- The monkey, which is holding the magazine picture, is pasted onto the branches.

Note: Modeling compound recipe courtesy of Linda Fisher.

- The next part of the illustration is completed at the Writing Center. At the bottom of the page the child writes or fills in the blank of this sentence:

Monkey monkey in a tree,

Don't you throw your ___[picture name]___ at me.

- The teacher binds all pages into a class book that the children read together.

Read the poem *Five Little Pumpkins Sitting on a Gate*. Provide a variety of craft supplies—paint, crayons, yarn, glue, lace, glitter—and allow children to illustrate the poem the way they wish. (This is a good activity for the Pumpkin Patch theme.)

Story Extensions for Big Books and Read-Alouds.
Read *Brown Bear, Brown Bear, What Do You See?* by Bill Martin Jr., illustrated by Eric Carle. Have children create their own page in a book entitled *Children, Children, What Do You See?*

- At the Art Center, each child decorates a page by gluing colored tissue paper squares around the page border.
- Children bring in photos of themselves. Each child glues the photo to the center of a page and writes his or her name on the page. Bind the class book and read it together. Refrain: "I see [child's name] looking at me!"

Read *Have You Seen My Cat?* by Eric Carle. At the Art Center, each child completes a tissue-paper collage of a predrawn cat—either a cat pattern or a cat drawn by the child.

Read *Smarty Pants* by Joy Cowley.

- At the Art Center, each child creates a page by drawing a picture of something he or she is good at doing.
- At the Writing Center, the child dictates or writes the answer consistent with the wording of the book. Bind the class book and read it together.

Words We Know.
The teacher writes a short paragraph on a piece of paper using familiar words—spelling, color, and number words, and words from the Word Wall (see page 78). The children read the sentences and illustrate the paragraph.

Alphabet Art. Children make alphabet letters in the following ways:

- Use cookie dough and bake the letters in a toaster oven.
- Form alphabet letters (especially those in the children's names) with playdough.
- Create letters from felt.
- Use clay to make letters.
- Write the alphabet using finger paint.

Farm Animal Book. Create a group of printed cards—each with the name of a different farm animal—and put the cards in a basket. Provide stencils for tracing the farm animals and pictures as examples for children who wish to draw their own animal.

- Each child draws or uses a stencil to trace an animal on drawing paper and writes the name of the animal at the bottom of the page. The printed word cards will help those who need help writing the words.
- Each time the children visit the Art Center, they make a new page (with a new animal). It will take them several days to do this.
- Create a farm animal book for each child by stapling the child's completed pages together.

Seasonal Patterns. Provide two baskets—one basket with die-cut apples (or any seasonal pattern) in four colors and one basket with letter patterns printed on index cards. Examples: AAB, ABC, ABBCD. The patterns' complexity should depend on the age and ability of the children.

- Each child chooses an index card and die-cut patterns that will match the letter pattern on the index card. Examples: AAB: red red yellow; ABC: yellow red green; ABBCD: green red red yellow pink. (It makes no difference what colors they choose, as long as the colors are arranged in the same pattern as the letters.)
- Children write one letter on each die-cut pattern and glue the die cuts onto a paper in the order of the letter pattern.

Seasonal Sewing. This activity is appropriate for any season and any theme. It works well with any simple drawing—pumpkin, heart, egg, and so on.

- For each child, cut a pumpkin from heavy material such as oak tag, construction paper, or wallpaper. With a hole punch, make holes evenly around the edge of the pumpkin.
- Children use twine, ribbon, or yarn to lace or sew through the holes. When the child has finished, tie the yarn into a knot.

Me, Myself, and I: Self-Portraits. Provide oak-tag cutout figures, about two feet high, one boy and two girls—one girl with long hair and one with short hair. In a whole-class activity, discuss skin tones and have children decide what skin tone fits them. Show the colors that will be available to paint the skin.

- At the first painting session, children choose an oak-tag figure (one that resembles them) and paint their skin-tone color on the face, arms, and legs.

- At the second session they use a mirror to check the color of their eyes and hair. They finish the self-portrait by designing and painting on their clothing—perhaps a favorite outfit.

- When the paint has dried, children write their name on a sentence strip or card. They also write (or dictate) the end of this statement: "This is what I like about myself: _____."

- Staple names and sentences to each finished self-portrait. Display, and enjoy.

Thumbprint Art. For each child, divide a piece of art paper into four equal parts; fold or draw. Provide an ink pad (stamp pad) for making thumbprints and thin (fine-point) markers for drawing.

- Have children choose and write a theme word in each section. For instance, for the Pumpkin Patch theme, the words could be *pumpkin, clown, scarecrow, face painting.* You can do this by having a basket of words from which to choose, or allowing the children to write the words themselves—standard or invented spelling.

- The child presses a thumb onto the ink pad and makes a thumbprint in each section.

- The thumbprint becomes part of the picture and the markers are used to embellish it by drawing arms, legs, faces, and so on.

Fall Leaf Creatures. Read a book about leaves to the class. Then let each child select a die-cut or real fall leaf and use art materials to create a creature from the leaf. Hold a class meeting during which each child answers the question: "What did your creature do when he or she fell from the tree?"

Fall Trees. This project uses the brown paper towels commonly found in school sink dispensers.

- Children trace or draw a tree trunk and limbs onto a brown paper towel.

- They cut the tree out and glue it onto sky-blue construction paper.

- The teacher provides paint in fall colors. The children sponge-paint the leaves with small, odd-shaped (rectangle, square, and so on) pieces of sponge.

- At the bottom of the picture children complete this sentence using standard or invented spelling: "My tree is _____."

Thanksgiving Home-School Connection.
Trace the profile of a turkey on tagboard for each child.

- Attach a letter to the tagboard stating: "This is a family project." List suggestions for various types of materials that may be used to decorate the turkey. Do not allow food items to be used. Children decorate the tagboard turkeys at home with their families.

- On a set date, children bring back the completed turkeys to display in the classroom.

Quill Writing.
Provide long feathers and black ink.

- Show children how to dip the quill into the ink for writing.

- On a piece of paper, have children write words or sentences, alphabet letters, numbers, or their names.

Tinsmith Art.
For each child, glue a five-inch by seven-inch piece of heavy-duty aluminum foil onto a piece of construction paper. Provide an opened paper clip to act as a design instrument. The child takes the open, pointed end of the paper clip and draws a design (or traces a pattern) on the foil.

Native American Clothing—Boys' Vests and Girls' Dresses.
Each child brings in a white or beige pillowcase; old pillowcases are fine. The teacher dyes the pillowcases brown and cuts each one into the shape of a vest or dress. The children decorate (sponge paint) their garments using Indian designs such as the ones in the November tepee theme.

Dyed pillowcases can also be made into cowboy vests using sponge-painted western designs. If you plan to do both projects, have each child bring two pillowcases and dye them all at the same time.

Winter Celebrations.
Discuss winter customs and celebrations—Christmas, Kwanza, Hanukkah. Talk about how Christmas and Hanukka are celebrated here and in other countries and how Kwanza is celebrated in America alone.

- Read books about the various celebrations.

- Children can use their journals for writing about the celebrations. If they are learning about the celebrations in other countries, they can write about and illustrate one idea for each country.

- Children illustrate their idea on a (pretraced) tagboard Christmas, Kwanza, and Hanukkah symbol.
- Read aloud several books on winter celebrations and discuss this question: "What makes the celebration special for me?"
- Children dictate or write their answers to this question.
- Children illustrate what they wrote or dictated.

Santa's Workshop. This is a fun way to make a Christmas list. Make a booklet for each child by stapling together four to five pieces of art paper. Provide seasonal toy advertisements and paste. Children cut out pictures of toys they want for Christmas, paste one picture per page, and on each page, complete this sentence:

Santa's little elf is making _____.

Classroom Giant. On a long piece of wrapping paper, trace the outline of a seven- to eight-foot giant and hang it on a wall for the children to see. During classroom morning meeting time, the children vote on the following:

- Whether it is a girl or boy giant
- The color of the giant's clothes
- Whether it should have hair or no hair, hair type and color
- What its facial expression should be

Lay the giant on the floor or on one or two tables pushed together. In small groups, the children paint the giant, based on colors and features chosen by the class. You might want to have them use different techniques, such as sponge painting or finger painting. When the painting is complete, the class decides on a name and lists how they would describe the giant. Hang for all to enjoy.

Painting Michelangelo-Style. In this activity, children experience what it would have been like to paint the ceiling of the Sistine Chapel as Michelangelo did—lying on his back! You will need a desk (or table), a small carpet square, a smock (buttoned in the back), and several different sizes of brushes and colors of paint.

- Tape a piece of easel paper to the underside of the desk or table.
- Children work in pairs to assist each other. First they button on the smocks. Then, one at a time, they lie on the carpet squares (on their backs) to paint—words or pictures.
- The paint, brushes, and assisting student should all be close by on the floor beside the painter. The assistant can help when necessary.
- Instruct children to wipe brushes to avoid drips and to keep their mouths closed in the process!

Thematic Activities

Activities appropriate for all kinds of themes include these:

- Illustrate big books and little books and LEA stories.
- Make and decorate covers for books written by students.
- Create puppets to illustrate writing, act out stories, or represent favorite characters.
- Build story settings in shoeboxes.
- Create a mural.
- Assemble and decorate class telephone directories, recipe books, and so on.
- Create and illustrate books about the classroom theme.
- Illustrate music and poetry.
- Create book jackets for favorite books. Include the names of the author, illustrator, and publisher.
- Illustrate greeting cards from the Writing Center—holiday, get-well, thank-you, birthday, special occasion.
- Make collages—glue pictures from catalogues and magazines.
- Illustrate words and word parts—initial sounds, rhyming words, consonant blends, opposites, and so on.
- Use playdough or modeling clay to create letters, words, characters, settings, and so on.
- Make mobiles—create characters, settings, or story events, and fasten with a piece of string to a coat hanger.

Here are some specific-theme activities:

- *School Days:* Decorate portfolios for storing work, create collages using newspaper ads for back-to-school clothing, decorate journal covers.
- *Pumpkin Patch:* Design covers for pumpkin recipe books; make pumpkins from playdough, clay, paper, or fabric; or make scarecrow puppets using ice cream sticks, fabric, and yarn.
- *Native American Tepee:* Make up totem pole stories. Create Native American necklaces from dyed macaroni. (See Section Four.)
- *Winter Wonderland:* Create playdough snowmen, paper snowflakes, and snowstorm jars.
- *Black History Month:* Create African masks.
- *Spaceship:* Create a class mural of the solar system. Use butcher paper or cloth and colored markers. Conduct research and construct a model of the solar system.

- *Springtime:* Create Earth Day posters.
- *Cinco de Mayo:* Create a Mexican flag.
- *Lunar New Year:* Make good-luck signs.
- *Restaurant:* Decorate menus, placemats, and recipe books. Make mobiles of favorite foods—make foods from playdough and hang on a coat hanger with yarn.
- *Roman Holiday:* Illustrate animal books, including the animals' names in both Latin and English.
- *Valentine's Day and Dental Health Month:* Make room decorations, valentines, and dental health posters.

THE WRITING CENTER

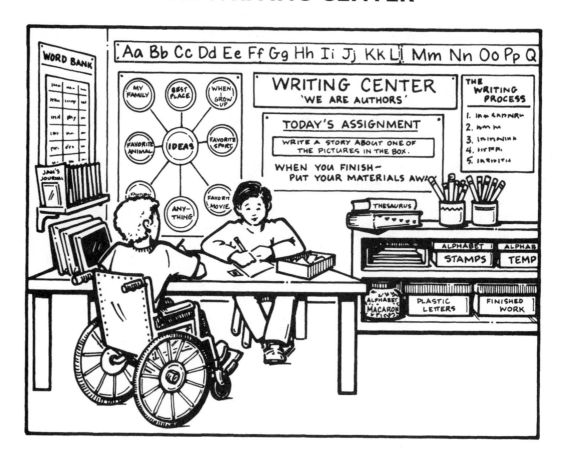

The Writing Center provides children with opportunities to create their own writings, to read what they have written, and to read what their classmates have written. At the Writing Center children engage in individual or partner writing, peer editing, shared reading, and book publishing. Partners may have the same or differing abilities. The grouping should be flexible and depend on the task at hand.

Children should write every day because writing and reading are learned together. Writing reinforces reading because a good writing program increases the amount of time that children spend with text—in fact, through writing, they learn the purpose of text (to be understood), that written language is different from spoken language, and that writing is used for many purposes: lists, labels, stories, newspapers, greeting cards (Soderman, Gregory, and O'Neill, 1999). And children can begin writing long before they learn all their letters. In fact, many start the process as toddlers—as soon as they can hold a pencil they begin writing. So there is no prescribed set of skills they need to begin the writing process.

Writing can be creative (journal writing, publishing books, and writing poetry) or practical (writing letters, writing reports, or making lists). It develops much like reading and speaking—through maturity, experience, and practice. Children usually enjoy writing if they feel their writing is valued, if they are given time to write, and if they are in an encouraging setting.

Awareness of writing begins early in life. Marie Clay (1975) found that three- to five-year-old children in literate societies are aware that people write passages on paper for a purpose. Some children have many experiences writing at home—notes to grandparents, messages to parents, grocery lists, greeting cards—they spell some words correctly and create ways to spell others. In fact, many begin to write before they begin to read. Children who haven't had opportunities to write may be at the very early stages of writing—scribbling, writing strings of letters, play letters, and so on (Schickendanz, 1999). Let them begin where they are; given a chance, they can become writers too.

Encourage all children to write what they can say, which means accepting invented spelling and less-than-perfect sentence structure—both are experimental and neither is in conflict with teaching standard spelling and sentence structure. (A Word Wall placed close to the Writing Center encourages good word use and conventional spelling.) The goal is to get children to experiment with writing because the more they write, the more accomplished they become at both reading and writing.

Frank Smith (1982) refers to children having membership in a club of writers. The teacher makes sure that everyone can join the club and can see the advantage of being in the club. Most researchers agree that simply grading a child's writing doesn't teach a child anything except that he or she is or is not a club member! Emphasis on mistakes usually results in less writing. What writers really need is the teacher's response, not a grade. For this reason, assessment at the primary level should be informal. For further information on informal assessment, see Miller (2000).

Each child needs a portfolio for keeping writing samples. One of the ways to assess growth in writing is to look at a child's writing over time. Can you see changes that indicate growth? Is the child's invented spelling phonetic? Are common classroom words or thematic words being used? Is it evident that the child is using the Word Wall, a word bank, game words, or classroom labels? Because it's important to talk to children about their writing, hold a periodic conference with each child to look at work in the portfolio and to give helpful feedback. Make sure that you celebrate progress!

Basic Equipment

You will need the following equipment to set up a Writing Center:

- Student seating—a table and chairs or a cluster of desks with chairs
- Storage for supplies
- A place to display student writing

In addition, you'll need these materials:

- Lined and unlined paper, pencils, pens, markers, crayons
- Materials for publishing books—construction paper, scissors, hole punch, brads, stapler and staples, yarn
- Manipulatives for letter formation—plastic and macaroni letters, letter stamps and ink pads, templates for tracing letters
- Material for making classroom labels and signs
- Stationery and envelopes for letter writing
- Posted alphabet, uppercase and lowercase
- Slates, magazines, and catalogues
- A Word Wall with list of high-frequency and descriptive words
- Dictionaries, picture dictionaries, and beginning thesauruses
- Boxes or folders for finished and unfinished work
- A poster or sign that reads: "Writing Center"
- A poster or sign with student directions: "When you finish, put your materials away."
- Student assignments (posted)

Place the student seating near the Word Wall. Arrange paper, slates, dictionaries, manipulatives, and jars of writing tools nearby. Put folders or boxes for finished and unfinished work on the table. Post student assignments and signs.

The Word Wall

The Word Wall is a large "wall dictionary" that displays words most often used in the reading and writing activities of a particular classroom. Words are taken from whatever the children are reading: literature, basal readers, language experience charts, trade books, or classroom labels. The wall provides a resource for reinforcing both newly acquired *and* high-frequency words. It also helps children become aware of the conventional spelling of each word. The Word Wall can display word patterns, such as rhyming words, on a separate chart.

Systematically practice and review words—with the whole class or in small groups—by using a pointer or yardstick to point to words as children read them. Let them take turns pointing to the words as the group reads each word. Practice helps children get used to using the Word Wall, and, of course, helps them learn the words. Model strategies for using the words in various genres and across content areas (Miller, 2000).

Children can use the Word Wall when they are at the Writing Center. As you add new words, make connections between each word, its meaning, and ways it may be used in writing. Praise children when they demonstrate correct word usage and spelling in their writing.

You may wish to set up two Word Walls—one with frequently used words and one with thematic words from board, card, sorting, and matching games (see Section Five).

Here's how to make the Word Wall:

- Print pairs of letters—capital and lowercase—on index cards. Display the letters in alphabetical order in left-to-right progression (see the illustration on page 80).

- Cut cards from light-colored paper or use index cards. Using a wide (thick-tip) marker and writing in large, bold letters, write one word on each card. Be sure the word is readable from all the learning centers in the room. Attach each word under the matching letter pair.

- Use words from high-frequency lists, LEA stories, basal readers, trade books, and literature. Allow children to suggest words. Add only a few new words each week.

- Display words with patterns (like rhyming words) separately, perhaps on a separate chart.

- Illustrate some words if you wish.

Activities

Process Writing. Process writing is for fluent writers who are able to go through the steps to publish a book (Miller, 2000). This usually means children at an upper-primary level. Process writing isn't a onetime thing—it's an ability that develops in phases.

1. The *prewriting phase* (brainstorming), usually done in a group, is for dialoguing, imagining, clarifying ideas, and choosing a topic.

2. The first step in the *shaping phase* is getting the topic onto paper. The author writes a rough draft (known as "sloppy copy"), then reads the draft to fellow students (holds a conference) to see how it sounds. The group helps the author make improvements and correct mechanical errors.

Feedback in the group is to be affirming, not dogmatic. If a problem isn't solved in the group, the author has a conference with the teacher. Then the author writes a draft that incorporates improvements and corrections (Calkins, 1994; Schwartz, 1988).

3. In the *editing phase,* the document is checked to see if changes were made. The teacher and peer group serve as the child's audience.

4. The *publishing phase* gives the author motivation to write for an audience. The author illustrates the work, signs it, and shares it from the Author's Chair (see "Children's Presentations" on page 35). The presentation includes a group discussion of the work. The author can discuss these or other questions: What was it I liked best about writing this piece? What gave me the most trouble? How do I feel about this piece? What would I have done differently?

Writing Workshop. If you really want to turn your children on to writing, set aside time each day for a writing workshop. The writing workshop features daily writing on ongoing projects and everyone writes at the same time. The teacher can circulate and interact with the children or write while the children are writing. Children don't have an assignment, but rather write on a topic of their choice. When children finish a project, they begin another. During the workshop, children are at different phases of the writing process. Some are brainstorming while others are editing or publishing. Children are encouraged to write what they can say, even if they are still in the beginning stages of writing.

The daily workshop usually begins with a mini-lesson designed to inspire or to teach. Mini-lessons are appropriate for the whole class or for a small group of students. Sometimes mini-lessons are held so that children can talk about their writing or share a published work. In other mini-lessons the teacher takes the opportunity to teach a particular writing strategy. Lucy Calkins has written extensively about the writing workshop in *The Art of Teaching Writing* (1994); see Chapter Twelve in particular.

Journal Writing. Journal writing is appropriate for children at all stages of the writing process—in fact, keeping a daily journal helps children identify themselves as writers. Setting aside a consistent journal time, perhaps while the child is at the Writing Center, will assure that journal writing is a regular activity. A journal can be a notebook or a few sheets of paper stapled together. A plain white or construction-paper cover is easy to decorate.

Process writing requires conferencing with peers or the teacher until the text is perfected, published, and shared publicly from the Author's Chair. Journals may consist of personal thoughts, shared only if the child so chooses. Because material written in journals is private, perhaps shown only to a teacher or parent, children are free to experiment with new writing or illustration techniques. Some teachers have children share their journals from the Author's Chair, but this is not a must, especially if children wish to keep their journals private (and store them in a private place).

Morning Sign-In. Each morning when children arrive, have them sign in, using information that they are learning about themselves. At the first of each month, change the morning signature to reflect the newly learned information. For example, the children may provide first name only, first and last names, birth month and day, telephone number, address, and so on.

Word Wall Word Bank. You will need a box or a self-sealing bag for each child, to hold his or her own word bank, and cards with words marked or printed on them.

- Create a game by making a "Word Wall Word Bank" (a box of words from the Word Wall).
- Use the word bank for sentence-building activities (Hall, 1981).
- Have children work in pairs or small groups to read the cards to each other.

- Children make individual "Word Wall Word Banks" to take home and practice with a family member.
- Children find the two most interesting words in their banks and tell why the word is interesting to them (Hall, 1981).
- Children work with a buddy to read each other's words (Hall, 1981).

Word Wall Buddies. Children work as partners pointing to the words as they read them. To use this as an assessment tool, observe the partners and make a written notation of words each student knows. Use a separate checklist for each child and keep track of words mastered and those that still need practice.

Alphabet Books. Have emergent readers write and illustrate their own personal alphabet book. They can use their own illustrations, magazine pictures, stencils, and so on.

Class Storybook. In a class meeting, select a theme for a class storybook—perhaps one of the themes outlined in Section Four—and tell the children that every group will write a story about that theme and then the stories will be bound together into a book. Discuss the "question words"—who, what, when, where, how—and explain how question words are used in writing a story. Tell the children that these words will be used in writing the class storybook.

- Divide the class into groups, with five or six children per group. Each group brainstorms what their story is going to be about, then creates a story using the question words as guides. They can dictate the story to the teacher or write it down themselves.
- As a group dictates the story, the teacher writes one sentence on each page. If children are doing their own writing, they write one sentence per page—if there are five children in the group, the story will have five pages, each with one sentence on it. (If needed, help younger writers add connecting words or phrases so that the story will flow smoothly.)
- Each child in the group illustrates one page of the story. The group creates a title and the teacher helps the group collate the pages.
- The teacher assembles all the stories together with a title on the cover and a table of contents. It helps to have a title page for each story to keep the stories separated. Here is an example of one table of contents:

Winter Wonderland: Mr. Smith's Kindergarten Class

Chapter 1. Winter Weather

Chapter 2. Winter Clothes

Chapter 3. Winter Sports

Chapter 4. Winter Celebrations

Children love to read their class storybooks again and again. Share them with other classes and the school media center.

Mailbox. Use this for every classroom theme. A classroom mailbox is fun and it encourages children to write to each other. Furnish stationery and envelopes—or have children create greeting cards at the Art Center. Decorate the mailbox to match any theme—see two suggestions following. Furnish stationery, envelopes, and a stamp or ink pad for canceling the stamps. The game cards for Black History Month are postage stamps. Photocopy them at a reduced size and let children cut and paste them on (or use stickers as stamps). For the mailbox, you will need these materials:

- A cardboard box, about eighteen inches square
- Construction paper
- Tape and glue
- Scissors

Cut the flaps from the top of the box. Turn the box over. Cut a slit in what is now the top. Cover the cardboard by taping construction paper to the box, and then decorate the box to fit the theme. Here are two examples.

Valentine Mailbox

1. Show children how to make a heart by folding a square of paper and drawing half a heart shape. Remind them to draw the heart "out" from the fold.
2. Distribute squares of construction paper and lace doilies.
3. Have the children make and decorate hearts any size they wish.
4. When the hearts are finished, have children glue their hearts to the box.

Black History Month Mailbox

1. Photocopy the game cards for Black History Month (replicas of postage stamps; see Section Four) and let children color and cut them out.
2. Glue the game cards to the mailbox.

Seasonal Mailbags. Use these for every classroom theme.

- Let each child decorate a white paper bag (or a manila folder stapled along the sides) for the theme or season; use stickers or die-cut construction paper markers, and so on. Children write their first and last names on their bags.
- Children create greeting cards at the Writing Center and the Art Center.
- On the day that seasonal cards are exchanged, set the open bags (or folders) on a table or at each child's seat.

- Let children act as mail carriers to deliver the cards.
- If these bags are made for the springtime theme, children can use their bags to collect their eggs at an Easter egg hunt.

Classroom Mail. For each child, provide a manila folder, stapled along the sides. The child or teacher writes the first and last names plainly across the top of the folder. Display these in an easily accessible location—on a table, bookcase, bulletin board, and so on. Set up a classroom post office. Ask parents to send unwanted paper, note cards, envelopes, stickers, stamps, and so on. Write each child's name on an index card or sentence strip. Put the names in a basket or box.

- Each child selects a name, writes a letter or card, puts it into an envelope, addresses and stamps it, and delivers it to the appropriate child's mailbox (folder).
- After the name card is used, keep it in a special place until every child has received mail. Then the process begins again.

Class Diary. Create a class diary based on the growth of an amaryllis bulb, other bulbs, or sunflower seeds.

- Plant an amaryllis bulb and watch the daily growth.
- As the bulb grows the children write or dictate what they see. The diary can include words, photos, and drawings of the plant; each part of the plant should be labeled.
- When the diary is complete, read it together. Share it with others by placing it in the school media center.

Story Extensions for Big Books and Read-Alouds. Read several books on a specific holiday. At the Writing Center, children dictate or write (and illustrate) their answer to this question: "What makes this holiday special for me?" If you wish, use the pages to create a class book and let the group read it together.

Let children choose their favorite book and write another story with the same characters, a different plot, or a different ending.

Step-by-Step Elf or Leprechaun. In a whole-class lesson, demonstrate how to draw an elf or a leprechaun, step by step. All the children have paper, pencil, and crayons for the illustration, and they draw as you demonstrate.

- Begin with the head—draw a circle or oval, then have them draw it.
- Draw the shoulders and wait for them to draw shoulders.
- Do this step by step until the elf is complete.

Under the drawing children write this sentence, filling in the blanks with their own ideas:

My little _____ can _____.

Children who are writing well can write additional words and sentences.

If the demonstration is how to draw a leprechaun, then have them write this sentence under the drawing, filling in the blanks, and writing additional sentences if they wish:

If a leprechaun gave me gold, I would _____.

Signs of Winter. You will need two baskets—one filled with winter stencils and one filled with matching seasonal words printed on index cards—and a four- to five-page stapled-paper booklet for each child.

- Each child selects a stencil, traces it onto a page, and decorates it.
- The child finds the corresponding word and writes it under the picture.
- Repeat until all pages of the booklet are complete.

Valentine's Day Candy-Heart Writing. This activity uses the packaged "conversation" hearts (small pastel-colored candy hearts with valentine messages). Empty the hearts into a bowl and provide a small scoop—a tiny cup or large spoon. Children spoon out several hearts (you determine how many) from the bowl and write the candy-heart message on a paper heart (one message per heart). Die-cut the hearts or teach children how to fold paper and cut them. (For directions, see the earlier Valentine Mailbox in the section.)

Thematic Activities

Here are activities that fit any theme:

- Write thematic books, stories, plays, raps, poems, and songs.
- Write in journals.
- Write letters to classmates.
- Create a class newspaper.
- Respond to reading—tell the best part of the book, describe characters and settings, tell the most exciting event, and so on.
- Summarize thematic books or stories.
- Write student versions of thematic literature and trade books.
- Write grocery lists for classroom food-preparation projects.
- Publish student-made picture dictionaries.

- Do process writing—brainstorming, rough draft, conferencing with teacher or peer, final draft, editing, publishing, Author's Chair (at the Teacher Center or in front of the class).
- Make lists—story facts, things to do, favorite foods, and so on.
- Make labels for thematic art projects.
- Write thematic skits or radio scripts to perform.
- Make thematic greeting cards or write letters, messages, or thank-you notes.
- Write announcements and make thematic posters.
- Publish a class newspaper.
- Study the writing style of a favorite author.

Here are some specific-theme activities that are appropriate for the Writing Center.

- *School Days:* Write and illustrate a book about favorite school activities.
- *Pumpkin Patch:* Keep journal records on the growth of pumpkin seeds. Write a book about pumpkins.
- *Native American Tepee:* Make up totem pole stories or write stories using symbols.
- *Winter Wonderland:* Write and illustrate winter activity books.
- *Black History Month:* Make a booklet about favorite African-American "heroes and sheroes."
- *Spaceship:* Create a booklet about space. Make a fact list about planets.
- *Springtime:* Create an Earth Day booklet. Write a spring skit.
- *Cinco de Mayo:* Write some Spanish words from those featured in the Cinco de Mayo theme in Section Four.
- *Lunar New Year:* Children write about their favorite activity for the Lunar New Year. They tell why it is their favorite.
- *Restaurant:* Create menus. Write a party invitation that includes a menu.
- *Roman Holiday:* Write a story about a Roman boy or girl trying to learn to speak English.
- *Valentine's Day and Dental Health Month:* Create valentine messages for pen pals and classmates. Create dental health booklets.

THE WORD PLAY CENTER

Children explore language through social interaction and creative play, and the Word Play Center allows them to do just that. At this center, children engage in active learning through role-play and interesting games. Students of mixed abilities work together sharing activities.

Dramatic Play and Reading Games

The Word Play Center has two functions: dramatic play and reading games.

Dramatic Play. Research shows that dramatic play increases oral language and story comprehension (Robinson, Ross, and Neal, 2000). Role-playing requires abstract thought that advances cognitive development and strengthens memory (Soderman, Gregory, and O'Neill, 1999). So why not set up a dramatic play area to create daily language opportunities? Each month the Word Play Center sets an imaginative new theme for both the play area *and* the entire classroom. The themes represent real-life situations that expand background knowledge and vocabulary. They provide language learning across content areas using problem solving, listening, speaking, art, music, and cooking. Props at the center stimulate children's imaginations; children expand vocabulary and language as they play characters in a restaurant, tepee, post office, or spaceship (Whitehead, 1999). Dramatic play allows them to use language that is not part of their daily conversation but will be encountered in many of the books they read. When they see these words, they will have had firsthand experience using them in their play. Role-play in imaginative settings is also called *sociodramatic play* (Owocki, 2001).

Dramatic play areas are easy to create if you do it in stages. The first year, choose three or four themes that are appropriate for your purposes. Use each theme for more than one month. Keep those same themes the next year, but also choose three more. Soon you will have enough props to have a new dramatic play set each month. Better yet, work with another teacher to create and exchange themes. If each teacher creates three different themes, both teachers have access to six. And many teachers have their students help them in both the planning and the setting up of the play sets. (For information on letting children help you plan dramatic play sets, see Soderman, Gregory, and O'Neill, [1999].)

Reading Games. If the dramatic play area is working well, you may want to continue to use it for more than a month. But it's easy to change the theme monthly without changing the dramatic play set. Section Four of this volume, "Learning Center Thematic Units," provides reproducible games for each month's theme. Section Four includes the following items for each theme:

- A board game pattern
- Cards for making one or two card games, a sorting game, and a matching game
- Sorting game labels
- Matching game patterns
- Bulletin board ideas
- A thematic calendar

The reproducible patterns are for two kinds of games:

- *Thematic games.* For each of the special themes this volume features, Section Four includes four or five games designed to fit the theme—a board game, one or two card games, a sorting game, and a matching game. The games help children learn new vocabulary related to the theme with engaging, hands-on practice activities. The games are at different levels to allow children of differing abilities to participate. Make several copies of the games so that several groups can play at the same time. For extra practice, produce copies of the games for children to take home and play with family members.

- *Skill games.* Hands-on games can teach word analysis, vocabulary, or spelling faster than most paper-and-pencil activities and without papers to grade! Section Five, "Learning Center Skill Games," provides reproducible game directions, answer keys, and game cards to create forty hands-on board games, card games, sorting games, and matching games. There are games involving abbreviations, antonyms, compound words, consonant blends, consonant digraphs, contractions, figurative language, homophones, syllables, and synonyms. Blank cards are provided so you can add your own words or produce your own games.

- In addition, an easy recipe is provided with each theme—you can print these out (and illustrate them) on a chart. While cooking, children follow instructions, measure ingredients, follow steps in sequence, and then eat what they've made. To extend the activity, you can send the recipes home, create a classroom cookbook, or have children illustrate or write about their cooking experience (Allen and Allen, 1982).

Basic Equipment

Here is the basic equipment you will need to set up a Word Play Center:

- Floor space for the dramatic play area
- Student seating for both the dramatic play and reading game areas— a table and chairs, floor pillows, mats, a group of desks or other suitable furniture for role-play, manipulatives and games
- A poster listing the names of children who will be in the dramatic play area; all others will play reading games while in the Word Play Center
- Storage space for games
- Labeled containers to store theme-related games and activities
- Enough wall space to post the student directions or management chart that relates to the theme

You will also need the following materials:

- Magnetic letters and board for "building" names and simple words
- Sentence strips with missing words and word cards to fill in the blanks
- Letter recognition and letter identification games
- Alphabet puzzles and matching games
- Sorting games (use the reproducible sorting-game patterns or create your own): rhyming words, beginning sounds, shapes, colors, animals, number words, action words, and so on

- Age-appropriate crossword puzzles, word hunts, and word scrambles that use Word Wall and thematic words
- Sorting games for words that have the same initial or ending sounds
- Activities for sequencing
- Activities and games that use riddles
- Activities for rhyming words

Assembling the Games

Board Games. Here's how to make board games. (See illustrations on page 91.)

1. Photocopy the game board and let the children decorate it.
2. Glue the two board game halves inside a file folder and trim protruding edges. Write the name of the game on the front of the folder.
3. Copy the game board directions and glue them on the back of the folder.
4. Copy the matching game cards on card stock. If you wish, photocopy the cards to enlarge the size. Have children decorate the cards. Then laminate the sheets and cut the individual cards apart.
5. Copy the answer key and glue it to a piece of tagboard. Add your extra words to the key.
6. Attach a small brown envelope to the back of the folder to hold game cards and the answer key. Laminate the game board and slit the film at the envelope's opening.

To play the game, choose two or three players. They will need a game board, game cards, an answer key, one die, and a marker for each player.

1. Each player picks a marker and places it on START.
2. Players roll the die. The player with the highest number goes first. Other players go in a clockwise direction.
3. Each player rolls the die, draws a card, and reads it. (Younger readers read only the underlined words. More fluent readers read the sentence.)
4. If the player reads the card correctly, the player moves ahead the number shown on the die. If the card is read incorrectly, the player does not move.
5. The player puts the card at the bottom of the pile.
6. The first player to reach FINISH wins!

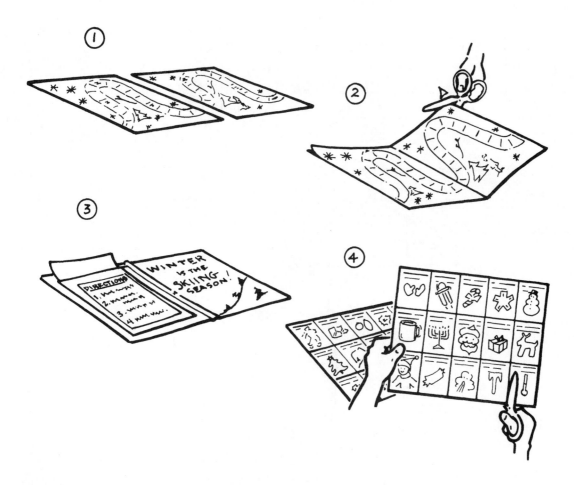

Card Games. Section Four includes one card game for the Cinco de Mayo, Lunar New Year, and Roman Holiday themes. All other themes have two card games.

The object of the game is to match pairs of cards. For that reason, copy each page of game cards (fifteen cards to a page) twice so you will have fifteen pairs of cards for each game. For the Cinco de Mayo, Lunar New Year, and Roman Holiday card games, make one copy of each page, one with the English word, the other with the matching Spanish, Chinese, or Latin word.

1. Select a page of game cards. Copy the page on two pieces of card stock to make fifteen pairs of cards. For the Spanish, Chinese, and Latin games, copy both pages so that one will show fifteen foreign language word cards and the other fifteen matching English word cards. If you wish, set the copy machine to enlarge the size of the cards. Let children decorate them. Then laminate the sheets and cut the individual cards apart.

2. Use a small box (such as a stationery box), a small brown envelope, or a self-sealing plastic bag to hold the cards. Decorate the top of the box on the front of the envelope or plastic bag.

3. Copy the card game directions and glue them inside the box top, on the back of the envelope, or glue on tagboard and place inside the plastic bag.

Two players may play.

1. Deal five cards to each player. Stack the rest of the cards facedown.

2. Player One draws one card from the stack. The player then discards one unwanted card face up beside the stack.

3. The other player draws one card—from the stack or from the top of the discard pile—and discards one unwanted card.

4. When players get a match, they put the pair down on the table.

5. The first player to lay down all cards on the table wins!

Sorting Games.   Here's how to make the games.

1. Copy and have children decorate the sorting game patterns. Attach each pattern to the top edge of a cylinder container with a clothespin or large paper clip.

2. Copy both pages of game cards on card stock and have children decorate them. If you wish, enlarge the cards on a photocopy machine. Laminate the sheets and cut the cards apart.

3. Use a small brown envelope or self-sealing plastic bag to store the cards.

4. Glue the game directions on the back of the envelope or glue on tagboard and place inside the plastic bag.

5. Copy the answer key and glue it onto tagboard. Place the key inside the envelope or plastic bag.

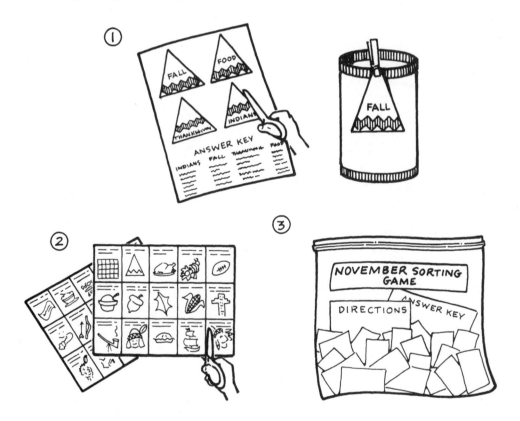

One or two players play this game.

1. Look at the game cards. Decide which category each card matches. Put the card in that container.

2. When you have sorted all the cards, get out the answer key and check your work.

3. Read the cards to a partner.

Matching Games. Here's how to make and play matching games.

1. Make enough copies of the matching game patterns so that there is one pattern for every word pair on the answer key. Write a word pair on each pattern.

2. On the back of the pattern, write matching numbers on each side of the matching pair. This will allow players to check for correct and incorrect matches by matching numbers. Have children decorate the patterns. Laminate, then cut them apart on the dotted lines.

3. Decorate a stationery box, envelope, or self-sealing plastic bag for storing the cards.

4. Copy the game directions and answer key and glue them to the box or envelope or laminate them and put them inside the plastic bag.

5. Players find pairs of words that match.

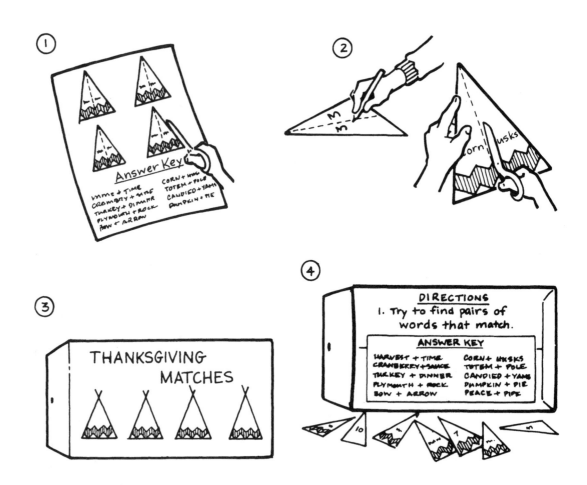

4 LEARNING CENTER THEMATIC UNITS

This section describes twelve thematic units for the classroom. Although the themes are arranged in monthly sections, many are interchangeable, and there are three extra themes provided for additional choice, summer school, or year-round schools. The description of each unit includes directions for setting up two areas in the Word Play Center: dramatic play and thematic games. Each suggests activities and children's books appropriate to the theme and includes relevant reproducible board, card, sorting, and matching games. *Note:* All cards can be enlarged, if you wish, when photocopying.

AUGUST AND SEPTEMBER: SCHOOL DAYS

Theme Decorations

Decorate based on the classroom theme.

Game and Dramatic Play Areas

You will need these materials for the thematic game area:

- Basic equipment (Section Three)
- School Days board game, card games, sorting game, and matching game
- Learning center skill games (Section Five)
- September vocabulary cards (game cards or index cards with underlined words from game cards written on them)
- A sign that says: "We practice reading."
- A poster or sign with student directions: "1. Read the September vocabulary cards to a partner. 2. Play a reading game."

You will need these materials for the dramatic play area (to create a schoolroom):

- Teacher desk (or table) and chair
- Props, such as a plastic apple, eyeglass frames, a stamp and stamp pad
- Song and story charts, a pointer
- Flannel board and story pictures (see flannel board directions in the Teacher Center activities, Section Three)
- Books (so children can read a story with the Teacher of the Day)
- Slates with chalk and erasers or whiteboard with markers
- A jar of pencils with erasers and blank paper or old workbook pages for "playing school"
- A Teacher of the Day chart, which lists children's names and which day of the week each will be teacher

Post the names of children who will be in the dramatic play area. All others will play reading games.

Theme Setup

1. Position the "teacher's desk" and props near the student seating. Put the pointer, pencils, and labeled boxes containing slates, workbooks, and vocabulary cards nearby.
2. Place the song and story charts and flannel board near the student seating.
3. Post student directions and the Teacher of the Day chart. The Teacher of the Day straightens the area before moving to another center.

Bulletin Boards

See the illustrations on page 102.

Whole-Group Activities

- Learn new vocabulary: *chalkboard, chart,* and so on.
- Role-play activities that students will use at the School Days learning center (thematic games, big books, vocabulary cards, flannel board).
- Role-play being Teacher of the Day at the Word Play Center.
- Visit the principal's office. Have the principal tell why he or she became a teacher.
- Have the special area teachers (music, art, physical education) tell the class why they became teachers.
- Have a child's grandparent or great-grandparent tell the class about his or her school days.
- Create and post a set of class rules.
- Learn the purpose of old-fashioned samplers. (Colonial children made these decorative pieces of needlework by embroidering numerals and their ABCs.)
- Create an alma mater by writing words to a familiar tune. Write the words on a song chart.
- Set up an overhead projector, screen, transparencies, and pointers. Let students use this activity in pairs.
- Complete the theme calendar (see the illustrations on pages 103 and 104).

Back-to-School Trail Mix Recipe*

One or two cups *each:*

> Peanuts
>
> Puffed-corn cereal or small pretzels
>
> Raisins
>
> Chewy fruit snacks or candy-coated chocolate pieces

Children measure and mix ingredients. Serve in small disposable cups.

Snacktime Fruit Recipe**

> Vanilla yogurt (one or two eight-ounce cups)
>
> Honey (one or two teaspoons)
>
> One piece for each child: strawberries (keep leaves intact); grapes; bananas (two or three whole bananas); apples (three or four whole apples)
>
> Apple core cutter
>
> Plastic knife (for slicing bananas)
>
> A large dish
>
> Toothpicks

1. Children mix one teaspoon honey into each eight-ounce cup of yogurt.
2. Children prepare the fruit—wash berries, apples, and grapes; slice bananas; core and slice apples.
3. Children arrange fruit on a dish with the yogurt in the middle. Serve with toothpicks. Use leaves to pick up a strawberry and dip it in the yogurt. Enjoy!

Note: Trail mix recipe courtesy of Allison Holland.
**Note: Fruit recipe courtesy of Lilibeth Oyama.*

Content Area Activities

- Study schools in colonial times.
- Learn about schools in other countries.
- Use an encyclopedia or the Internet to gather information about early books such as the hornbook *Blueback Speller,* or *McGuffey's Readers.*
- Provide math story problems. (Dan brought the teacher an apple. Bill brought her two pears. How many snacks did she have in all?)
- Gather information about the children's favorite school activities. Use the results to create a graph.
- Create a map of the school.
- Create a day's schedule. (What time do we visit centers, have recess, go to the lunchroom, and go home?)

Word Play Center Activities

- Reread stories with the Teacher of the Day.
- Take turns role-playing teacher and students.
- Play skill games that reinforce skills being taught at the Teacher Center.
- Play the School Days board game, card games, sorting game, and matching game.
- Read School Days vocabulary cards made by the teacher.

Thematic Books

For additional thematic books, see Joanne Sullivan's (2004) *The Children's Literature Lover's Book of Lists*.

Emergent and Early Readers

Baer, Edith. (1992). *This Is the Way We Go to School.* Describes the many different ways children all over the world get to school.

Calmenson, Stephanie. (1989). *The Principal's New Clothes.* Illustrated by Denise Brunkus. A new version of Hans Christian Andersen's classic story, with an elementary school principal cast in the role of emperor.

Carlson, Nancy. (2004). *Henry's Show-and-Tell.* Henry doesn't like show-and-tell because he's too shy to speak, but his teacher helps out.

Carlson, Nancy. (2004). *Look Out Kindergarten, Here I Come!* When Henry gets to school he's not so sure he's ready for kindergarten, but finds that the only thing he's not ready for is how much fun he's going to have!

Cohen, Miriam. (1983). *First Grade Takes a Test*. The first grade is worried by a test that fails to measure true aptitude.

Cohen, Miriam. (1996). *Starring First Grade: Welcome to First Grade*. Illustrated by Lillian Hoban. The first-grade play production is a lesson in cooperation when Jim overcomes his dissatisfaction with his part and helps a friend with his stage fright.

Cousins, Lucy. (1992). *Maisy Goes to School*. This book has both flaps and tabs that show all the wonderful things Maisy does at school.

Crews, Donald. (1993). *School Bus*. A bright yellow school bus takes children to school.

Danneberg, Julie. (2000). *First-Day Jitters*. Illustrated by Judith Dufour Love. Sarah Jane is afraid on her first day of school.

Freeman, Don. (2002). *Corduroy Goes to School*. A delightful flap book that describes an interesting day at school for Corduroy.

Grant, Jim, and Richardson, Irv. (1997). *What Teachers Do When No One Is Looking*. Illustrated by Patrick Belfiori. Funny illustrations show all those "extra things" that teachers do.

Hallinan, P. K. (1987). *My First Day of School*. A first-day kindergartner finds out about name tags, safety, manners, bathrooms, snacks, games, and more.

Hallinan, P. K. (2001). *My Teacher's My Friend*. A story about the friendship between child and teacher.

Hest, Amy. (1999). *Off to School, Baby Duck*. Illustrated by Jill Barton. Baby Duck is helped through a new experience by her family in this book about first-day jitters.

Maccarone, Grace. (1995). *The Lunch Box Surprise*. Sam's mother forgets to pack his lunch, but first-grade friends help out by sharing their lunches with him.

Shalleck, Margaret and Alan J. (1989). *Curious George Goes to School*. Curious George makes a mistake in the art room but finds a missing painting in time for the open house.

Developing and Fluent Readers

Bemelmans, Ludwig. (1958). *Madeline*. Madeline goes to a boarding school in France. This is the first book in a series that celebrates over fifty years of success.

Brimneer, L. (1990). *Cory Coleman, Grade 2*. Cory has to invite his whole class, even the bully, to his birthday party.

Creech, Sharon. (2001). *A Fine, Fine School*. When Mr. Keene met with the students and teachers and said, "This is a fine, fine school! From now on, let's have school on Saturdays too!" it was up to Tillie to show her principal that it's not fine to be at school all the time.

Giff, Patricia Reilly. (1986). *Kids of the Polk Street School*. Describes a year in Mrs. Rooney's class.

Giff, Patricia Reilly. (1988). *B-E-S-T Friends*: *New Kids at the Polk Street School*. Stacy's new friend says potatoes are for breakfast. When Stacy eats some, she discovers it is fun to be different.

Haywood, Carolyn. (1990). *"B" Is for Betsy*. Betsy has an interesting first year in school and looks forward to summer at her grandfather's farm.

Haywood, Carolyn. (1990). *Back to School with Betsy*. Betsy and her friend Billy seem to be always getting into scrapes. (See also other books in this series.)

Levy, Elizabeth. (2002). *The Principal's on the Roof*. The principal promised to spend time on the roof if children read one thousand books during their reading marathon—and they did!

Marzollo, Jean. (1988). *Red Ribbon Rosie*. Rosie cheats to win a race against Sally with disastrous results, until her older sister helps her learn an important lesson about winning races and keeping friends.

Peterson, P. J. (1998). *The Sub*. Friends switch seats to fool a substitute teacher.

August/September Bulletin Boards

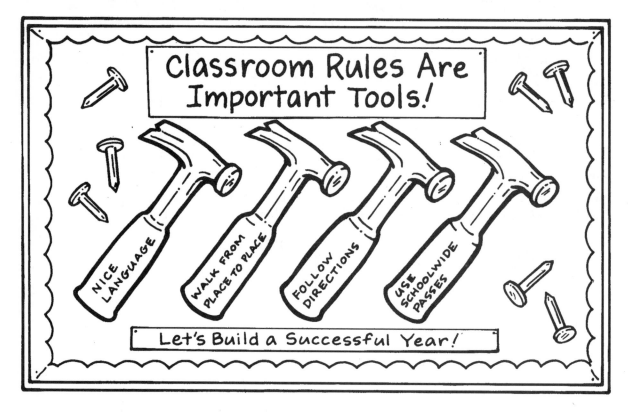

Classroom Rules Are Important Tools!

NICE LANGUAGE

WALK FROM PLACE TO PLACE

FOLLOW DIRECTIONS

USE SCHOOLWIDE PASSES

Let's Build a Successful Year!

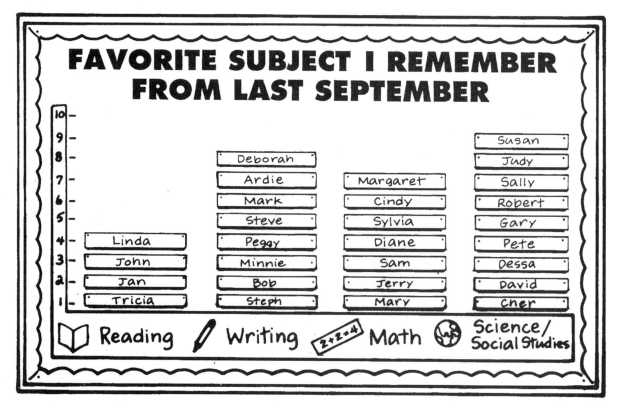

FAVORITE SUBJECT I REMEMBER FROM LAST SEPTEMBER

Reading   Writing   Math   Science/Social Studies

AUGUST

SUNDAY	MONDAY	TUESDAY	WEDNESDAY	THURSDAY	FRIDAY	SATURDAY

SEPTEMBER

SUNDAY	MONDAY	TUESDAY	WEDNESDAY	THURSDAY	FRIDAY	SATURDAY

August/September Sorting Game

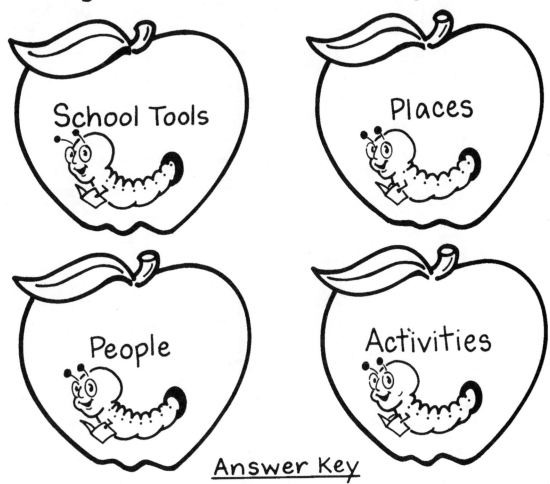

School Tools

Places

People

Activities

Answer Key

School Tools	Places	Activities	People
lead pencil	art room	reading books	teacher
paper	music class	writing stories	student
eraser	classroom	science	principal
color crayons	playground	social studies	safety patrol
desk	office	ride the school bus	cafeteria
chalkboard	clinic	physical	worker
sticky glue	media center	education	
lunch box			
sharp scissors			
dictionary			
atlas			
computer and CDs			

Take a Ride

START →

A⁺
on your test!
Roll again.

FINISH
YOU WIN!

Forgot your lunch! Lose one turn.

LUNCH

on the School Bus

The cafeteria workers make lunch.

The phone is in the office.

OFFICE

We use the dictionary.

DICTIONARY

We have fun on the playground.

I use the computer and CDs.

When you're sick, go to the clinic.

Our classroom is big.

The principal is nice.

PRINCIPAL
COME IN

The safety patrol helps us.

The student learns.

A+

The media center is quiet.

PLEASE WHISPER

NEWSPAPER

Look at maps in the atlas.

ATLAS

I have a smart teacher.

I have a lunch box.

The sharp scissors can cut.

Sit at the desk.

Science is interesting.

Physical education is outside.

I have some color crayons.

He loves writing stories.

Music class is fun.

The eraser is important.

Reading books is fun.

Walk to the art room.

Write on the paper.

We ride the school bus.

Use the sticky glue.

I see a lead pencil.

The chalkboard is big.

Social Studies is important.

August/September Matching Game

Answer Key

art + room

Sticky + glue

lead + pencil

color + crayons

chalk + board

school + bus

reading + books

writing + Stories

Social + studies

media + center

music + class

physical + education

play + ground

cafeteria +workers

lunch + box

Computer + CDs

Sharp + scissors

Safety + patrol

atlas + maps

OCTOBER: PUMPKIN PATCH

Theme Decorations

Decorate to look like a pumpkin patch.

Game and Dramatic Play Areas

You will need these materials for the thematic game area:

- Basic equipment
- Pumpkin Patch board game, card games, sorting game, and matching game
- Learning center skill games (Section Five)
- October vocabulary cards (game cards or index cards with underlined words from the game cards written on them)

Note: Fall festival ideas courtesy of Addie and Nathan Washington.

- A sign that says: "We read with a scarecrow."
- A poster or sign with student directions, "1. Read the October vocabulary cards to a partner. 2. Play a reading game with a partner."

You will need these materials for the dramatic play area (to make a scarecrow and a field):

- Lightweight broom
- Small-sized Christmas-tree stand or bucket of damp sand
- Yardstick
- Shirt, blue jeans, straw hat, gloves, boots, eyeglasses
- Masking tape
- Large safety pins
- Construction paper and white glue
- One bale of hay (can be found at a feed store or garden shop)
- Pumpkins (real, plastic, or made of construction paper)

Post the names of the children who will be in the dramatic play area. All others will play reading games.

Making the Scarecrow

1. Insert broom and secure it into the stand or bucket. If you are using a Christmas-tree stand, wrap the broomstick with a thick cloth before tightening the screws. This makes the broom handle thicker and prevents slipping.
2. Slip the yardstick through the shirt sleeves. Don't button the shirt.
3. Using masking tape, secure the yardstick horizontally below the broom head. Wrap masking tape around the broom several times. Then hold the yardstick against the tape on the broomstick and wrap the tape diagonally (about ten times in each direction) around both sticks.
4. Button the shirt and attach the back of the shirt to the blue jeans with safety pins. (The front of the shirttail will hang out over the pants.) Stuff the pants into a pair of boots. If you wish, stuff the legs of the blue jeans with crumpled newspaper. Pin the gloves to the shirt cuffs.
5. Stick hay or pine needles around the cuffs and neck, in the boots, and so on.
6. Using white glue, apply construction paper eyes, nose, and other features to the broom head. Add a pair of eyeglasses; poke them in the straw.

Theme Setup

1. Stand the scarecrow next to a wall (for stability).
2. Place the bale of hay next to the scarecrow.
3. Arrange pumpkins on top of the hay and on the floor near the scarecrow.
4. Post the signs.

Bulletin Boards

See the illustrations on page 117.

Whole-Group Activities

1. Learn new vocabulary: *pumpkin, smile,* and so on.
2. Use the pumpkin activity sheet shown on page 125 to create a bulletin board.
3. Cook winter squash.
4. Collect pumpkin and winter-squash recipes and assemble into a class book.
5. Dry gourds to make musical instruments or birdhouses.
6. Visit a local farmer who grows pumpkins, winter squash, or uses a scarecrow.
7. Look for pumpkins in literature: Cinderella's coach, "Peter, Peter, Pumpkin Eater," and so on.
8. Create a class book about pumpkins or a scarecrow.
9. Make pumpkin pies (see recipe). Then list and display words that describe pumpkin pies.
10. Decorate the October calendar (see page 124).

Pumpkin Pie Recipe*

Graham crackers (two per child)

Plastic sandwich bags (one per child)

Rolling pins

Sugar (one teaspoon per child)

Margarine (one tablespoon per child)

Foil muffin cups (one per child)

Note: Pumpkin pie recipe courtesy of Patricia Tolbert.

Plastic bowls (one per child)

Measuring spoons

Eggbeaters

Packages of instant vanilla pudding (two tablespoons per child)

Milk (half-cup per child)

Canned pumpkin (one to two teaspoons per child)

Candied orange slices (one per child)

To make the crust:

1. Have each child place two graham crackers in a plastic bag.
2. Seal bag and crush crackers into crumbs with a rolling pin.
3. Add one teaspoon sugar and one tablespoon margarine and mix right in the bag.
4. Press mixture into a foil cup to form the crust.

To make the filling:

1. Measure two tablespoons vanilla pudding into bowl.
2. Add a half-cup cold milk.
3. Mix with beater until pudding starts to thicken.
4. Add one to two teaspoons pumpkin to pudding and stir.
5. Pour into each crust and decorate with candied orange slice.

Content Area Activities

- Grow pumpkin vines from seeds.
- Study the nutrient value of the squash family.
- Study ways that farmers protect crops from birds, rabbits, and other pests.
- Count the ribs on several different sizes of pumpkins. Is the number of ribs always the same or different?
- Estimate the number of seeds in a small pumpkin. Then cut the pumpkin and count the seeds.
- Create cookbooks using pumpkin and squash recipes.
- Estimate the number of pumpkin seeds in a jar.

Word Play Center Activities

- Play skill games that reinforce skills being taught at the Teacher Center.
- Play the Pumpkin Patch board game, card games, sorting game, and matching game.
- Read October vocabulary cards made by the teacher.

Thematic Books

Emergent and Early Readers

Brown, Ken. (2001). *The Scarecrow's Hat*. Chicken likes Scarecrow's hat, and Scarecrow is willing to trade his hat for a walking stick. Chicken begins to trade among all her farm friends to get the walking stick to trade for the hat.

Brown, Margaret Wise. (1998). *The Little Scarecrow Boy*. Illustrated by David Diaz. A delightful story about a little scarecrow and his family.

Dillon, Jana. (1995). *Jeb Scarecrow's Pumpkin Patch*. Jeb Scarecrow invents a plan to keep the crows from throwing their October harvest celebration in his pumpkin patch.

Kantor, Sue. (2002). *Tiny Tilda's Pumpkin Pie*. Illustrated by Rick Brown. Tilda, the hippo, plants, tends, harvests, and bakes an amazing pumpkin pie.

King, Elizabeth. (1996). *The Pumpkin Patch*. Text and photographs describe a pumpkin patch, with seeds developing into pumpkins.

Maass, Robert. (1992). *When Autumn Comes*. A photo book with simple text tells about the fall season in New England.

Preston, Tim. (1999). *The Lonely Scarecrow*. Illustrated by Maggie Keen. A winter snow changes a scarecrow into a friendly-looking snowman, no longer frightening to the local animals.

Rylant, Cynthia. (2001). *Scarecrow*. The world is a wonderful place when seen through the eyes of a scarecrow.

Sloat, Teri P. (1999). *Patty's Pumpkin Patch*. Both a story, told in the main text and illustrations, and an introduction to the alphabet, presented in smaller illustrations along the bottom of each page.

Titherington, Jeanne. (1990). *Pumpkin, Pumpkin*. Jamie plants a pumpkin seed in the spring and watches it grow.

White, Linda. (1997). *Too Many Pumpkins*. Illustrated by Megan Lloyd. Rebecca, who had only pumpkins to eat as a child, buries a load that accidentally fell off a truck, only to reap a bumper crop that she doesn't want.

Developing and Fluent Readers

Elhert, Lois. (1991). *Red Leaf, Yellow Leaf.* A young child examines the life of a sugar maple tree in this beautiful book.

Fowler, Allan. (1992). *How Do You Know It's Fall?* The many signs of fall—geese flying south, squirrels hiding acorns, and football—are presented.

Gibbons, Gail. (2000). *The Pumpkin Book.* The book explains the planting, cultivating, and harvesting of pumpkins.

Maestro, Betsy. (1994). *Why Do Leaves Change Color?* This book explains how leaves change their color and describes simple activities and places to visit to enjoy the fall leaves.

Potter, Tessa. (1999). *Digger: The Story of a Mole in the Fall.* Digger escapes the fall rains that flood her tunnels but finds new danger aboveground.

Robbins, Ken. (2003). *Autumn Leaves.* This is a color-photo book about fall leaves that gives some scientific information, such as on photosynthesis and the chemicals that make the leaves turn colors.

Taylor, Mark. (1975). *Henry Explores the Mountains.* Illustrated by Graham Booth. Henry goes to the woods with his dog and experiences a forest fire, heroism, and a helicopter ride.

Tresselt, Alvin R. (1990). *Autumn Harvest.* Illustrated by Roger Duvoisin. A book about all the features of fall—the first frost, migrating geese, burning leaves, and a big harvest.

Van Allsburg, Chris. (1986). *The Stranger.* The stranger that Farmer Bailey hit with his truck comes home with him to recuperate—and while trees to the north of the farm turn fall colors, Bailey's farm is still experiencing summer. Does the stranger have a mysterious relation to the weather?

October Bulletin Boards

PUMPKIN PATCH PLACES

A place a story occurs is called a <u>setting</u>. What is one of your favorite settings?

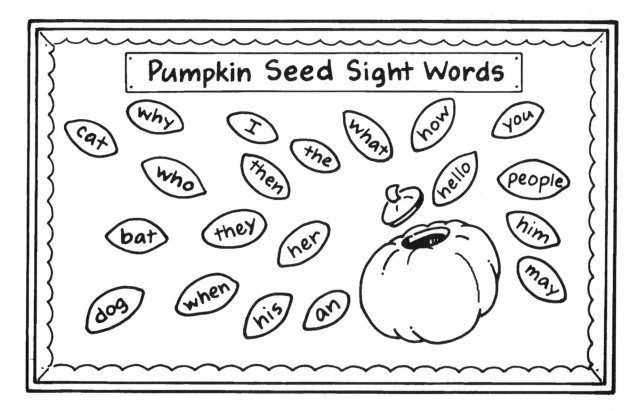

Pumpkin Seed Sight Words

cat • why • I • what • how • you • who • then • the • hello • people • bat • they • her • him • dog • when • his • an • may

START

You rake leaves.

Move ahead two spaces.

Game Cards

Take one more turn.

Forgot your jacket!

Go back one space.

Miss a turn.

Move ahead one.

FE

FALL STIVAL

Go back one space and eat pumpkin pie.

Columbus Day!

Move ahead two.

Move ahead one.

FINISH

You Win!

Eat a big red apple.

Pick up acorns.

Eat candy corn.

I drink warm cocoa.

See the orange pumpkin.

We like hay rides.

Face painting is fun.

I love to bob for apples.

Sit by a haystack.

See the moon?

I made pumpkin pie.

They won the three-legged race.

Pumpkin contest!

Wear your warm mittens.

She won the sack race!

We can rake the fall leaves.

Please wear your cap.

Eat a hot breakfast.

I drink apple cider.

We celebrate Columbus Day.

I like to see the red leaves.

I can carve a pumpkin.

See the scarecrow.

Listen to the blackbird.

I ate the candied apple.

Don't forget to put on a jacket.

Smile!

The pie-eating contest is yummy.

Clowns are funny.

Build a fire.

October Sorting Game

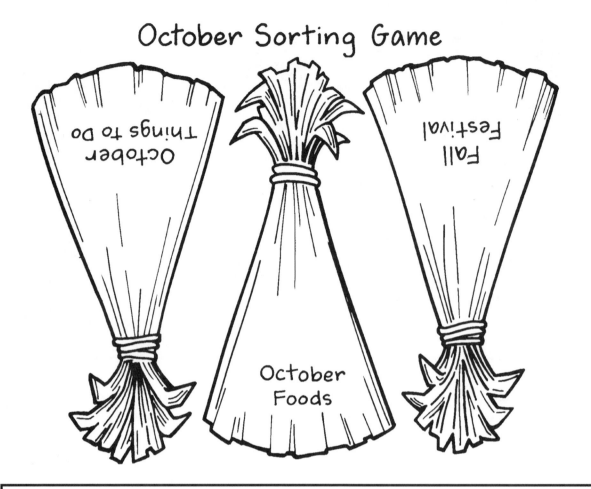

October Things to Do

October Foods

Fall Festival

Answer Key

October Things to Do

carve a pumpkin
rake fall leaves
put on a jacket
wear your cap
build a fire
Smile!
see the red leaves
pick up acorns
see the moon
sit by a haystack
listen to the blackbird
celebrate Columbus Day
wear your warm mittens
make a pumpkin pie
see the scarecrow

October Foods

candied apple
apple cider
orange pumpkin
cocoa
candy corn
red apple
candy treats
pumpkin pie
hot breakfast

Fall Festival

face painting
hay ride
bob for apples
biggest pumpkin contest
sack race
three-legged race
pie-eating contest
clowns

October Matching Game

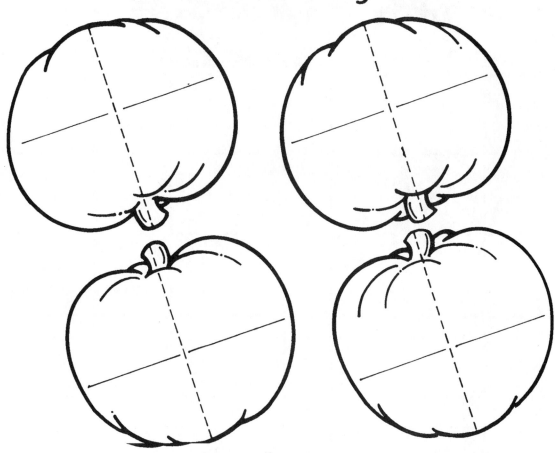

Answer Key

funny + clowns	bob + for apples
hay + stack	candied + apples
apple + cider	black + bird
hot + breakfast	rake + leaves
pie-eating + contest	candy + corn
face + painting	three-legged + race
Columbus + Day	warm + jackets
Sack + race	hot + cocoa
hay + ride	orange + pumpkin
pumpkin + pie	red + apple

OCTOBER

SUNDAY	MONDAY	TUESDAY	WEDNESDAY	THURSDAY	FRIDAY	SATURDAY

Pumpkin Sheet
for Bulletin Board

Name _____   _____ Date

_____
Book Title

_____
Author

Describe the setting: _____

_____

_____

_____

_____

_____

_____

_____

_____

NOVEMBER: NATIVE AMERICAN TEPEE

Theme Decorations

Decorate based on the Native American tepee theme.

Game and Dramatic Play Areas

You will need these materials for the thematic game area:

- Basic equipment
- Tepee board game, card games, sorting game, and matching game

- Learning center skill games (Section Five)
- November vocabulary cards (game cards or index cards with under-lined words from game cards written on them)
- "Native American Partners" chart—a list of pairs of students and the date they will have dramatic play in the tepee
- A poster or sign with student directions: "1. Read the November vocabulary cards to a partner. 2. Play a reading game with a partner."

You will need these materials for the dramatic play area (the tepee):

- See the following directions and illustrations. If electric drills are foreign to you, ask a handy friend to help.
- To store the tepee, remove the paper, untie the bottom sections, and fold up the poles.

Post the names of the children who will be in the dramatic play area. All others will play reading games.

YOU WILL NEED—

- 8–1" X 3" BOARDS:
  4–6' AND 4–4'
- 2–ROLLS BROWN WRAPPING PAPER OR BUTCHER PAPER
- STRONG THIN ROPE
- ELECTRIC DRILL WITH 3/4" BIT
- COLORED MARKERS

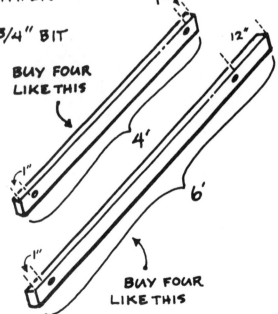

BUY FOUR LIKE THIS

BUY FOUR LIKE THIS

Note: Tepee pattern courtesy of Diane Holman.

- TIE THE TEPEE TOGETHER, STARTING WITH THE TOP OF THE 6' POLES.

- SPREAD THE BOTTOMS OF THE 6' POLES APART AND TIE A 4' POLE BETWEEN EACH.

- COVER WITH PAPER AND DECORATE.

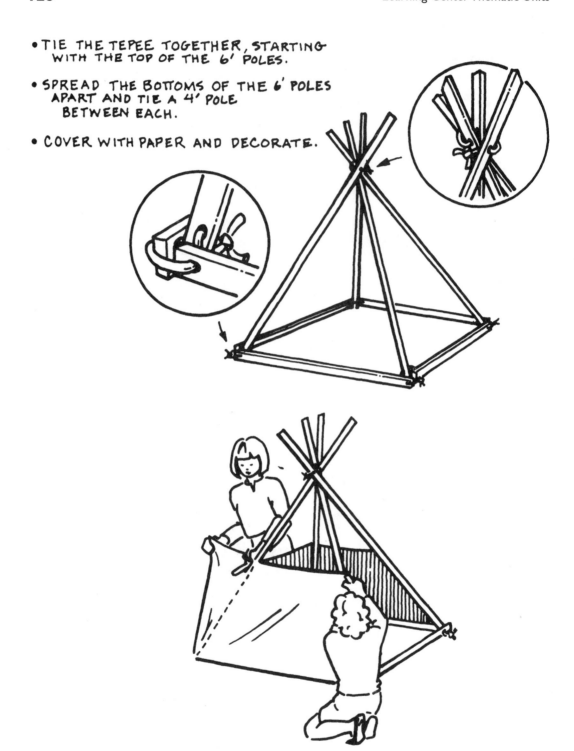

Theme Setup

1. Arrange student seating.
2. Set the tepee near the student seating.
3. Post student directions and Native American Partners chart.

Bulletin Boards

See the illustrations on page 133.

Whole-Group Activities

- Learn new vocabulary: *Native American, Indian, tepee, Thanksgiving,* and so on.
- Role-play the Thanksgiving story.
- Visit a turkey farm.
- Create a Thanksgiving song; write the words on your song chart.
- Make totem poles (see activity sheet on page 141).
- Glue totem-pole symbols (photocopy those on the activity sheet) to small magnets. Children can tell stories by moving the magnets on metal trays or cookie sheets. Have activity sheet handy as a reference.
- Make cranberry sauce, then list and display words that describe cranberry sauce.
- Make macaroni necklaces.
- Decorate the November calendar (see page 140).

Cranberry Sauce Recipe

Four cups fresh cranberries

Two cups sugar

Two cups water

A hot plate and saucepan

1. Combine ingredients.
2. Boil on hot plate until skins of berries pop (about four minutes).
3. Cool and serve in tiny paper cups.

Native American Necklaces

Food coloring

Water

Rubbing alcohol

Small cups

Macaroni (uncooked)

Aluminum foil

String or yarn

1. Mix food coloring, water, and a teaspoon of alcohol in each cup.
2. Quickly dip macaroni into colored water and place on foil to dry.
3. Have children string the macaroni pieces to make necklaces.

Content Area Activities

- Learn the Thanksgiving story.
- Using reference materials, find the route of the Pilgrims.
- Estimate the number of cranberries in a cellophane package, then count them.
- Gather information about the children's favorite Thanksgiving foods; use the results to create a graph.
- Learn about different Native American groups.
- Create a Thanksgiving menu.

Word Play Center Activities

- Experience dramatic play in the tepee.
- Play skill games that reinforce skills being taught at the Teacher Center.
- Play the tepee board game, card games, sorting game, and matching game.
- Read November vocabulary cards made by the teacher.

Teacher Resource Book

Tibbett, Teri. (2004). *Listen to Learn: Using American Music to Understand Language Arts and Social Studies.* Although this resource book is designed for grades five to eight, it includes excellent information about Native American music—including traditional singing, Native American instruments, Native American music regions, and contemporary Native American music (see Unit 1).

Thematic Books

Emergent and Early Readers

Bruchac, Joseph. (1998). *The First Strawberries: A Cherokee Folktale.* Illustrated by Anna Vojtech. This book tells a Cheyenne legend that explains the origins of strawberries, which help the first man and woman patch a quarrel.

Bruchac, Joseph, and Ross, Gayle. (1995). *The Story of the Milky Way: A Cherokee Tale.* Illustrated by Virginia Stroud. This tells a Cherokee tale of how the Milky Way came to be.

de Paola, Tomie. (1996). *The Legend of the Indian Paintbrush.* Little Gopher, smaller than the other young Indians, could not do what the others did. However, he grows up to be an artist who paints wonderful pictures of his tribe.

Grossman, Virginia. (1995). *Ten Little Rabbits.* Illustrated by Sylvia Long. This is an entertaining counting book that celebrates Native American culture.

Joosse, Barbara. (1991). *Mama, Do You Love Me?* This illustrated book tells the story of a daughter's attempt to find how much her mother loves her. The Inuit characters and settings are beautifully rendered!

London, Jonathan. (1997). *Fire Race: A Karuk Coyote Tale of How Fire Came to the People.* Illustrated by Sylvia Long. A carefully researched and beautifully illustrated retelling of the Karuk tale.

McGovern, Ann. (1993). *If You Sailed on the Mayflower in 1620.* This book is about the life of the Pilgrims, both on the ship and after they reached America.

McGovern, Ann. (1993). *The Pilgrims' First Thanksgiving.* Illustrated by Elroy Freem. The Pilgrims' first Thanksgiving lasted three days. This book introduces the hardships during the first year at Plymouth Colony and the events leading to the first Thanksgiving.

Nelson, S. D. (1999). *Gift Horse: A Lakota Story.* The story tells how Flying Cloud matured from a boy to a man in the Lakota society of the 1800s.

Oughton, Jerrie. (1996). *How the Stars Fell into the Sky: A Navajo Legend.* A Navajo folktale tells how First Woman tried to write the laws of the land using stars in the sky.

Ross, H. L. (1995). *The Story of the Pilgrims.* The dangerous voyage across the Atlantic, the first harsh winter, and the first Thanksgiving feast. A great history book!

Rylant, Cynthia. (2000). *In November.* Poetic language and oil paintings tell the traditional activities that happen in November.

Steptoe, John. (1989). *The Story of Jumping Mouse.* Magic Frog gives courage to a young mouse on his long, dangerous journey to reach the land of legend.

Van Laan, Nancy. (1989). *Rainbow Crow: A Lenape Tale.* Illustrated by Beatriz Vidal. The Lenape fable tells how the crow lost his beautiful plumage when he interceded for friends who were being buried in a snowstorm.

Developing and Fluent Readers

Ancona, George. (1995). *Earth Daughter: Alicia of Acoma Pueblo.* A beautiful essay about the traditions of the Keres Indians of New Mexico.

Blood, Charles, and Link, Martin. (1990). *The Goat in the Rug.* Geraldine, a goat, describes the way she and her friend make a Navajo rug, from the hair clipping and carding to the dyeing and actual weaving.

Bruchac, Joseph. (1998). *The Boy Called Slow: The True Story of Sitting Bull.* Illustrated by Rocco Baviera. This biography is a picture book about the boyhood of Sitting Bull, a Lakota (Sioux) Indian, who grew up in the 1830s.

Bruchac, Joseph, and London, Jonathan. (1997). *Thirteen Moons on a Turtle's Back: A Native American Year of Moons.* Illustrated by Thomas Locker. Myths or legends of different Native American tribes are told in poetry and paintings.

Bunting, Eve. (2002). *Cheyenne Again.* Illustrated by Irving Toddy. The story of Young Bull, a Cheyenne boy who struggles to hold onto his heritage.

Caduoto, Michael, and Bruchac, Joseph. (1991). *Keepers of the Animals: Native American Stories and Wildlife Activities for Children.* A book of Native American stories and creative nature activities.

Devlin, Wende and Harry. (1971). *Cranberry Thanksgiving.* Grandmother's cranberry bread was wonderful and Maggie was careful that no one stole the recipe. Cranberry bread recipe included.

Francis, Lee. (Editor). (1999). *When the Rain Sings: Poems by Young Native Americans.* This anthology consists of thirty-seven beautiful poems by young Native American writers from across the United States.

Morris, Ann. (2003). *Grandma Maxine Remembers: A Native American Family Story.* This is the story of an eight-year-old Shawnee girl of the Shoshone tribe who lives on the Wind River Reservation, in Wyoming, with her mother, siblings, and grandmother. This photo-essay shows life on a reservation.

Stamper, Judith Bauer. (1996). *New Friends in a New Land: A Thanksgiving Story.* Illustrated by Chet Jezierski. A young Pilgrim girl is afraid of her new home. Then she becomes friends with Native American neighbors and they celebrate Thanksgiving together.

Stock, Catherine. (1993). *Thanksgiving Treat.* Everyone is busy with Thanksgiving preparations, leaving out the youngest child, until Grandpa has an idea.

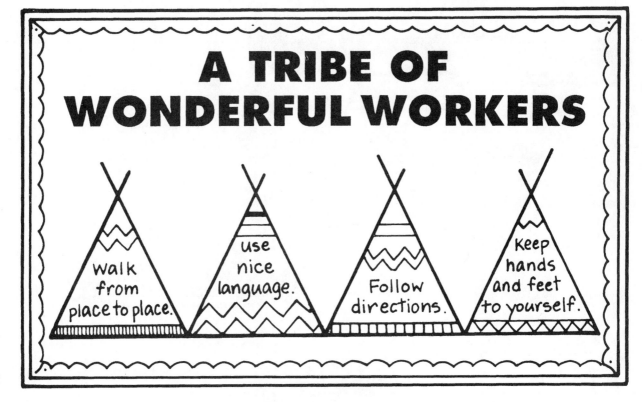

A TRIBE OF WONDERFUL WORKERS

Walk from place to place.

Use nice language.

Follow directions.

Keep hands and feet to yourself.

A CORNUCOPIA OF SUPER WORKERS

134

Happy Family Feast! Move ahead 2.

Game Cards

Too much turkey! Lose 1 turn.

Hit with an arrow! Move back 1.

Spilled your cranberry sauce. Move back 2.

Good Harvest Move ahead 3.

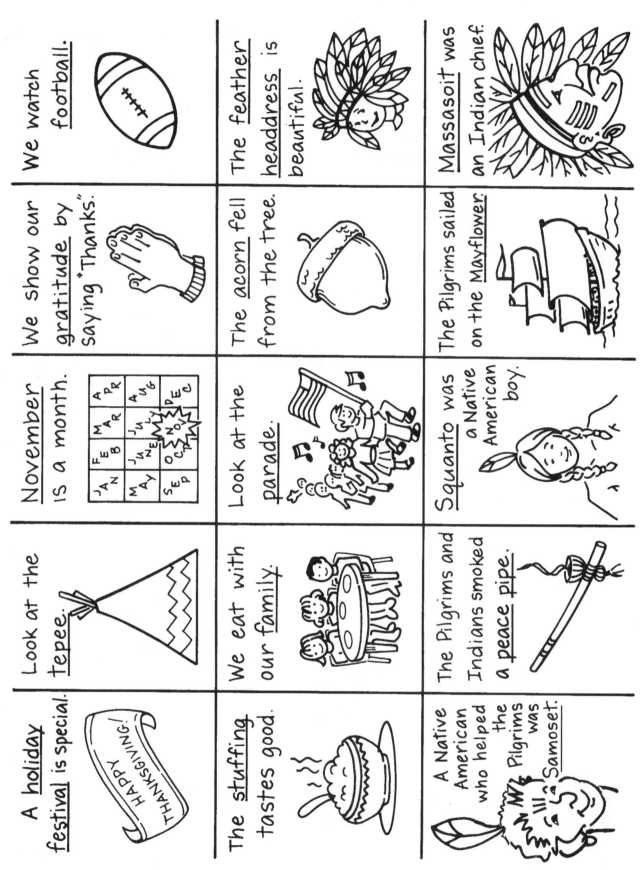

We watch football.

The feather headdress is beautiful.

Massasoit was an Indian chief.

We show our gratitude by saying "Thanks."

The acorn fell from the tree.

The Pilgrims sailed on the Mayflower.

November is a month.

Look at the parade.

Squanto was a Native American boy.

Look at the tepee.

We eat with our family.

The Pilgrims and Indians smoked a peace pipe.

A holiday festival is special.

The stuffing tastes good.

A Native American who helped the Pilgrims was Samoset.

HAPPY THANKSGIVING!

Settlers landed on Plymouth Rock.

A totem pole reminds us of Indians.

Thanksgiving is on the third Thursday in November.

Look at the cornucopia of fruit.

The corn husks are pretty.

The autumn season is also called fall.

Eat a yummy turkey dinner.

Look at the colored leaves.

We eat pumpkin pie.

Eat the cranberry sauce.

Indians used a bow and arrow.

The Pilgrims and Indians celebrated.

It is harvest time.

We eat turkey on Thanksgiving Day.

Candied yams taste good.

November Sorting Game

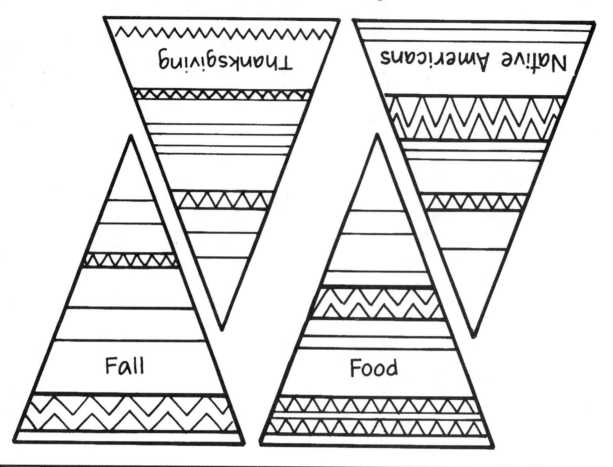

Thanksgiving

Native Americans

Fall

Food

Answer Key

Native Americans
- bow and arrow
- totem pole
- tepee
- Samoset
- peace pipe
- Squanto
- Massasoit
- feather headdress

Fall
- harvest time
- colored leaves
- corn husks
- autumn season
- November
- acorn
- football
- Cornucopia of fruit

Thanksgiving
- Plymouth Rock
- third Thursday
- holiday festival
- gratitude
- family
- parade
- Mayflower
- Thanksgiving Day
- Pilgrims and Native Americans

Food
- pumpkin pie
- candied yams
- turkey dinner
- stuffing
- cranberry sauce

November Matching Game

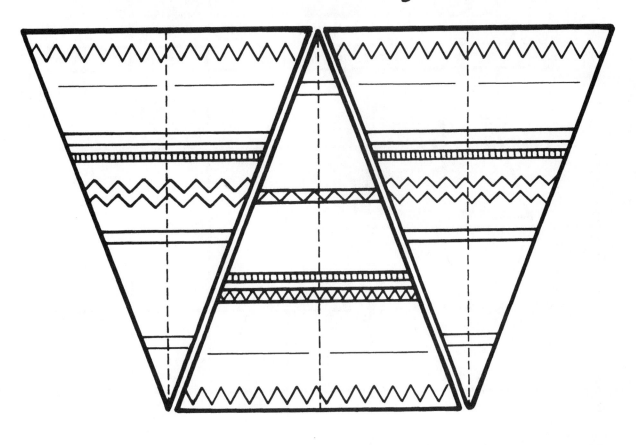

Answer Key

harvest + time	totem + pole
cranberry + sauce	candied + yams
turkey + dinner	peace + pipe
cornucopia + of fruit	pumpkin + pie
Plymouth + Rock	autumn + season
Thanksgiving + Day	third + Thursday
bow + and arrow	holiday + festival
colored + leaves	feather + headdress
corn + husks	Pilgrims + and Indians

NOVEMBER

SUNDAY	MONDAY	TUESDAY	WEDNESDAY	THURSDAY	FRIDAY	SATURDAY

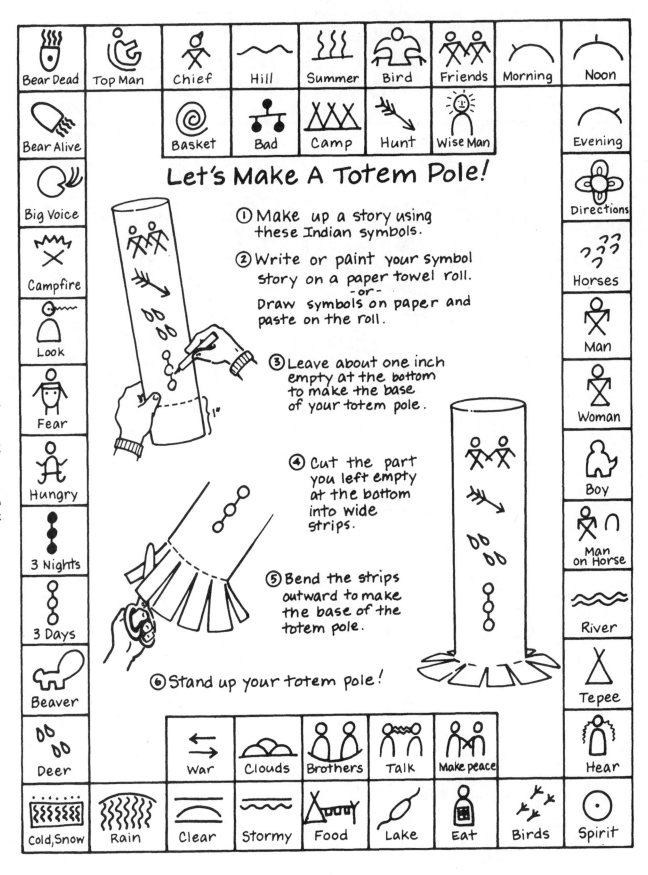

Let's Make A Totem Pole!

① Make up a story using these Indian symbols.

② Write or paint your symbol story on a paper towel roll.
-or-
Draw symbols on paper and paste on the roll.

③ Leave about one inch empty at the bottom to make the base of your totem pole.

④ Cut the part you left empty at the bottom into wide strips.

⑤ Bend the strips outward to make the base of the totem pole.

⑥ Stand up your totem pole!

Bear Dead · Top Man · Chief · Hill · Summer · Bird · Friends · Morning · Noon

Basket · Bad · Camp · Hunt · Wise Man

Bear Alive · Evening · Directions · Horses · Man · Woman · Boy · Man on Horse · River · Tepee · Hear

Big Voice · Campfire · Look · Fear · Hungry · 3 Nights · 3 Days · Beaver · Deer

War · Clouds · Brothers · Talk · Make peace

Cold, Snow · Rain · Clear · Stormy · Food · Lake · Eat · Birds · Spirit

DECEMBER AND JANUARY: WINTER WONDERLAND

Theme Decorations

Create a winter snow scene.

Game and Dramatic Play Areas

You will need these materials for the thematic game area:

- Basic equipment
- Winter Wonderland board game, card games, sorting game, and matching game
- Learning center skill games (Section Five)
- Winter vocabulary cards (game cards or index cards with underlined words from game cards written on them)
- A sign that says "Winter is a great time to read!"
- A poster or sign with student directions: "1. Read the winter vocabulary cards to a partner. 2. Play a reading game with a partner."

You will need these materials for the dramatic play area (the snow scene):

- Wall space
- A solid-color bed sheet, blue or white
- White cotton batting and glitter or artificial snow spray
- A winter pond made of white or light blue construction paper
- Hand-drawn ice skaters, evergreens, and snowmen (and women) made by children
- Thumbtacks and straight pins
- Bare branches planted in clay flowerpots
- Small tree lights (optional)
- White or light blue snowflake cutouts (see following illustration)
- Snowcaps, mittens, scarves, boots, jackets, skis, sled

Post the names of the children who will be in the dramatic play area. All others will play reading games.

Snowflake Directions

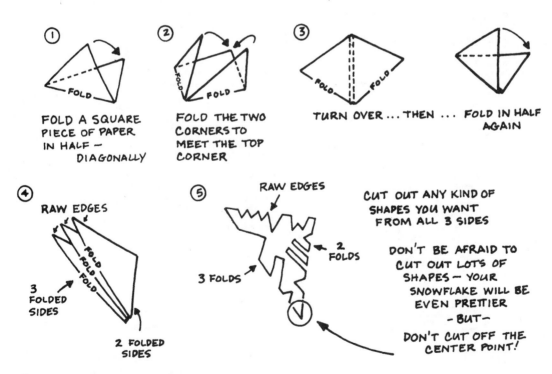

① FOLD A SQUARE PIECE OF PAPER IN HALF — DIAGONALLY

② FOLD THE TWO CORNERS TO MEET THE TOP CORNER

③ TURN OVER ... THEN ... FOLD IN HALF AGAIN

④ RAW EDGES   3 FOLDED SIDES   2 FOLDED SIDES

⑤ RAW EDGES   3 FOLDS   2 FOLDS

CUT OUT ANY KIND OF SHAPES YOU WANT FROM ALL 3 SIDES

DON'T BE AFRAID TO CUT OUT LOTS OF SHAPES — YOUR SNOWFLAKE WILL BE EVEN PRETTIER – BUT – DON'T CUT OFF THE CENTER POINT!

⑥ UNFOLD GENTLY AND FLATTEN IN A THICK BOOK FOR A DAY OR SO

⑦ HANG YOUR SNOWFLAKES FROM THE CEILING WITH WHITE THREAD AND TAPE – OR – STICK THEM TO THE WINDOW FOR AN INSTANT SNOW SCENE!

Theme Setup

1. Using thumbtacks, hang the sheet on the wall.

2. Tack or pin the cotton batting onto the bottom half of the sheet. Sprinkle with glitter or spray with snow.

3. Attach the pond and cutouts to the sheet with straight pins.

4. Stand the pots of bare branches on each side of the scene. Wrap lights around the bare branches (optional).

5. Place a box of winter clothing—snowcaps, mittens, scarves, boots, jackets—and the skis and sled nearby.

6. Post student directions.

Bulletin Boards

See the illustrations on page 148.

Whole-Group Activities

- Learn new vocabulary: *snowflake, hibernate, migrate,* and so on.
- Role-play winter stories.
- Make a winter bird feeder for the playground.
- Decorate the December and January calendars.
- Make snowstorm jars (see following illustration).

Snowstorm Jars

YOU WILL NEED—
- I SMALL JAR WITH A TIGHT LID
- I SMALL PLASTIC FORM SUCH AS A SNOWMAN
- HOT GLUE GUN, GLUE OR FLORAL CLAY
- SILVER GLITTER
- LIQUID DETERGENT
- WATER

DIRECTIONS—

1. USING THE HOT GLUE GUN (OR GLUE OR FLORAL CLAY) STICK THE PLASTIC FORM TO THE JAR LID.

2. PUT ONE TEASPOON OF GLITTER IN THE JAR AND SLOWLY FILL WITH WATER. ADD ONE DROP OF DETERGENT.

3. SCREW THE LID TIGHT, INVERT THE JAR AND SHAKE GENTLY TO MAKE A SNOWSTORM.

Hot Apple Cider Recipe

A bottle of apple cider (46 ounces)

Two to three cinnamon sticks

A slow-cooker (such as a Crock-Pot)

1. Combine ingredients.
2. Simmer in the Crock-Pot.
3. Serve in small drinking cups.

Content Area Activities

- Study how snowflakes form and why each is unique.
- Use reference materials to find out how igloos are made.
- Keep a daily record of high and low temperatures.
- Learn about winter animal habits—migration, hibernation, and so on.
- Find out how evergreens differ from deciduous plants and trees.

Word Play Center Activities

- Play skill games that reinforce skills being taught at the Teacher Center.
- Play the Winter Wonderland board game, card games, sorting game, and matching game.
- Read winter vocabulary cards made by the teacher.

Thematic Books

Emergent and Early Readers

Benjamin, Alan. (1993). *Hanukkah.* This book introduces children to the traditions and artifacts of this Jewish holiday, including the dreidel and menorah.

Blades, Ann. (1990). *Winter.* A brother and sister have fun playing in the snow.

Briggs, Raymond. (1989). *The Snowman.* In this wordless book, a little boy runs out into the wintry day to build a snowman, which comes alive in his dreams that night (ALA Notable).

Burton, Virginia. (1988). *Katy and the Big Snow.* Katy, a tractor, pushes a bulldozer in the summer and a snowplow in the winter so that townspeople can do their jobs. (Audiocasette is also available for the Listening Center.)

Brown, Margaret Wise. (1994). *The Winter Noisy Book*. Illustrated by Charles G. Shaw. A little dog listens to the indoor and outdoor sounds of winter—sneezes, rattling branches, a crackling fire, and the tinkling of iced tree branches.

Cartwright, Ann. (1993). *The Winter Hedgehog*. Illustrated by Reg Cartwright. Rather than hibernate, a young hedgehog travels to find winter and discovers the season to be beautiful but cold and dangerous.

Chocolate, Deborah M. Newton. (1999). *My First Kwanzaa Book*. Illustrated by Cal Massey. This book introduces the holiday during which African Americans celebrate their cultural heritage.

Coleridge, Sara. (1986). *January Brings the Snow*. Illustrated by Jenni Oliver. In this poem about the changing seasons, each month brings something new and different.

Goffstein, M. B. (1986). *Our Snowman*. When a girl and her young brother build a snowman, their father creates a companion for the snowman.

Joosse, Barbara M. (2001). *A Houseful of Christmas*. Illustrated by Betsy Lewin. A family finds out that, even during a blizzard, Granny's house is the best place for Christmas.

Keats, Ezra Jack. (1962). *The Snowy Day*. A boy wakes up to discover that snow has fallen during the night. (A CD version is available for the Listening Center; Caldecott Medal.)

Lobe, Mira. (1984). *The Snowman Who Went for a Walk*. Illustrated by Winfried Opgenoorth. A wandering snowman decides to find a place where he can live and never melt.

McCully, Emily A. (2003). *First Snow*. A family of mice goes sledding, and when the smallest sister conquers the big hill she wants to go again and again.

Morgan, Allan. (1987). *Sadie and the Snowman*. Illustrated by Brenda Clark. When Sadie makes a snowman, animals eat the eyes, nose, and mouth, and then the snowman melts. This happens several times, but Sadie doesn't give up.

Munsch, Robert. (1985). *Thomas's Snowsuit*. Thomas won't wear his new snowsuit despite the urging of his mother, his teacher, and the principal.

Developing and Fluent Readers

Bancroft, Henrietta. (1997). *Animals in Winter*. An Asian-American girl and boy find out how animals in a country neighborhood prepare for winter.

Bartoli, Jennifer. (1979). *In a Meadow, Two Hares Hide*. Illustrated by Takeo Ishida. When a Japanese boy and an American girl compare sounds of animals in their own languages they find that one animal says the same thing to them both.

Cole, Joanna. (1973). *Plants in Winter*. Illustrated by Kazue Mizumura. This book explains what happens to various plants in winter.

Devlin, Wende and Harry. (1991). *Cranberry Christmas*. Mr. Whiskers faces a gloomy Christmas, but Maggie and her grandmother help him clean house and find the deed to the nearby pond.

Duncan, Jane. (1975). *Brave Janet Reachfar*. During a snowstorm, Janet goes out to a hill to rescue a lost sheep but winds up needing help herself.

Fain, Moira. (1998). *Snow Day*. Maggie Murphy is happy when school is let out because of snow. She thinks she is avoiding an assignment, but she meets her teacher on the sledding hill.

Freedman, Russell. (1981). *When Winter Comes*. This book describes how various animals prepare for and survive the winter season.

George, Jean Craighead. (2003). *Snow Bear*. Bessie meets a polar bear cub, and they become friends. Watched over by mother bear and Bessie's wary older brother, they enjoy each other's company until a large male bear appears.

Johnston, Tony. (1993). *The Last Snow of Winter*. Illustrated by Friso Henstra. Gaston Pompicard creates a large snow sculpture of all the children in his neighborhood. One day, as he hears children laughing outside, he and his dog look out to see a snow sculpture of him!

Joosse, Barbara M. (1999). *Snow Day!* This is about a great family snowball fight; includes cartoon-style illustrations.

Lapp, Eleanor. (1976). *The Mice Came in Early This Year*. Illustrated by David Cunningham. A boy observes winter preparations made by his family and by the wild creatures outdoors.

Moore, Clement C. (1998). *The Night Before Christmas*. Illustrated by Christian Birmingham. A new rendition of the 1822 Clement Clarke Moore poem.

Pinkney, Andrea Davis, and Pinkney, Brian. (1993). *Seven Candles for Kwanzaa*. This book is an introduction to the holiday. It explains the meaning of the weeklong African-American winter holiday and the way each day is celebrated.

Potter, Teresa. (1999). *Fang: The Story of a Fox in Winter*. A fox experiences his first winter, looking for food and interacting with other animals in the woods.

Rau, Dana M. (2000). *Kwanzaa*. This holiday lasts seven days. Each day is centered around a different principle: unity, self-determination, collective work and responsibility, cooperative economics, purpose, creativity, and faith. The holiday reminds people of African descent of the harvest festivals of long ago.

Silverman, Maida. (1999). *Festival of Lights*. This book explains the origin and importance of Hanukka and includes a holiday game, a song, and instructions for the candle-lighting ceremony.

December/January Bulletin Boards

DECEMBER

SUNDAY	MONDAY	TUESDAY	WEDNESDAY	THURSDAY	FRIDAY	SATURDAY

JANUARY

SUNDAY	MONDAY	TUESDAY	WEDNESDAY	THURSDAY	FRIDAY	SATURDAY

December/January Sorting Game

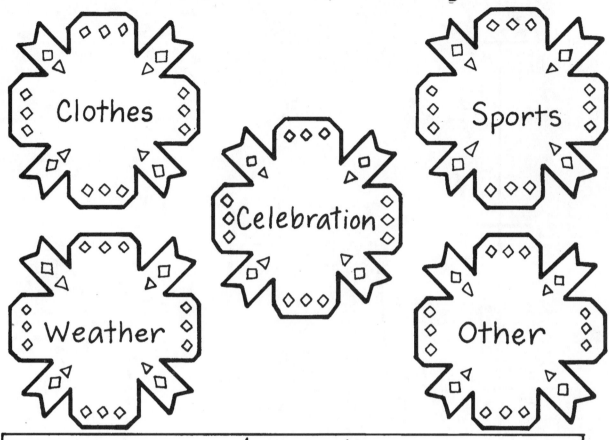

Clothes

Sports

Celebration

Weather

Other

Answer Key

Celebration	Clothes	Sports
Christmas tree	stockings	ice hockey
presents	mittens	downhill skiing
Santa Claus	winter coat	ice skating
Hanukka	hat	sledding
Kwanzaa	wool scarf	snowmobile
reindeer	boots	**Weather**
New Year	sweater	snowflake
candy cane	**Other**	ice
mistletoe	hot chocolate	freezing cold
ornaments	snowman	windy
holly wreath	fireplace	

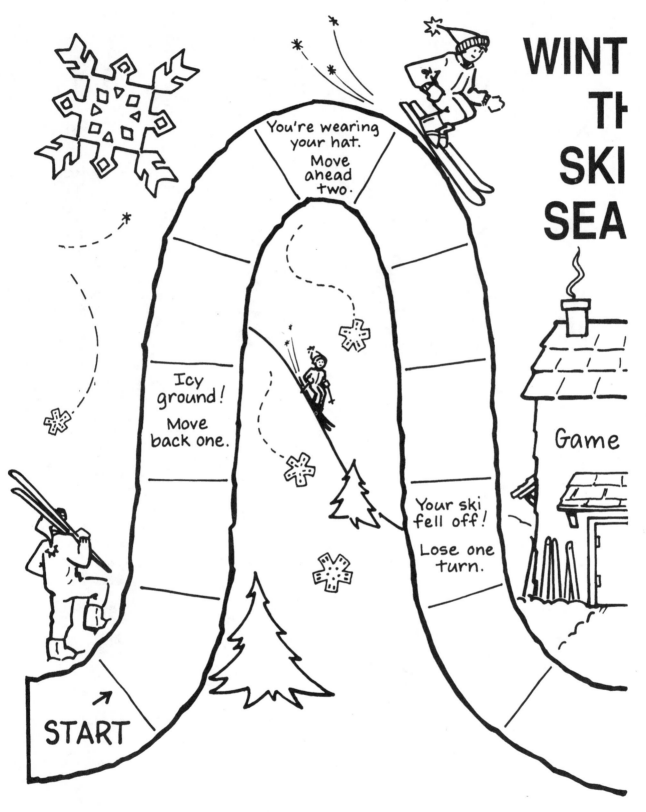

WINT
TH
SKI
SEA

You're wearing your hat. Move ahead two.

Icy ground! Move back one.

Your ski fell off! Lose one turn.

Game

START

ER IS

HE

ING

SON

Blizzard!
Move back
two.

Lots of
good snow
for skiing.
Roll
again!

Cards

You won the
ski race!

Move
ahead
one.

You
Win!
FINISH

Let's build
a snowman.

The reindeer
has antlers.

It is freezing
cold outside.

The snowflake
is pretty.

Presents
are gifts.

Water turns
to ice.

I see a
candy cane.

Santa Claus
brings toys.

It is windy.

Sledding
is fun.

Hanukka is a
Jewish holiday.

We celebrate
the New Year.

Look at the
mittens.

Hot chocolate
tastes good.

Celebrate
Kwanzaa.

See the <u>mistletoe</u>.

Let's sit by the <u>fireplace</u>.

<u>Ice</u> hockey is a sport.

The <u>holly</u> <u>wreath</u> is pretty.

Look at the wool scarf.

The <u>sweater</u> is warm.

<u>Ornaments</u> are decorations.

See the winter <u>coat</u>.

Ride on the <u>Snowmobile</u>!

Look at the <u>boots</u>.

This is a <u>hat</u>.

<u>Stockings</u> are warm.

<u>Ice</u> skating is fun.

Look at the <u>Christmas</u> tree.

<u>Downhill</u> skiing is fun.

155

December/January Matching Game

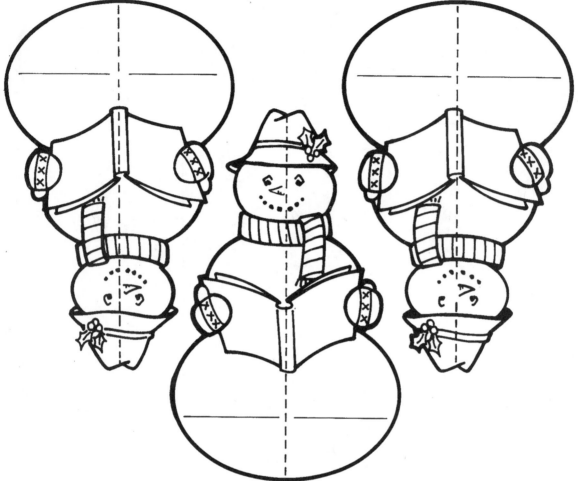

Answer Key

downhill + skiing	wool + scarf
ice + skating	winter + coat
Christmas + tree	New + Year
Santa + Claus	candy + cane
freezing + cold	holly + wreath
snow + flake	hot + chocolate
celebrate + Kwanzaa	snow + man
rein + deer	snow + mobile
ice + hockey	fire + place

FEBRUARY: BLACK HISTORY MONTH AND VALENTINE'S DAY

Theme Decorations

Have students make African art and African masks to display as decorations.

Game and Dramatic Play Areas

You will need these materials for the thematic game area:

- Basic equipment
- Black History/Valentine's Day board games, card games, sorting games, and matching games
- Learning center skill games (Section Five)
- Black History/Valentine's Day vocabulary cards (game cards or index cards with underlined words from game cards written on them)
- A sign that says: "Celebrate Black History Month and Valentine's Day."
- A poster or sign with student directions: "1. Read the February vocabulary cards to a partner. 2. Play a reading game with a partner."

In the dramatic play area have students dress up and play the parts of African-American heroes and "sheroes." *For dramatic play set in the slavery era:* you will need kerchiefs for the head, aprons, and long skirts for the girls; denim overalls and straw hats for the boys. *For play set in the civil rights era:* you will need fashionable straw hats, high heels, and gloves for the girls; and suits, shirts, neckties, and bow ties for the boys.

Theme Setup

1. Place clothing in separate boxes marked "Slavery Era" and "Civil Rights Era."
2. Add other props, such as a toy kitchen and farm equipment for the slavery era, and briefcases and office equipment for the civil rights era.

Post the names of the children who will be in the dramatic play area. All others will play reading games.

Bulletin Boards

See the illustrations on page 167. (See also page 266 on Valentine's Day).

About the Game Cards

Since 1940, the U.S. Postal Service has issued stamps to commemorate black heroes and heroines who have contributed to America's history. The February game cards show copies of some of the stamps that have been issued; new ones are issued each February. The following list of the individuals depicted on the game cards includes a word or group of words that describe each one. Two matching games are provided—one matches first and last names (for beginning readers), the other matches the name of the person and what he or she is famous for (for developing and fluent readers). In the spirit of Black History Month, it is important to talk about the groundbreaking work that each of these heroes and heroines did. Emerging and early readers can learn this information, even though they might not be able to play the more advanced matching game.

Musicians

Louis Armstrong, trumpeter

Nat King Cole, popular music singer

Duke Ellington, jazz ambassador

Mahalia Jackson, gospel singer

James Weldon Johnson, author of the hymnal *Lift Every Voice and Sing*

Scott Joplin, ragtime composer

Ma Rainey, "Mother of the Blues"

Athletes

Joe Louis, boxer

Jesse Owens, Olympic track star

Satchel Paige, baseball player

Jackie Robinson, baseball player

Scientists and Mathematicians

Benjamin Banneker, mathematician

George Washington Carver, scientist

Bessie Coleman, aviation pioneer

Percy Lavon Julian, chemist

Ernest E. Just, marine biologist

Historical and Political Figures

Mary McCleod Bethune, educator

Ralph Bunche, winner of the Nobel Peace Prize

Dr. Allison Davis, anthropologist

Benjamin O. Davis Sr., Army general

Frederick Douglass, abolitionist

W.E.B. DuBois, educator and the first black American to receive a Ph.D. from Harvard University

Patricia Roberts Harris, U.S. ambassador

Dr. Martin Luther King Jr., civil rights leader

Thurgood Marshall, Supreme Court justice

Bill Pickett, cowboy

A. Philip Randolph, civil rights leader

Harriet Tubman, abolitionist

Booker T. Washington, educator

Carter G. Woodson, "Father of Black History"

Many additional stamps are available, including one representing Kwanza, and stamps depicting the following individuals.

Musicians

Count Basie, Big Band leader

Eubie Blake, pianist

John Coltrane, saxophonist

Erroll Garner, composer

W. C. Handy, "Father of the Blues"

Coleman Hawkins, saxophonist

Billie Holiday, jazz singer

James P. Johnson, pianist

Robert Johnson, blues singer

Huddy "Leadbelly" Ledbetter, guitarist

Roberta Martin, gospel singer

Clyde McPhatter, rhythm and blues musician

Charles Mingus, bassist

Thelonious Monk, jazz pianist

Jelly Roll Morton, pianist

Charlie Parker, saxophonist

Otis Redding, popular music singer

Jimmy Rushing, jazz singer

Bessie Smith, jazz singer

Sonny Terry, folk musician

Sister Rosetta Tharpe, guitarist

Clara Ward, leader of the Ward Singers gospel group

Dinah Washington, rhythm and blues singer

Ethel Waters, blues singer

Muddy Waters, blues singer

Josh White, folksinger

Howlin' Wolf, blues singer

Athlete

Roberto Clemente, baseball player

Scientist

Dr. Charles R. Drew, researcher of blood plasma

Historical and Political Figures

Jim Beckwourth, fur trader

Matthew Henson, explorer

Langston Hughes, writer

Salem Poor, soldier

Paul Robeson, activist, actor, and singer

Sojourner Truth, abolitionist

Ida B. Wells, cofounder of the NAACP

Roy Wilkins, civil rights leader

Malcolm X, civil rights leader (originally named Malcolm Little)

Whitney Young, civil rights leader

Whole-Group Activities

- Learn new vocabulary: *demonstration, segregation, integration, prejudice, slave,* and so on.
- Make African masks. Color and display the masks. You may want to have a "Color the Mask" contest.
- Visit an African-American museum.
- Choose a school in Africa to visit on the Internet.
- Have students explore their family roots.
- Read storybooks about African-American children.
- Invite an African-American speaker to the class.
- Choose pen pals from another culture and send valentine cards to them.
- Create an African rhythm dance.
- Write a rap song using rhyming words.
- Have a fashion show of African attire.
- Decorate the calendar on page 175.

Cornbread Recipe

Corn muffin mix

Eggs and milk, if recipe requires

Mixing bowl, measuring cups, and spoon for stirring; knife for slicing muffins

Nonstick spray

Muffin tins (or individual custard cups) that will fit into a toaster oven

Toaster oven

Butter or margarine

1. Prepare batter by following muffin-mix directions.
2. Spray muffin tins with nonstick cooking spray. Pour batter into tins.
3. Heat toaster oven to temperature muffin-mix suggests.
4. Bake muffins in toaster oven.
5. Cut each muffin into two or three sections and serve with butter.

Content Area Activities

- Study the lives of Dr. Martin Luther King Jr. and Malcolm X.
- Have a Martin Luther King Jr. birthday party: send invitations, bake a cake (using a cake mix and canned icing), make birthday cards, count candles to show how old he would be if alive today.
- Plan an African-American "Food Tasting Fair."
- Have daily "Moments in Black History."
- Locate the seven continents on a map of the world, then locate the continent of Africa.
- Study an African country and the people who live there.

Word Play Center Activities

- Play skill games that reinforce skills being taught at the Teacher Center.
- Play the Black History Month board game, card games, sorting game, and matching game.
- Read February vocabulary cards made by the teacher.

For Further Study

Study the year 1619, when the first Africans were brought to America as slaves, or find out more about the following famous people:

Muhammad Ali, boxing champ (originally named Cassius Clay)

Arthur Ashe, tennis champ

Henry Blair, one of earliest black inventor to receive a patent

Shirley Chisolm, politician

Bill Cosby, entertainer

Althea Gibson, first black person to play in the Wimbleton Tennis Tournament

Whoopi Goldberg, actress, entertainer

Alex Haley, author of the book *Roots*

Reverend Jesse Jackson, political leader

Maynard Jackson, first black mayor of Atlanta

Mae C. Jemison, physician and first black female astronaut in space

Barbara Jordan, the South's first black congresswoman

Michael Jordan, basketball champ

Ronald E. McNair, black astronaut who died in *Challenger* explosion, posthumously awarded the Congressional Space Medal of Honor

Rosa Parks, the woman who famously refused to give up her bus seat to a white man

Sidney Poitier, actor

Wilma Rudolph, track star, Olympic Gold Medalist

Harriet Beecher Stowe, author of *Uncle Tom's Cabin*

Madam C. J. Walker, designer of the hot comb for black hair

Phillis Wheatley, first black woman to be published

Oprah Winfrey, entertainer

Venus and Serena Williams, tennis champs

Tiger Woods, golf pro

You may also want to study these black institutions and organizations:

Bethune-Cookman College

Clark Atlanta University

Essence, the magazine of today's black woman

Fisk University

Florida A&M University

Howard University

Morehouse College

National Association for the Advancement of Colored People (NAACP)

Here are some ideas for additional matching games:

Soul + Food

Black + Power

Soul + Brother

African + American

Slave + Owner

Civil + Rights

Segregation + Integration

Teacher Resource Book

Tibbett, Teri. (2004). *Listen to Learn: Using American Music to Understand Language Arts and Social Studies.* Although this resource book is designed for grades five to eight, it includes excellent information about African-American music, including the music of the slaves, spirituals, and the blues (see Unit 3).

Thematic Books

Emergent and Early Readers

Bang, Molly. (1996). *Ten, Nine, Eight.* Numbers from ten to one are part of this lullaby between a daddy and his little girl (Caldecott Honor Book).

Bunting, Eve. (1999). *Smoky Night.* During a night of rioting in Los Angeles, amid fires and looting, neighbors come together (Caldecott Medal).

Davol, Marguerite. (1993). *Black and White, Just Right!* Illustrated by Irene Trivas. The story is about an interracial child who explores the different skin colors of the members of her family.

Flournoy, Valerie. (1992). *The Best Time of Day.* Illustrated by George Ford. As he goes through his busy day, William decides what time of day he likes best.

Hoffman, Mary. (1998). *Amazing Grace.* Illustrated by Shay Youngblood. A classmate says that Grace cannot play Peter Pan in the school play because she is black, but Grace finds that she can do anything she sets her mind to do.

Hoffman, Mary. (2000). *Boundless Grace.* Illustrated by Caroline Binch. Grace feels strange about visiting her father's new family in Africa, but Nana says families are what you make them.

Johnson, Angela. (2000). *Daddy Calls Me.* Illustrated by Rhonda Mitchell. Four poems about the happy home life of a young African-American boy.

Kates, Bob. (1992). *We're Different, We're the Same.* The colorful characters from Sesame Street teach young children about racial harmony.

Klingel, Cynthia. (2001). *Rosa Parks.* Illustrated by Robert Noyed. A phonics-based book about Rosa Parks, who played a major role in the civil rights movement.

Kroll, Virginia L. (1998). *Faraway Drums.* Illustrated by Floyd Cooper. Two sisters are frightened by the city noises at their new apartment, but then they remember the stories about life in Africa that their great-grandmother had told.

Nikola-Lisa, W. (1995). *Bein' with You This Way.* Illustrated by Michael Bryant. This playground rap shows children how people are different, yet the same.

Rappaport, Doreen. (2001). *Martin's Big Words: The Life of Martin Luther King, Jr.* This book sums up Martin Luther King Jr.'s life and work.

Steptoe, John. (1986). *Stevie.* Robert, an African-American child, resents and then misses a little foster brother (ALA Notable Book).

Steptoe, John. (1987). *Mufaro's Beautiful Daughters.* Mufaro's two beautiful daughters—one bad-tempered and one kind—go before the king, who is choosing a wife.

Yarbrough, Camille. (1979). *Cornrows.* The book shows how the cornrows hair style—an ancient symbol in Africa—can currently symbolize the courage of outstanding African Americans (Coretta Scott King Award Book).

Developing and Fluent Readers

Adedjouma, Davida. (Editor). (1999). *The Palm of My Heart: Poetry by African-American Children.* Illustrated by Gregory Christie. A collection of poems by children who participated in a writing workshop (Coretta Scott King Illustrator Award).

Adler, David A. (1993). *A Picture Book of Harriet Tubman.* Illustrated by Samuel Byrd. A biography of the black woman who escaped from slavery to become famous as a conductor on the Underground Railroad.

Adler, David A. (1995). *A Picture Book of Frederick Douglass.* Illustrated by Samuel Byrd. A biography of the man who escaped slavery and became a speaker, writer, and leader in the abolitionist movement.

Adler, David A. (1995). *A Picture Book of Rosa Parks.* Illustrated by Robert Casilla. Another look at Rosa Parks, who helped spark the civil rights movement by keeping her seat on a Montgomery bus.

Adler, David A. (1996). *A Picture Book of Sojourner Truth.* Illustrated by Gershom Griffith. About the life of the woman born into slavery who became a famous abolitionist.

Adler, David A. (1997). *A Picture Book of Jackie Robinson.* Illustrated by Robert Casilla. A brief look at Jackie Robinson's life—his childhood, athletic accomplishments, and the bigotry and prejudice he faced as the first African American to play in the major leagues.

Adler, David A. (1999). *A Picture Book of Thurgood Marshall.* Illustrated by Robert Casilla. The life story of Thurgood Marshall, who became a highly regarded Supreme Court justice.

Adler, David A. (2000). *A Picture Book of George Washington Carver.* Illustrated by Dan Brown. The book includes important facts about slavery and racial prejudice as well as documenting the botanist's significant contributions.

Farris, Christine King. (2003). *My Brother Martin: A Sister Remembers Growing Up with the Rev. Dr. Martin Luther King, Jr.* Illustrated by Chris Soentpiet. This is an informational story told by King's sister that shows how he got many of his ideas and courage—from his dad!

Gavin, Curtis. (2001). *The Bat Boy and His Violin.* Illustrated by Earl B. Lewis. In this book, a young violin player—whose father manages the Negro National League's worst team—plays his violin in the dugout and inspires the Dukes to make it to the playoffs (Coretta Scott King Illustrator Honor Book).

Grimes, Nikki. (2003). *Talkin' About Bessie: The Story of Aviator Elizabeth Coleman.* Illustrated by E. B. Lewis. The story of the early African-American aviator is revealed in snapshots, free-verse poetry, and watercolors (Coretta Scott King Illustrator Award; Coretta Scott King Author Award).

Nelson, Vaunda Micheaux. (2003). *Almost to Freedom.* Illustrated by Colin Bootman. A beloved rag doll tells how Lindy's family escapes on the Underground Railroad to find freedom. (Coretta Scott King Honor Book).

Orgill, Roxane. (1997). *If I Only Had a Horn.* Illustrated by Leonard Jenkins. This is the story of beloved Louis Armstrong—a boy who grew up to be a giant of jazz.

Pinkney, Andrea Davis. (1998). *Duke Ellington.* Illustrated by Brian Pinkney. A picture-book biography of jazz musician Edward Kennedy Ellington—better known to all as the Duke (Caldecott Honor Book).

Pinkney, Andrea Davis. (2002). *Ella Fitzgerald: The Tale of a Vocal Virtuosa.* Illustrated by Brian Pinkney. Illustrations and words create a portrait of the jazz star (ALA Notable).

Rappaport, Doreen. (2000). *Freedom River.* Illustrated by Bryan Collier. John Parker repeatedly risked his life to help other slaves escape to freedom. This book describes one of the exciting incidents (Coretta Scott King Honor Book).

Ryan, Pam Muñoz. (2002). *When Marian Sang: The True Recital of Marian Anderson, Voice of a Century.* Illustrated by Brian Selznick. This is about the life of famed African-American contralto Marian Anderson. It tells of her perseverance in overcoming the barriers to both train and perform because of her race (Sibert Honor Book).

February Bulletin Boards

STAMPS OF

START "

You learn about the Olympics! Go again!

APPROVAL

Jackie Robinson
Black Heritage USA 20c

OLYMPIAN
USA 25

USA 33
SATCHEL PAIGE

MAHALIA JACKSON
32

GAME CARDS

You listen to some jazz! Go ahead one!

W.E.B.DuBois
29
Black Heritage USA

Scott Joplin
Black Heritage USA 20c

32
LOUIS ARMSTRONG
USA

"Ma" Rainey

USA 29 'MA' RAINEY — BLUES SINGER, 1886-1939

Percy Lavon Julian

Percy Lavon Julian 29 — Black Heritage USA

Satchel Paige

USA 33 — SATCHEL PAIGE

Frederick Douglass

FREDERICK DOUGLASS 25c U.S. POSTAGE

Mahalia Jackson

32 USA MAHALIA JACKSON — GOSPEL SINGER

Bill Pickett

USA 29 BILL PICKETT

Ralph Bunche

Ralph Bunche USA 20c

George Washington Carver

32 USA George Washington Carver

Bessie Coleman

BLACK HERITAGE USA 32 BESSIE COLEMAN

Booker T. Washington

UNITED STATES POSTAGE 10c 10c

Jessie Owens

OLYMPIAN Jesse Owens 1936 USA 25

Scott Joplin

Scott Joplin Black Heritage USA 20c

Louis Armstrong

USA 32 LOUIS ARMSTRONG — JAZZ COMPOSER AND TRUMPETER

W.E.B. DuBois

W.E.B. DuBois 29 Black Heritage USA

Nat "King" Cole

USA NAT "KING" COLE 29 — POPULAR SINGER, 1917-1965

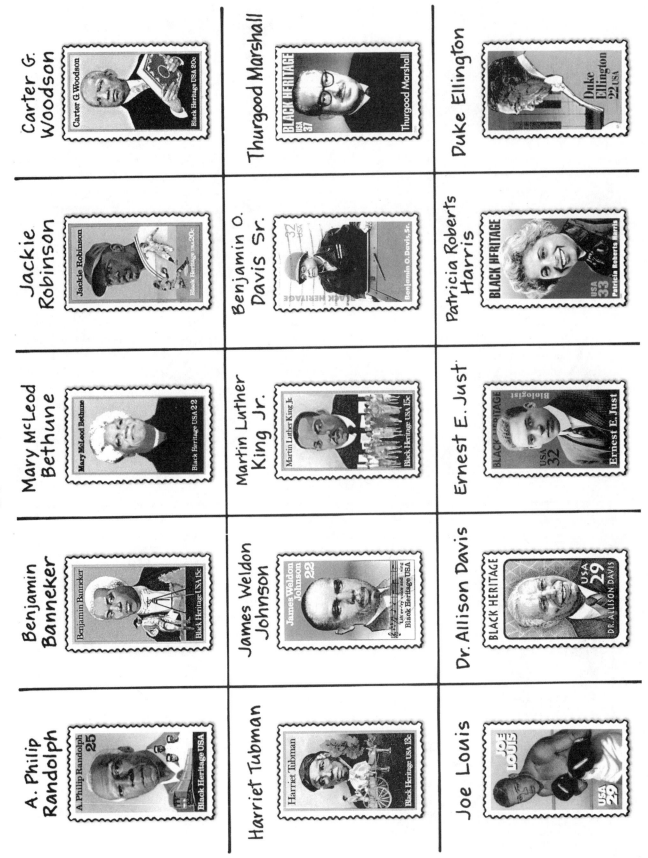

Carter G. Woodson

Thurgood Marshall

Duke Ellington

Jackie Robinson

Benjamin O. Davis Sr.

Patricia Roberts Harris

Mary McLeod Bethune

Martin Luther King Jr.

Ernest E. Just

Benjamin Banneker

James Weldon Johnson

Dr. Allison Davis

A. Philip Randolph

Harriet Tubman

Joe Louis

February Sorting Game

| Music | Science |
| History | Sports |

History

Mary McLeod Bethune
Ralph Bunche
Dr. Allison Davis
Benjamin O. Davis
Frederick Douglass
Martin Luther King Jr.
Bill Pickett
A. Philip Randolph
Harriet Tubman
Booker T. Washington
Carter G. Woodson
Patricia Roberts Harris
W.E.B. Du Bois
Thurgood Marshall

Science

Bessie Coleman
Percy Lavon Julian
Ernest E. Just
Benjamin Banneker
George Washington
   Carver

Sports

Joe Louis
Jessie Owens
Jackie Robinson
Satchel Paige

Music

Louis Armstrong
Nat "King" Cole
Duke Ellington
Mahalia Jackson
Scott Joplin
James W. Johnson
"Ma" Rainey

Answer Key

February Matching Game

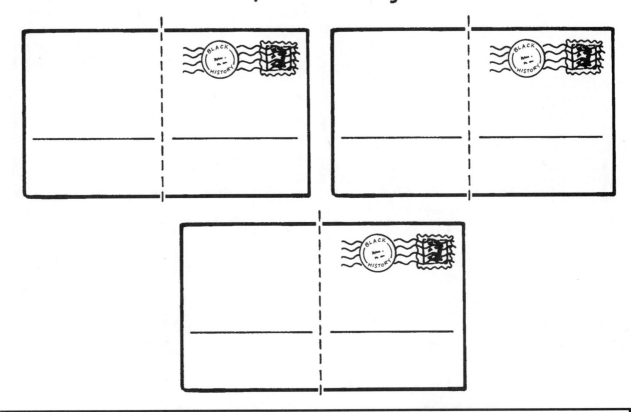

Answer Key

A. Philip + Randolph

Benjamin + Banneker

Mary McLeod + Bethune

Jackie + Robinson

Harriet + Tubman

James W. + Johnson

Martin + Luther King Jr.

Benjamin O. + Davis

Joe + Louis

Dr. Allison + Davis

Ernest E. + Just

Thurgood + Marshall

Duke + Ellington

Louis + Armstrong

Patricia Roberts + Harris

Booker T. + Washington

Ralph + Bunche

Frederick + Douglass

"Ma" + Rainey

W.E.B. + DuBois

Jessie + Owens

George Washington + Carver

Mahalia + Jackson

Percy Lavon + Julian

Nat "King" + Cole

Scott + Joplin

Bessie + Coleman

Satchel + Paige

Bill + Pickett

Carter G. + Woodson

February Matching Game

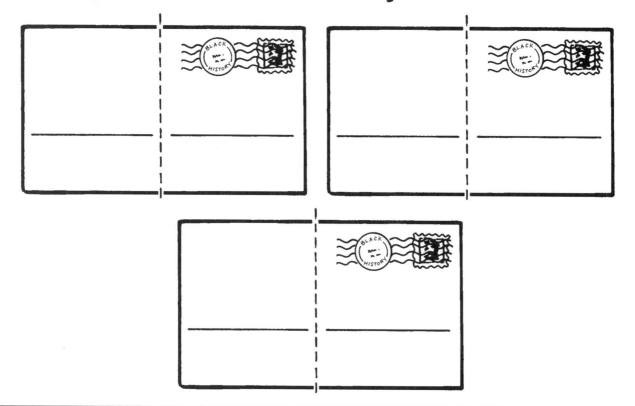

Answer Key

A. Philip Randolph + Civil Rights
Benjamin Banneker + Mathematics
Mary McLeod Bethune + Educator
Jackie Robinson + Baseball Player
Harriet Tubman + Liberator
James W. Johnson + Hymn Writer
Martin Luther King Jr. + Civil Rights
Benjamin O. Davis + General
Joe Louis + Boxer
Dr. Allison Davis + Anthropologist
Ernest E. Just + Marine Biologist
Thurgood Marshall + Supreme Court
Duke Ellington + Jazz Ambassador
Louis Armstrong + Trumpeter
Patricia Roberts Harris + U.S. Ambassador

Booker T. Washington + Educator
Ralph Bunche + Nobel Peace Prize
Frederick Douglass + Abolitionist
"Ma" Rainey + Mother of the Blues
W.E.B. DuBois + Educator
Jessie Owens + Olympic Track Star
George Washington Carver + Peanut Scientist
Mahalia Jackson + Gospel Singer
Percy Lavon Julian + Chemist
Nat "King" Cole + Popular Singer
Scott Joplin + Ragtime
Bessie Coleman + Aviation Pioneer
Satchel Paige + Baseball Pitcher
Bill Pickett + Black Cowboy
Carter G. Woodson + Father of Black History

BLACK HISTORY MONTH

SUNDAY	MONDAY	TUESDAY	WEDNESDAY	THURSDAY	FRIDAY	SATURDAY

Make an African Mask!

Punch
holes
here.

Cut out
some
holes
to see!

1. Color the
   mask in
   your colors.

2. Cut out
   your mask.

3. Attach strings or
   pipecleaners
   for wearing.

4. Wear your mask
   and talk about
   Black History
   and Africa.

MARCH: SPACESHIP

Theme Decorations

Decorate to fit the spaceship theme.

Game and Dramatic Play Areas

You will need these materials for the game area:

- Basic equipment
- Spaceship board game, card games, sorting game, and matching game
- Learning center skill games (Section Five)
- March vocabulary cards (game cards or index cards with underlined words from game cards written on them)
- A sign that says: "It's spectacular to read in a spaceship."
- A poster or sign with student directions: "1. Read the March vocabulary cards to a partner. 2. Play a reading game."

You'll need these materials for the dramatic play area (to create a spaceship):

- A large appliance box with top (such as a box for a refrigerator or washing machine)
- Silver spray paint
- A mural of the solar system
- A throw rug

Post names of children who will be in the dramatic play area. All others will play reading games.

Theme Setup

1. Let the children paint a mural of the solar system. Hang it on a wall in the Word Play Center.
2. Spray-paint the appliance box and box top. Stand the box upright and use a sharp knife or box cutter to cut a door tall enough for children to see out when they sit in the box. Place the throw rug in the bottom.

Bulletin Boards

See the illustrations on page 183.

Whole-Group Activities

- Learn new vocabulary: *planet, galaxy, space capsule,* and so on.
- Build models of the moon and planets.
- Make space helmets. *Use plastic gallon milk jugs:* Cut the top off the jug, cut an arch in one side for the face, and spray-paint silver or cover with foil. *Use grocery bags:* Cut a hole in the bag for the face; decorate with paint and foil.
- Create a mural of the solar system for the theme setup.
- Make a class book of astronauts: take a photo of each child sitting in the spaceship. Have children write a story about their "spaceship ride." Glue the children's photos to their stories and bind together for a class book.
- Make Zero-Gravity Space Pudding (recipe follows). Then list and display words that describe the pudding.
- Decorate the March calendar on page 190.

Zero-Gravity Space Pudding Recipe*

Instant pudding (each package makes eight servings)

Milk

Self-sealing plastic bags (one per child)

1. Put one tablespoon instant pudding and a quarter-cup milk in each bag. Zip the bags closed.
2. Squeeze the bags to make pudding. Let them stand several minutes.
3. Cut a corner off each bag. Children sip the pudding through the hole.

Content Area Activities

- Study the solar system.
- Study the history of rockets.
- Read about the U.S. space program.
- Learn about constellations.
- Find longitude and latitude lines on a globe.
- Identify continents and oceans on a map.
- Find out how many miles the earth is from the sun, moon, Mars, and so on.
- Line planets up, smallest to largest.
- List which planets have moons and which do not.
- Find the length of day and year on each planet.
- Define meteoroids, asteroids, comets, and galaxies.
- Answer this question: *What is an orbit?*

Word Play Center Activities

- Sit in the spaceship and play reading games.
- Play skill games that reinforce skills being taught at the Teacher Center.
- Play the spaceship board game, card games, sorting game, and matching game.
- Read March vocabulary cards made by the teacher.

Note: Pudding recipe courtesy of Diane Holman.

Thematic Books

Emergent and Early Readers

Agee, Jon. (1996). *Dmitri the Astronaut*. Dmitri returns to Earth with Lulu, his companion during a visit to the moon, and becomes an overnight sensation when he begins drawing pictures of a mysterious figure. This is a science fiction fantasy.

Anderson, Joan. (1993). *Richie's Rocket*. Illustrated by George Ancona. Richie blasts off in his cardboard spaceship for an adventurous journey of exploration to the moon.

Barton, Byron. (1988). *I Want to Be an Astronaut*. Would-be astronauts sleep in zero gravity, put on space suits, help fix a satellite, and then come back to Earth.

Fox, Christyan. (2002). *Astronaut Piggy Wiggy*. Illustrated by Diane Fox. Piggy Wiggy imagines what it would be like to be a daring astronaut.

Coffelt, Nancy. (1996). *Dogs in Space*. Dogs in space visit each of the planets in the solar system.

Collicott, Sharleen. (1996). *Seeing Stars*. Junkyard animals build a "junkbird" and fly up to what they think are the stars.

Fuchs, Erich. (1970). *Journey to the Moon*. Describes a trip to the moon.

Kroll, Steven. (1992). *The Magic Rocket*. Illustrated by Will Hillenbrand. Felix loves his toy rocket, but when his dog is captured by aliens, he flies it on a rescue mission.

Kuskin, Karla. (1978). *A Space Story*. This book introduces the characteristics of the sun and planets.

Leedy, Loreen. (1996). *Postcards from Pluto: A Tour of the Solar System*. A group of children tour the solar system with Dr. Quasar, who describes each of the planets from Mercury to Pluto.

Loomis, Christine. (2001). *Astro Bunnies*. Illustrated by Ora Eitan. Astro Bunnies fly rockets, explore space, and return home.

Lorenz, Lee. (1983). *Hugo and the Spacedog*. A dog is refused a post to guard farm animals until a visitor from space proves that a watchdog is needed.

Maisner, Heather. (1997). *Planet Monsters*. Illustrated by Alan Rowe. This is an adventure and puzzle story with Planet Monster. The main job is to find a way through the planet's ten zones to the Underground City and stop the Mad Mathematician from destroying the universe.

Mitton, Tony. (2000). *Roaring Rockets*. This is a simple explanation of how space rockets work, where they travel, and what they do.

Oxenbury, Helen. (1989). *Tom and Pippo See the Moon*. A boy asks questions about the moon and imagines himself and his toy monkey flying there.

Pinkney, Brian. (2000). *Cosmo and the Robot*. Cosmo lives on Mars with his sister and a broken robot. When his parents give him a new Solar System Utility Belt with ten supersonic attachments, his luck changes.

Rabe, Tish. (1999). *There's No Place Like Space: All About Our Solar System*. Beginning readers-astronomers take a wild trip to visit the planets with the Cat in the Hat, Thing One, Thing Two, and Dick and Sally.

Stott, Carole. (2003). *I Wonder Why Stars Twinkle and Other Questions About Space*. Curious young astronomers find the answers to such questions as "What are stars made of?" and "Why do astronauts float in space?"

Developing and Fluent Readers

Blocksma, Mary. (1983). *Easy-to-Make Spaceships That Fly*. Illustrated by Dewey Blocksma. The book gives directions for making spaceships from paper plates, straws, styrofoam cups, and other materials available in supermarkets.

Branley, Franklyn. (1983). *The Sky Is Full of Stars*. Children learn about star colors and brightness, locating constellations, and making planetariums from coffee cans and flashlights.

Branley, Franklyn. (1988). *Journey into a Black Hole*. Illustrated by Marc Simont. Readers go on an imaginary trip to a black hole.

Branley, Franklyn. (1998). *Floating in Space*. The book looks at life on a space shuttle and describes how astronauts deal with weightlessness, how they eat and exercise, and some of their work.

Branley, Franklyn. (1998). *The Planets in Our Solar System*. The book describes the nine planets and other bodies of the solar system. It includes directions for making models showing the size of the planets and their distance from the sun.

Branley, Franklyn. (1999). *Is There Life in Outer Space?* This book details ideas and misconceptions about life in outer space in light of recent space explorations.

Branley, Franklyn. (2000). *What the Moon Is Like*. Features information and photos from the Apollo space missions, with a description of how the moon's composition, terrain, and atmosphere differ from Earth's.

Cole, Joanna. (1992). *The Magic School Bus Lost in the Solar System*. Illustrated by Bruce Degen. On an exciting field trip in a magic school bus, Ms. Frizzle's class visits each planet.

Graham, Ian. (1998). *The Best Book of Spaceships*. The book shows how we have tried to learn about space. Some of the equipment and vehicles are described.

Greene, Carol. (1997). *Astronauts Work in Space*. Jobs that astronauts do aboard a space shuttle and how they prepare on the ground are described.

Hopkins, Lee Bennett. (1996). *Blast Off! Poems About Space*. Illustrated by Melissa Sweet. Poems about the moon, stars, planets, and astronauts are included in this book.

Jones, Brian. (1990). *Practical Astronomer*. This is a step-by-step guide to the basic techniques of astronomy.

Lauber, Patricia. (1996). *You're Aboard Spaceship Earth!* The earth is like a spaceship in orbit. It has everything onboard that we need to survive—water, food, and air with oxygen—and it is able to renew its resources.

Oxlade, Chris. (1999). *Space Shuttle (Take It Apart!).* Illustrated by Mike Grey. The book describes different parts of a space shuttle and how they work.

Petty, Kate. (1997). *The Sun Is a Star and Other Amazing Facts About Space.* Provides an introduction to the solar system—planets, stars, comets, meteorites, black holes—and other information about outer space.

Rey, H. A. (1976). *Find the Constellations.* This is a beginner's guide to locating and identifying constellations in the Northern Hemisphere. It includes an index, a glossary, and a timetable for looking at the sky.

Ride, Sally. (1986). *To Space and Back.* U.S. astronaut Sally Ride shares her outer-space adventure.

Ride, Sally, and O'Shaughnessy, Tam. (2003). *Exploring Our Solar System.* Describes what we learn about the solar system by using telescopes and spacecraft.

March Bulletin Boards

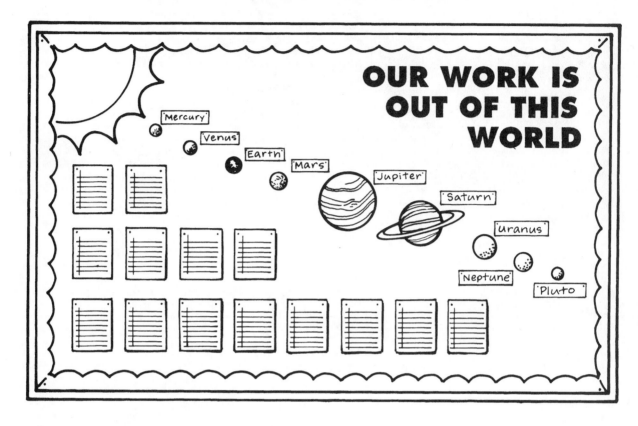

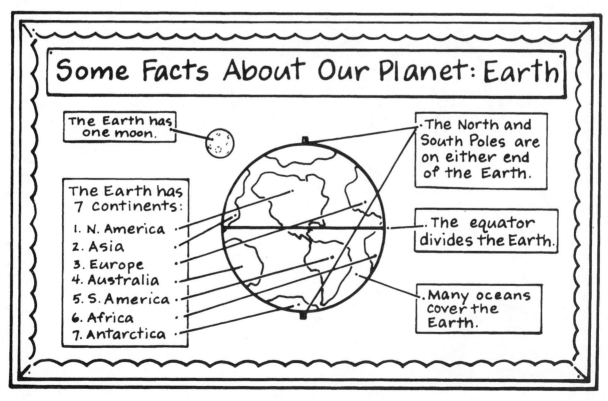

WEATHER

Saw a shooting star! Move ahead 2.

START

Game Cards

Walk on the moo Roll again.

184

TAKE A TRIP ON THE BIG DIPPER

No gravity! Lose 1 turn.

FINISH You Win!

USA

Blast Off! Move ahead 1.

Too far from Earth! Go back 1.

Saturn's rings surround it.

An astronaut explores space.

The Earth has one moon.

Neighborly Mars is close to Earth.

Neptune is closer than Pluto.

Constellations are groups of stars.

Venus is a cloudy planet.

Uranus is closer than Neptune.

A flying saucer is make-believe.

Big Jupiter is a planet.

Tiny Pluto is far away.

Look through a telescope.

We live on Earth.

Mercury is close to the Sun.

The spaceship goes fast.

We live in the United States.

U.S.A.

Astronauts put satellites in space.

WEATHER

There are no real Martians.

M

The North and South Poles are on each end of the Earth.

N. Pole

S. Pole

All the planets make up the Solar system.

A U.F.O. is pretend.

The equator divides the Earth.

There are many blue oceans.

An alien is not real.

The bright Sun is hot.

There are seven continents.

Cape Canaveral is in Florida.

CAPE CANAVERAL

See the shooting star.

Longitude and latitude lines divide the Earth.

YOU ARE HERE

The rocket will orbit the moon.

March Sorting Game

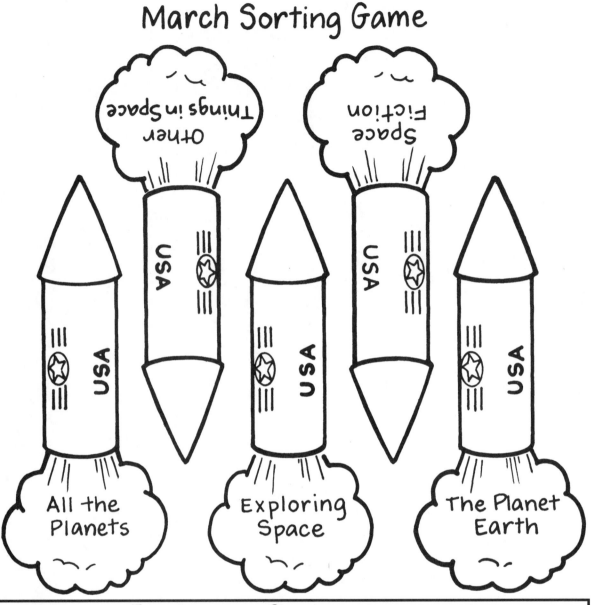

All the Planets	Exploring Space	The Planet Earth	Space Fiction	Other Things in Space
Earth	astronaut	seven continents	alien	constellations
Big Jupiter	Cape Canaveral	blue oceans	flying saucer	moon
Venus	spaceship	United States	Martian	shooting star
Saturn's rings	orbit	equator	U.F.O.	solar system
Mercury	satellite	North/South Pole		bright sun
Tiny Pluto	telescope	longitude and latitude		
Uranus				
Neptune				
Neighborly Mars				

Answer Key

March Matching Game

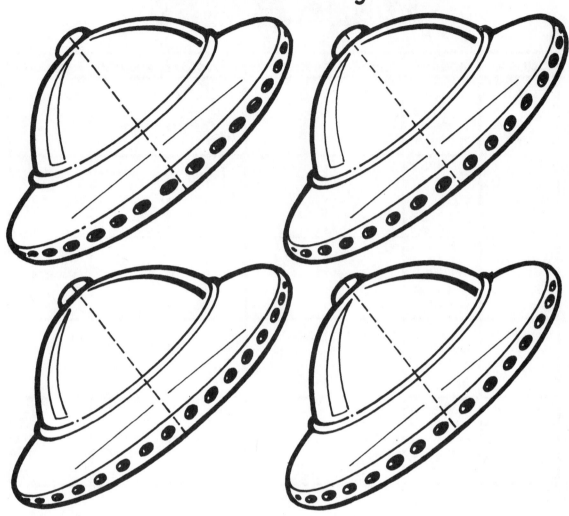

Answer Key

latitude + longitude	big + Jupiter
space + ship	solar + system
Saturn's + rings	flying + saucer
tiny + Pluto	North and South + Poles
seven + continents	shooting + star
blue + oceans	bright + Sun
United + States	neighborly + Mars

MARCH

SUNDAY	MONDAY	TUESDAY	WEDNESDAY	THURSDAY	FRIDAY	SATURDAY

APRIL: SPRINGTIME

Theme Decorations

Decorate to resemble a patio.

Game and Dramatic Play Areas

You will need these materials for the game area:

- Basic equipment
- April board game, card games, sorting game, and matching game
- Learning center skill games (Section Five)
- April vocabulary cards (game cards or index cards with underlined words from game cards written on them)
- A sign that says: "Spring into good reading."
- Poster or sign with student directions: "1. Read the April vocabulary cards to a partner. 2. Play a reading game with a partner."

You will need these materials for the dramatic play area (to create a patio setting):

- A large umbrella, or several small ones and strong cord
- Table and chairs or other patio furniture
- Toy food: hamburgers, hot dogs, condiments (and other foods appropriate for outdoor eating)
- Toy grill, apron, spatulas, and tongs for outdoor cooking
- Cloth napkins, plastic dishes, glasses, mugs, and silverware for outdoor eating
- Dish gardens and grass. *For dish gardens:* Use large plastic butter tubs, potting soil, pebbles, and green plants. *For Hairy Harry:* With markers, draw a face on the side of a disposable cup. Fill cup with potting soil, plant grass seed in the top, and keep moist. When the grass seed sprouts, you will have Hairy Harry.

Post the names of children who will be in the dramatic play area. All others will play reading games.

Theme Setup

1. Tie cord to the tip of the umbrella or umbrellas.
2. Open the umbrellas and hang them from the ceiling or light fixture.
3. Arrange patio furniture, grill, and plants nearby.
4. Keep toy food, dishes, napkins, apron, and so on in a box.

Bulletin Boards

See the illustrations on page 196.

Whole-Group Activities

- Learn new vocabulary: *seeds, blossoms, Earth Day,* and so on.
- Celebrate Earth Day.
- Plant a tree in the schoolyard.
- Make "delicious" bird nests—decorate cupcakes with green icing, coconut, and jelly beans.
- Dye eggs.
- Decorate construction-paper eggs with glitter, yarn, and paint.
- Visit a farm.

- Plant seeds using potting soil and disposable cups.
- Decorate the April calendar on page 197.

Egg Salad Sandwich Recipe*

For each child, you will need:

> One disposable cup
>
> Mayonnaise, mustard, milk
>
> One hard-boiled egg
>
> Celery or pickle relish
>
> Two slices bread
>
> A plastic serrated knife
>
> Waxed paper or clear wrap

1. Measure two teaspoons mayonnaise into cup.
2. Measure one-quarter teaspoon mustard into cup.
3. Measure one teaspoon milk into cup. Stir the mixture.
4. Crack and peel the egg.
5. Put the egg on a piece of waxed paper or clear wrap. With the knife, cut the egg into small pieces and place in the cup.
6. Add one teaspoon chopped celery or pickle relish.
7. Stir and spread on bread. Enjoy!

Content Area Activities

- Keep a log of weather patterns—note rain, lightning, thunder, and rainbows.
- Study the life cycles of frogs and butterflies.
- Using a science textbook, conduct a unit on flowers—the parts of a flower, the role of bees and other insects in pollination.
- Plan a garden. Measure length and width, plan number of rows, and decide what flowers and vegetables will be planted in each row.
- Find out why rainbows appear.
- Learn to measure. Use measuring spoons to make egg salad sandwiches (see recipe above).

Note: Egg salad sandwich recipe courtesy of Ardyth Ann Stanley.

Word Play Center Activities

- Play skill games that reinforce skills being taught at the Teacher Center.
- Play the April board game, card games, sorting game, and matching game.
- Read April vocabulary cards made by the teacher.

Thematic Books

Emergent and Early Readers

Bruce, Lisa. (2000). *Fran's Flower.* Illustrated by Rosalind Beardshaw. A little girl finds a flowerpot containing a tiny green shoot. She tries feeding it pizza and chocolate chip cookies, but when it still won't grow and bloom, she throws it out the door. The plant then grows and surprises Fran with a big, beautiful flower.

Carle, Eric. (2001). *Tiny Seed.* Colorful illustrations and a simple text tell the fascinating story of the life cycle of a flower by way of the adventures of a tiny seed.

Clifton, Lucille. (1988). *The Boy Who Didn't Believe in Spring.* Illustrated by Brinton Turkle. Two city boys decide to find spring, which, they've heard, is "just around the corner."

Cole, Henry. (1997). *Jack's Garden.* A delightful guide to creating a garden: "This is the garden that Jack planted." The ending page features gardening suggestions.

Domanska, Janina. (1976). *Spring Is.* A little dog explores fields during each of the four seasons.

Heller, Ruth. (1999). *Plants That Never Ever Bloom.* Wonderful illustrations and rhyming verse tell about mushrooms and seaweed that have no flowers.

Heller, Ruth. (1999). *The Reason for a Flower.* Flowers create seeds, but the author also discusses parts of plants and their functions—all in rhythmic verse.

Horton, Barbara Sawadge. (1994). *What Comes in Spring.* A mother tells her daughter how she grew inside her as the seasons changed.

Kuchalla, Susan. (1982). *All About Seeds.* Illustrated by Jane McBee. The author presents several kinds of seeds and shows how they grow into plants.

Kraus, Robert. (1982). *The First Robin.* Richard hopes to be the first robin of spring. He arrives a day early and catches a terrible cold. Kindly Groundhog cares for him.

Moncure, Jane B. (1975). *Spring Is Here.* The sights, smells, sounds, and activities of spring are described in verse.

Rockwell, Anne. (1985). *First Comes Spring.* Bear Child notices that everything changes with the seasons—the clothes he wears, the things everyone does at work and play, and other aspects of his world.

Developing and Fluent Readers

Barklem, Jill. (1995). *Spring Story*. The story of the little mice of Brambly Hedge.

Blos, Joan W. (1992). *A Seed, a Flower, a Minute, an Hour*. Illustrated by Hans Poppel. This poem praises of the beauty of growth: tadpole to frog, puppy to dog, seed to flower, minute to hour, and so on.

Cohen, Carol L. (1975). *Wake Up, Groundhog!* A pigeon tries a variety of ways to wake up the sleeping groundhog.

Fisher, Aileen Lucia. (1977). *And a Sunflower Grew*. Farmer Jones plants a sunflower that grows all summer and becomes food for the birds during the winter.

Gibbons, Gail. (1993). *From Seed to Plant*. The author shows the relationship between seeds and the plants that they produce.

Hirschi, Ron. (1996). *Spring*. Illustrated by Thomas D. Mangelsen. Text and photographs show how nature looks in spring.

Hopkins, Lee Bennett. (1993). *Easter Buds Are Springing: Poems for Easter*. Illustrated by Tomie de Paola. A collection of nineteen Easter poems.

Hughes, Monica. (1996). *A Handful of Seeds*. Illustrated by Luis Garay. After Grandmother dies, Concepcion and her family move to the city, where no garden grows. But Concepcion envisions a way to keep her grandmother's legacy—a seed collection.

Jordan, Helen J. (1992). *How a Seed Grows*. The author demonstrates the growth of seeds to plants with the story of bean seeds planted in eggshells.

Krensky, Stephen. (1990). *Lionel in the Spring*. Lionel has lots to do in spring—plant a vegetable garden, help celebrate his parents' anniversary, play with a friend, and help with spring cleaning.

Kroll, Steven. (1987). *I Love Spring!* Illustrated by Kathryn E. Shoemaker. A young boy describes all the things he loves about spring—spring birds, flowers, gardening, outdoor activities, and springtime celebrations.

Kroll, Steven. (1991). *It's Groundhog Day*. Illustrated by Jenni Bassett. Roland Raccoon is worried that an early spring will ruin his ski-lodge business, so he tries to prevent Godfrey Groundhog from looking for his shadow on Groundhog Day.

Simon, Seymour. (1996). *Spring Across America*. Photographs show the changes in spring, follows its movement from the southern to the northern United States, and describes its impact on the plants and animals in nature.

Tresselt, Alvin R. (1977). *Hi, Mister Robin*. This book shows the world of spring with color illustrations, many of them two-page spreads.

Watson, Mary. (1995). *Butterfly Seeds*. Jake brings special seeds to America that remind him of his grandfather.

April Bulletin Boards

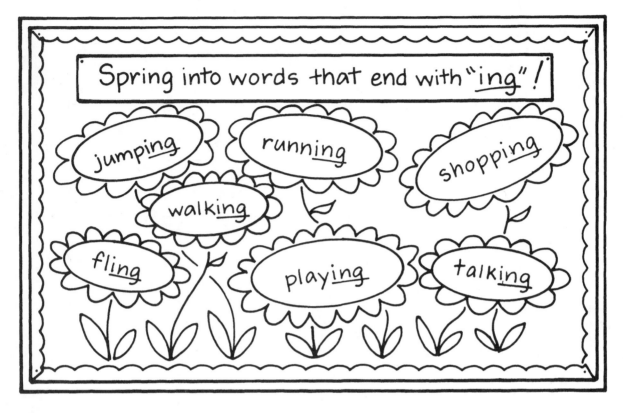

Spring into words that end with "_ing_"!

jumping

running

shopping

walking

fling

playing

talking

WHAT'S YOUR FAVORITE SPRING THING?

APRIL

SUNDAY	MONDAY	TUESDAY	WEDNESDAY	THURSDAY	FRIDAY	SATURDAY

START

LET'S GO FLOWER HOPPING

See a rainbow. Roll again.

Found some Easter eggs. Move ahead one.

Game Cards

Stung by a bee! Lose one turn.

Caught
in a
thunderstorm.
Go back
two.

FINISH
You
Win!

Your
garden grew.
Move ahead
one.

See the rosebud.

Look at the grass.

See the snake.

A rainbow comes at the end of a storm.

See the blossoms.

Jump in the mud puddle.

Thunder and lightning can be scary.

The flower basket is pretty.

The Easter bunny hops.

HAPPY EASTER!

Put on your hat.

See the green tree.

Seeds grow to be plants.

BEANS

See the drop of rain.

A daisy is pretty.

Plant in the garden.

The buzzing bee flies.

See the basket of goodies.

Look at the storm clouds.

Look at the bunny rabbit.

I like colored eggs.

Wear your rain boots.

Chirping birds sound good.

Look at the duck.

See the umbrella.

The white lamb is soft.

Look at the frog.

I like Earth Day.

See the fluffy chick.

See the butterfly.

Celebrate Arbor Day.

April Sorting Game

Answer Key

<u>Animals</u>	<u>Holiday</u>	<u>Rain Things</u>	<u>Plants & Flowers</u>
fluffy chick	Easter bunny	drop of rain	rose bud
white lamb	colored eggs	umbrella	daisy
chirping birds	basket of goodies	rain boots	green tree
bunny rabbit	Arbor Day	hat	flower basket
buzzing bee	Earth Day	mud puddle	blossoms
butterfly		storm clouds	grass
frog		rainbow	garden
duck		thunder and	seeds
snake		lightning	

April Matching Game

Answer Key

chirping + birds
bunny + rabbit
buzzing + bee
butter + fly
drop + of rain
mud + puddles
storm + clouds
thunder + lightning
rain + bow
white + lamb

Easter + bunny
Arbor + Day
colored + eggs
basket + of goodies
Earth + Day
rose + bud
green + tree
flower + basket
fluffy + chick

MAY: CINCO DE MAYO

Theme Decorations

Decorate as a background for a Mexican band.

Game and Dramatic Play Areas

You will need these materials for the game area:

- Basic equipment
- Cinco de Mayo board game, card games, sorting game, and matching game
- Learning center skill games (Section Five)
- May vocabulary cards (game cards or index cards with underlined words from game cards written on them)
- A sign that says: "We celebrate Cinco de Mayo."
- A poster or sign with student directions: "1. Read the Cinco de Mayo vocabulary cards to a partner. 2. Play a reading game with a partner."

You will need these materials for the dramatic play area:

- Mexican flags: children draw and color Mexican flags as decorations
- Instruments: maracas, guitar, accordion (or toy instruments)
- Mexican clothing: sombrero, poncho, dress, beads, and so on
- Mexican toy foods: tacos, salsa, tortillas
- Tables

Theme Setup

1. Make a cozy corner in your classroom and decorate it with Mexican flags.
2. On a small table, place a set of maracas, a guitar, and an accordion.
3. In another area of that corner place a poncho and a Mexican hat.
4. Place "play" food, including tacos, chips, salsa and tortillas, on a second table.

Post the names of the children who will be in the dramatic play area. All others will play reading games.

Bulletin Boards

See the illustrations on page 211. Both bulletin boards are vocabulary games for two or three players. *For the piñata bulletin board:* Use thumbtacks to attach the candy (word) pieces around the piñata. Each player says the word, unhooks it, and places it into the pocket of the piñata. *For the sombrero bulletin board:* Students use a pointer to "read the sombreros" in both Spanish and English.

Card Game and Matching Game

Cinco de Mayo features one card game; photocopy both pages. Children match the Spanish card with the English card. For the Cinco de Mayo matching game, make a *tapete* (a Mexican rug) by photocopying the diamond-shaped game pieces on light tan paper. Then have children play the game on a blue or burgundy cloth place mat or rectangular piece of material. As the children put the game pieces together, the mat will start to look like a Mexican rug.

Whole-Group Activities

- Learn new vocabulary (English and Spanish).
- Talk about piñatas.
- Bring Mexican food items for every day of the week: tacos, quesadillas, enchiladas, tamales, frijoles, salsa, empanadas, churros, and so on.
- Make a contest between two groups to find out which group knows more Spanish.
- Read greeting cards in Spanish and English.
- Make a piñata and have students fill it with candy.
- Have students make tapetes out of construction paper. Laminate them, if possible.
- Decorate the Mayo calendar on page 218. Fill in the days and mark Cinco de Mayo.
- Learn the days of the week in Spanish (point them out on the calendar): Sunday: *domingo;* Monday: *lunes;* Tuesday: *martes;* Wednesday: *miercoles;* Thursday: *jueves;* Friday: *viernes;* Saturday: *sabado.*

Nacho Beef Hot Dip Recipe*

One pound lean ground beef

Hot plate and heavy skillet

One cup shredded sharp cheese

One cup mild salsa

Salt and pepper

Crock-Pot

One large bag dipping-style corn chips

1. Brown beef in heavy skillet, drain, and combine with cheese, salsa, and salt and pepper.
2. Pour meat mixture into a small Crock-Pot to keep warm for serving.
3. Dip directly into pot with large corn chips. *(Be sure this is done under adult supervision.)*

---

*Note: Nacho dip recipe courtesy of Faith Whitesides.

Content Area Activities

- Learn the Cinco de Mayo story.
- Learn to count to ten in Spanish: one: *uno;* two: *dos;* three: *tres;* four: *quatro;* five: *cinco;* six: *sies;* seven: *siete;* eight: *ocho;* nine: *nueve;* ten: *diez.*
- Visit a Mexican Web site with students to see pictures and learn about the culture in Mexico (for example, see www.AltaVista.com).
- Gather information about students' favorite foods.
- Introduce math and science with the following activity (see illustration). Bring in guacamole sauce (green sauce) and chunky salsa (red sauce). Have students try both sauces and choose their favorite. Make a graph of the results and discuss which sauce the students liked the most. Ask the following questions: What sauce did the children like the most? What sauce did the children like the least? Compare the totals—how many more students would be needed to make both totals even? If all the students voted for the same sauce, how many total votes would that sauce get?

Word Play Center Activities

- Play skill games that reinforce skills being taught at the Teacher Center.
- Play the Cinco de Mayo board game, card games, sorting game, and matching game.
- Read May vocabulary cards made by the teacher.

For Further Study

The following sentences and matching pairs of words are included for those children who know some Spanish and for those who are fluent Spanish speakers.

Mexico is located to the south of the U.S.	Mexico esta localizado al sur de los E.U.
Mexicans have a different culture.	Los Mexicanos tienen una cultura differente.
Red, green, and white are the Mexican flag colors.	Rojo, verde y blanco son los colores de la bandera Mexicana.
The Mexican flag has an eagle.	La bandera Mexicana tiene un aguila.
Cinco de Mayo is celebrated every year.	Cinco de Mayo se celebra todos los años.
Cinco de Mayo symbolizes the strength of the Mexicans.	Cinco de mayo simboliza la fuerza de los Mexicanos.
The families are united.	Las familias estan unidas.
The mariachis sing happy songs.	Los mariachis cantan alegre.
Dance the Mexican hat dance.	Baila el jarabe tapatio.
Piñatas are filled with candy.	Las piñatas son llenas de dulce.
There are many kinds of piñatas.	Hay muchas clases de piñatas.
The Mexican rugs are new.	Los tapetes son nuevos.
May is a month.	Mayo es un mes.
Spring is in May.	La primavera es en Mayo.
May has thirty-one days.	Mayo tiene triente-uno dias.
Mexican hats are big.	Los sombreros Mexicanos son grandes.

Teacher Resource Book

Tibbett, Teri. (2004). *Listen to Learn: Using American Music to Understand Language Arts and Social Studies.* Although this resource book is designed for grades five to eight, it includes excellent information about Latin American music—including mariachi music, salsa music, and popular Latin music (see Unit 4, Lesson 20).

Thematic Books

Emergent and Early Readers

Ada, Alma Flor. (2001). *Gathering the Sun: An Alphabet Book in Spanish and English.* Simple poems in Spanish and English, one for each letter of the Spanish alphabet, describe the wonder of the vegetable and fruit farms where many Hispanic people work.

Brown, Tricia. (1987). *Hello Amigos!* Illustrated by Fran Ortiz. This book tells of a Mexican-American child's birthday.

Campbell, Geeslin. (1996). *In Rosa's Mexico.* Illustrated by Andrea Arroyo. A young Mexican girl is able to magically make things better when she meets a wolf, a rooster, and a burro. Each story uses some Spanish words, which are included in a Spanish-English glossary.

Campbell, Geeslin. (2004). *Elena's Serenade.* Illustrated by Ana Juan. A little Mexican girl goes on a journey—dressed as a boy—to learn to be a glassblower.

Declare, Lulu. (1992). *Arroz Con Leche.* This book is an illustrated bilingual nursery rhyme and music book of popular Hispanic selections.

Morales, Yuyi. (2004). *Just a Minute: A Trickster Tale and Counting Book.* This Mexican counting book features Grandma Beetle and Señor Calavera (Pura Belpré Illustrator Medal Book).

Orozco, Jose-Luis. (1994). *De Colores and Other Latin American Folk Songs for Children.* Illustrated by Elisa Klevin. This is an illustrated collection of twenty-five Latin American songs, chants, and musical games with both Spanish and English lyrics. It includes musical arrangements for piano, voice, and guitar.

Orozco, Jose-Luis. (2002). *Diez Deditos: Ten Little Fingers and Other Play Rhymes and Action Songs from Latin America.* Illustrated by Elisa Klevin. This bilingual collection includes more than thirty finger rhymes, play rhymes, and action songs and games for children of various ages and cultures.

Wade, Mary Dodson. *Cinco de Mayo.* (2003). Illustrated by Nanci Reginelli Vargus. The book describes events leading to the Battle of Puebla and shows various aspects of contemporary festivities—a mariachi band, dancers, parades, and so on.

Winter, Jonah. (2003). *Frida.* Illustrated by Ana Juan. Frida Calvo overcomes suffering to become a wonderful Mexican artist (ALA Notable).

Developing and Fluent Readers

Ancona, George. (1994). *The Piñata Maker—El piñaterto.* Describes how a craftsman from southern Mexico makes piñatas for all the village birthday parties and other fiestas.

Garza, Carmen Lomas. (1990). *Cuadros de Familia / Family Pictures.* In bilingual text, the author describes growing up in a Hispanic community in Texas (ALA Notable).

Garza, Carmen Lomas. (2000). *In My Family / En Mi Familia.* The author tells her memories of growing up in the traditional Mexican-American community of her hometown in Texas.

Johnston, Tony F. (1999). *My Mexico / Mexico Mio.* Illustrated by John Sierra. This is an English-Spanish book of poems about Mexico.

Harvey, Miles. (1999). *Look What Came from Mexico.* The author tells about things that originated in Mexico—foods, arts and crafts, music, sports, holidays, and more.

Haskins, Jim. (1989). *Count Your Way Through Mexico.* Illustrated by Helen Byers. The text presents numbers one to ten in Spanish, and uses each number to tell something about Mexico and its culture.

Kalman, Bobbie. (1999). *Mexico from A to Z.* Illustrated by Jane Lewis. This is a pictorial tour of Mexico. From the ancient Mayan civilization to modern Mexico City, discover people, festivals, food, and so on.

MacMillan, Dianne M. (1997). *Mexican Independence Day and Cinco de Mayo.* The author tells of the people and events that are celebrated on these two important Mexican holidays and describes how the holidays are celebrated.

Olawsky, Lynn A. (1997). *The Colors of Mexico.* Illustrated by Janice Lee Porter. An exploration—in English and Spanish—of the different colors in Mexico's nature and history.

Ryan, Pam Muñoz. (2002). *Mice and Beans.* Illustrated by Joe Cepeda. Rosa Maria gets ready for her granddaughter's birthday. The book includes some Spanish words (ALA Notable).

Cinco de Mayo Bulletin Boards

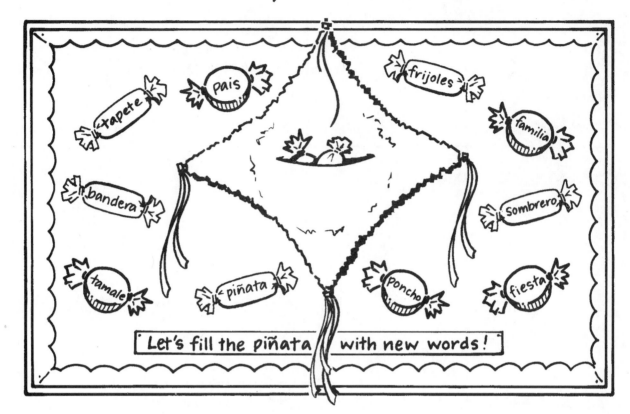

Let's fill the piñata with new words!

Let's read English and Spanish too!

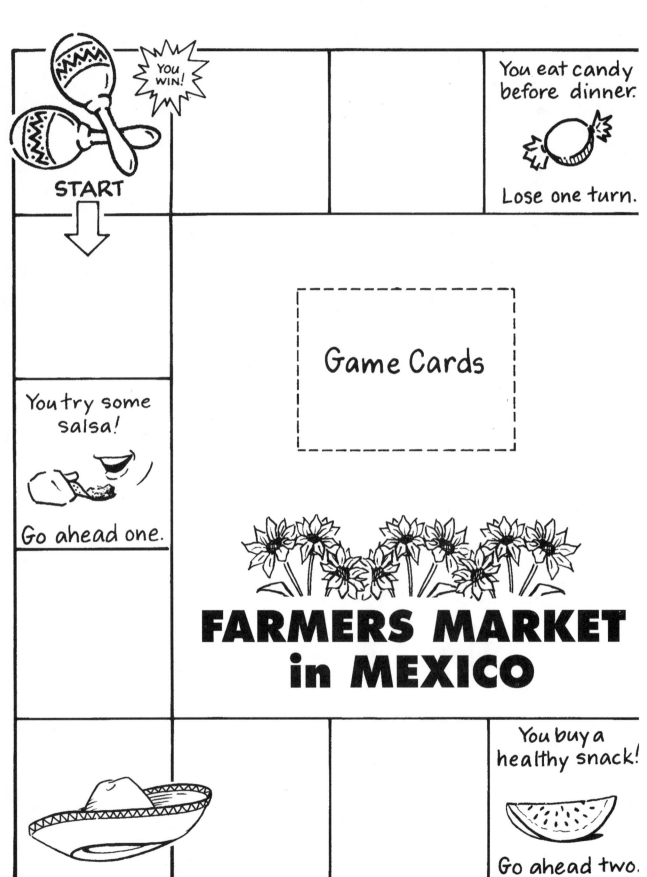

START

YOU WIN!

You eat candy before dinner.

Lose one turn.

You try some salsa!

Go ahead one.

Game Cards

FARMERS MARKET in MEXICO

You buy a healthy snack!

Go ahead two.

The parties are fun.

Eat tamales.

We eat beans.

Wear a poncho.

Piñatas are fun.

Mexicans speak Spanish.

HOLA!

The tapete is a Mexican rug.

Look at the Mexican flag.

Mexico is a country.

USA

MEXICO

Cinco de Mayo is a patriotic party.

The mariachis play the big guitar.

Wear a Mexican hat.

Play the maracas.

The maracas are instruments.

We all eat quesadillas.

Las fiestas son divertadas.

Come tamales.

Comemos frijoles.

Usa un poncho.

Las piñatas son divertadas.

Los Mexicanos hablan Espanol.

HOLA!

El tapete es una alfombra mexicana.

Observa la bandera Mexicana.

Mexico es un pais.

USA

MEXICO

Cinco de Mayo es una fiesta patriotica.

Los mariachis tocan el guitarron.

Usa un sombrero Mexicano.

Toca las maracas.

Las maracas son instrumentos.

Todos comemos quesadillas.

Cinco de Mayo Sorting Game

Answer Key

Mexico

piñatas
flag
rug
Spanish
party
country
Cinco de Mayo

Food

tamales
quesadillas
beans

Music

big guitar
maracas
play

Clothes

poncho
hat

Cinco de Mayo Matching Game

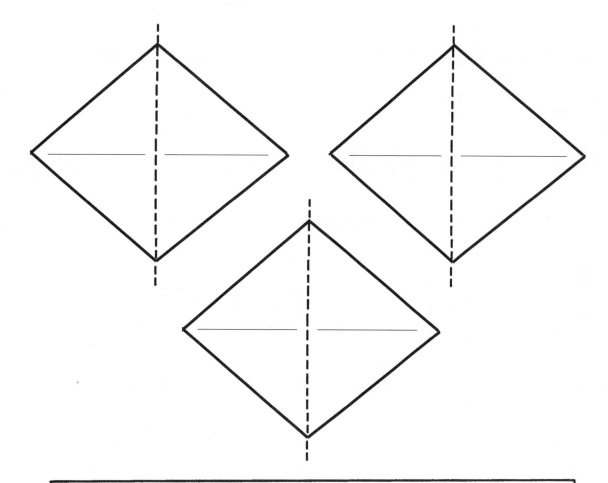

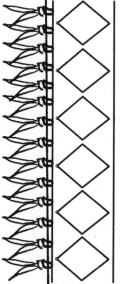

Answer Key

flag + bandera
rug + tapete
Spanish + Espanol
party + fiesta
country + pais
patriotic + patriotica
Mexican + Mexicano

big guitar + guitarron
play + toca
instruments + instrumentos
eat + come
beans + frijoles
hat + sombrero
May the 5th + Cinco de Mayo

MAYO

DOMINGO	LUNES	MARTES	MIERCOLES	JUEVES	VIERNES	SABADO

ADDITIONAL LEARNING CENTER THEMATIC UNITS

You may wish to use these themes in addition to or instead of one or more of those given earlier.

LUNAR NEW YEAR

About Lunar New Year

Lunar New Year marks the beginning of the year on the Chinese lunar calendar. The date, which is different each year, occurs sometime between late January and late February. The two-week celebration begins on the first day of the lunar month. Preparations for New Year include spring cleaning (a good time for children to help clean the classroom), fireworks, festive parades, lion dances, visits to relatives and friends, good-luck signs, red money packets (for children), and wearing lucky colors.

Theme Decorations

Hang Chinese lanterns, lion masks, and good-luck signs in red, yellow, and gold (the "good luck" colors).

Game and Dramatic Play Areas

You will need these materials for the game area:

- Basic equipment
- Lunar New Year board game, card game, sorting game, and matching game
- Learning center skill games (Section Five)
- Lunar New Year vocabulary cards (game cards or index cards with underlined words from game cards written on them)
- A sign that says: "We celebrate Lunar New Year."
- A poster or sign with student directions: "1. Read the Lunar New Year vocabulary cards to a partner. 2. Play a reading game with a partner."

You will need these materials for the dramatic play area:

- Lion masks (see directions below).
- Chinese lanterns (see directions on page 221).
- Good-luck signs (see directions on page 221).
- Chopsticks, Chinese teacups, bowls, spoons.
- Musical instruments: cymbals (pie pans), drums, and gongs (pie pan and spoon). Note that foil pie pans are a little quieter than regular metal pie pans.

Post the names of children who will be in the dramatic play area. All others will play reading games.

Making the Lion Masks

1. Provide each child with a brown-paper grocery bag.
2. Help each child measure where eyes are to be cut.
3. Have children use fabric strips, yarn, paint, glue, sequins, and other trim to decorate the bag to look like a lion's head.

Making the Lanterns

1. Children paint art paper or tissue paper with pastel watercolor designs. Let the paint dry.
2. Fold tissue paper accordion-style. Roll like a cylinder and tape together along the seam.
3. Hang by a string from the top.

Making Good-Luck Signs

1. Give each child a piece of red construction paper.
2. With black markers, have children write good-luck messages. *Optional:* Decorate with gold-foil paper.

Theme Setup

1. Display the lion masks on a table. Hang good-luck signs and lanterns around the room.
2. Place the musical instruments—cymbals (pie pans), drums, and gongs (pie pans and spoons)—in a box.
3. On a table nearby, put chopsticks, teacups, bowls, spoons.
4. Post the signs.

Bulletin Boards

See the illustrations on page 226.

Card Game

Lunar New Year features one card game—photocopy both pages. Children match each Chinese language card with an English card. (*Please note:* The illustrations of Chinese language characters are an artist's rendering of an archaic style and are used here for decorative rather than scholarly purposes.)

Whole-Group Activities

- Learn new vocabulary: *lion, firecracker, lantern,* and so on.

- The teacher gives out lucky money packets, or *hong bao.* These are small red envelopes or bags with two bright coins. Children can receive red packets at any time during the fifteen days of the Lunar New Year. For a fun packet, wrap two gold-foil chocolate coins (these are common) in red tissue paper. Give them out after lunch and let children enjoy a treat. The procedure is this: Children come up one at a time to receive their hong bao. The child extends two open hands and says "Happy New Year." The teacher extends the coin packet in two open hands and places it into the child's open hands.

- Conduct a classroom lion parade. Children wear their lion masks and play instruments—cymbals, gongs, drums, and so on. This is a great activity for the playground because the real Chinese New Year parades have lots of noise.

- Children use chopsticks to pick up small objects and foods—unshelled peanuts, tiny marshmallows, candy or cereal with a hole in the center (through the center), small pretzels (through the hole), and so on.

- Make lanterns, lion masks, firecrackers, and good-luck signs. Firecrackers, lion dances, and dragon parades can take place on any of the fifteen days of the holiday.

- Prior to the New Year, conduct a traditional Chinese New Year spring cleaning. Clean out desks, learning centers, bookshelves, and other storage areas. No cleaning is done on New Year's Day.

- Wear lucky colors—red for happiness, gold for wealth. Everyone who has new clothes wears them.

- Hold an open house. Invite the principal, the school staff, parents, or children and teachers from other classrooms. Visit friends in other classrooms, return borrowed books, and forgive your enemies.

- Decorate the Lunar New Year calendar on page 227.

Easy Fried Rice Recipe*

Two eggs

Nonstick cooking spray

An electric skillet and a spatula or large spoon

One to two cups frozen green peas

Note: Fried rice recipe courtesy of P. Ann Pan.

One cup frozen diced carrots (or use frozen peas and carrots)

One cup chopped ham (sandwich-type ham works well)

Five cups of cooked rice, standard or instant

One tablespoon oil

One to two tablespoons soy sauce (optional)

1. Beat eggs and scramble in pan coated with nonstick spray. Add peas, carrots, and ham. Simmer.
2. Add rice and fry.
3. Stir in oil and soy sauce.
4. Serve in disposable cups with plastic spoons or chopsticks.

Chinese Tea Eggs Recipe*

Six tea bags—three regular tea and three green tea (or use any types of tea in any combination)

Hot pot or hot plate and large saucepan for boiling the water for the tea

Crock-Pot

Two teaspoons salt

One tablespoon soy sauce

Four- or five-star anise

Enough hard-boiled eggs so that each child can have half an egg

Plastic sandwich bags

1. Steep tea bags in three cups of boiling water for five minutes. Transfer tea bags and water to Crock-Pot along with salt, soy sauce, and star anise. (Keep tea-bag labels out of the mixture.)
2. Place each egg in a plastic sandwich bag. Let the children gently tap each egg on a table top, gently turning the egg round and round after each tap so the shell develops a crackle pattern all over it. Do not peel the shells off the eggs. (The plastic bag prevents the shell from falling off onto the table.)
3. Remove the eggs from the bags, place in the Crock-Pot, and add enough water to cover the eggs (at least double the existing liquid).
4. Cook at low temperature for a minimum of one hour and a maximum of twenty-four hours.
5. Cool, peel, slice, and serve.

Note: Chinese egg recipe courtesy of Regina Pan and Linda Fox.

Content Area Activities

- Calculate on what day the Lunar New Year falls for the current year. The dates change from year to year. It begins on the first day of the first lunar month that occurs between late January and late February.
- Research the origin of firecrackers. Make paper firecrackers for decorations.
- Plant a Chinese garden. Use a pretty dish, narcissus or amaryllis bulb, potting soil, and pebbles to decorate the soil.
- Learn how an abacus is used.
- Eight and twelve are considered lucky numbers. Conduct some math activities using these numbers.
- Find China on a world map. Find out how many miles it is from where you are to where China is.

Word Play Center Activities

- Play skill games that reinforce skills being taught at the Teacher Center.
- Play the Lunar New Year board game, card games, sorting game, and matching game.
- Read Lunar New Year vocabulary cards made by the teacher.

Thematic Books

Emergent and Early Readers

Chinn, Karen. (1997). *Sam and the Lucky Money.* Illustrated by Cornelius Van Wright and Ying Hwa Hu. Sam decides how to spend the lucky money he received for Lunar New Year—he donates it to a barefoot homeless man.

Compestine, Ying Chang. (2001). *The Runaway Rice Cake.* After chasing the special rice cake Mother made for Lunar New Year, three brothers share it with an old woman and have their generosity richly rewarded.

Flack, Marjorie. (1977). *The Story About Ping.* Illustrated by Kurt Wiese. Ping, a little duck, finds adventure on the Yangtze River.

Holub, Joan. (2003). *Dragon Dance: A Chinese New Year Lift-the-Flap Book.* Illustrated by Benrei Huang. The book introduces the customs of Chinese New Year: shopping for flowers, eating dinner with the family, receiving red envelopes from Grandma and Grandpa, and watching the Lunar New Year parade.

Thong, Roseanne. (2000). *Round Is a Mooncake: A Book of Shapes.* Illustrated by Grace Lin. The author gives a rhyming lesson about shapes—circle, square, and rectangle—and Chinese culture.

Thong, Roseanne. (2001). *Red Is a Dragon: A Book of Colors.* Illustrated by Grace Lin. A Chinese-American girl describes colors she sees—a red dragon, firecrackers, lychees, and others.

Waters, Kate. (1990). *Lion Dancer: Ernie Wan's Chinese New Year.* Illustrated by Madeline Slovenz-Low. Ernie Wan, a six-year-old, prepares for the Lunar New Year celebrations and his first public performance of the lion dance.

Developing and Fluent Readers

Behrens, Terry. (1982). *Gung Hay Fat Choy! Happy New Year.* The author explains Chinese New Year and describes its celebration by Chinese Americans.

Brown, Tricia. (1997). *Chinese New Year.* Illustrated by Fran Ortiz. The book tells about the celebration of Lunar New Year by Chinese Americans living in San Francisco's Chinatown.

Demi. (1999). *Happy New Year! Kung-Hsi Fa-Ts'Ai.* The author tells about customs, traditions, foods, and lore of the Lunar New Year.

Holt-Goldsmith, Diane. (1999). *Celebrating Chinese New Year.* Illustrated by Lawrence Migdale. A San Francisco boy and his family prepare for Lunar New Year, their most important holiday.

Lin, Grace. (2001). *Dim Sum for Everyone.* A child describes the various little dishes of dim sum that she and her family enjoy on a visit to a restaurant in Chinatown.

Mahy, Margaret. (1992). *Seven Chinese Brothers.* Illustrated by Jean Mou-Sier Tsang. In this classic Chinese folktale, seven brothers use their supernatural gifts to triumph over a cruel emperor.

Mosel, Arlene. (1968). *Tiki Tiki Tembo.* A traditional legend of why the Chinese decided to give all their children short names.

Sing, Rachael. (1994). *Chinese New Year's Dragon.* Grandmother tells her granddaughter about dragons, and the girl finds herself on a dragon's back soaring over ancient China.

Tucker, Kathy. (2003). *The Seven Chinese Sisters.* Illustrated by Grace Lin. When a dragon snatches the youngest of seven Chinese sisters, the other six use their talents to come to her rescue.

Vaughan, Marcia K. (1996). *The Dancing Dragon.* Illustrated by Stanley Wong Hoo Foon. A typical Chinese New Year celebration is described in this rhyming story.

Wong, Janet S. (2000). *The Next New Year.* Illustrated by Yangsook Choy. A family prepares to celebrate the Lunar New Year and looks forward to the good luck it brings.

Lunar New Year Bulletin Boards

Let's Count in Chinese!

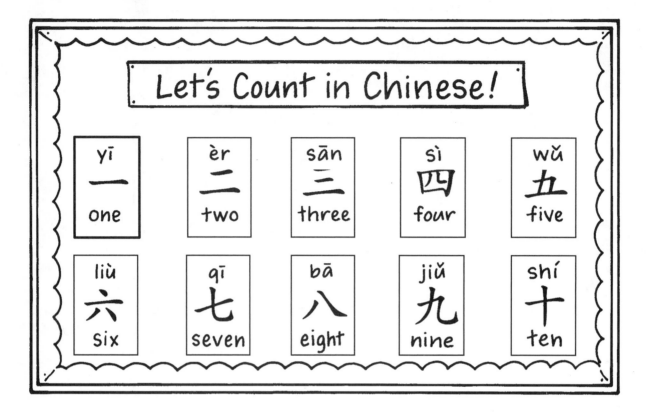

yī 一 one	èr 二 two	sān 三 three	sì 四 four	wǔ 五 five
liù 六 six	qī 七 seven	bā 八 eight	jiǔ 九 nine	shí 十 ten

What's Your Favorite Chinese Color?

hēi 黑 black	hóng 红 red	lǜ 绿 green
lán 蓝 blue	bái 白 white	huáng 黄 yellow

LUNAR NEW YEAR

SUNDAY	MONDAY	TUESDAY	WEDNESDAY	THURSDAY	FRIDAY	SATURDAY

CHINA

You eat your whole lunch with chopsticks! Go again.

Let's Celebra Lunar New Year!

You try chopsticks! Go ahead one!

START HERE!

Dress in red and gold. LUCKY COLORS!

Fish for lunch. GOOD FORTUNE!

All the relatives come to visit! FUN!

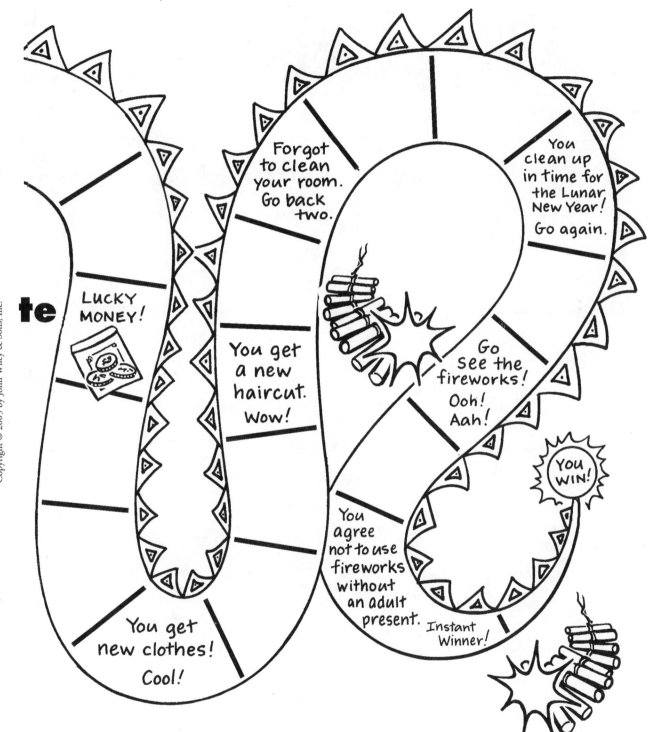

te

LUCKY MONEY!

Forgot to clean your room. Go back two.

You clean up in time for the Lunar New Year! Go again.

You get a new haircut. Wow!

Go see the fireworks! Ooh! Aah!

YOU WIN!

You get new clothes! Cool!

You agree not to use fireworks without an adult present. Instant Winner!

Good-luck signs are red.

We make a paper lantern.

Firecrackers are loud.

The lion dance is fun.

We wear new clothes.

Mandarin oranges are Chinese.

We get lucky money.

We clean our house.

We watch the dragon parade.

We visit relatives.

Lunar New Year lasts 15 days.

Lunar means moon.

New Year cake tastes good.

We eat fish for good fortune.

Long noodles mean long life.

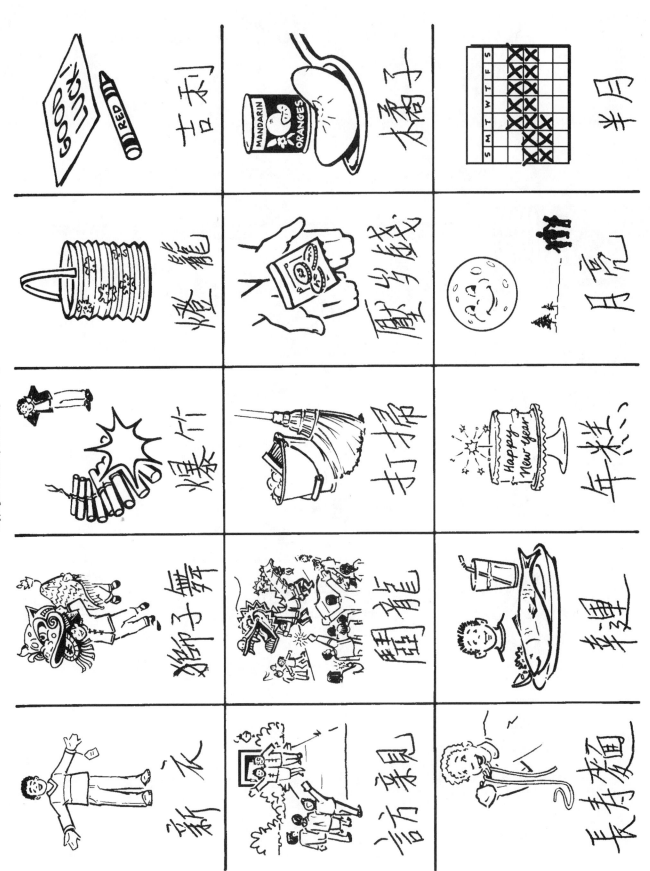

Lunar New Year Sorting Game

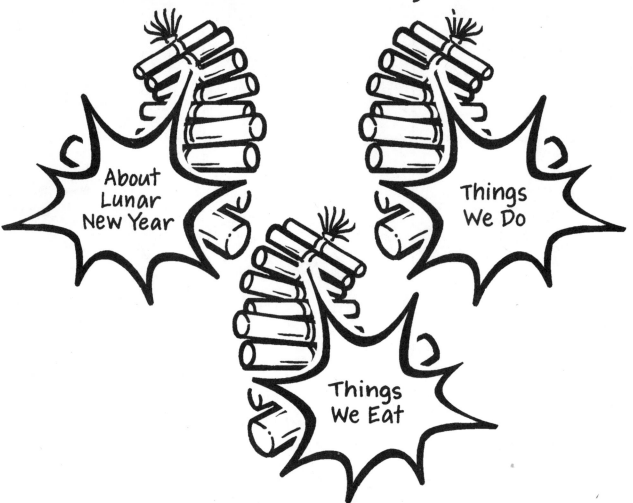

About Lunar New Year

Things We Do

Things We Eat

Things We Do

new clothes
lion dance
firecrackers
paper lantern
good-luck signs
visit relatives
dragon parade
clean house
lucky money

Things We Eat

mandarin oranges
long noodles
good fortune
New Year cake

About Lunar New Year

moon
15 days

Answer Key

Lunar New Year Matching Game

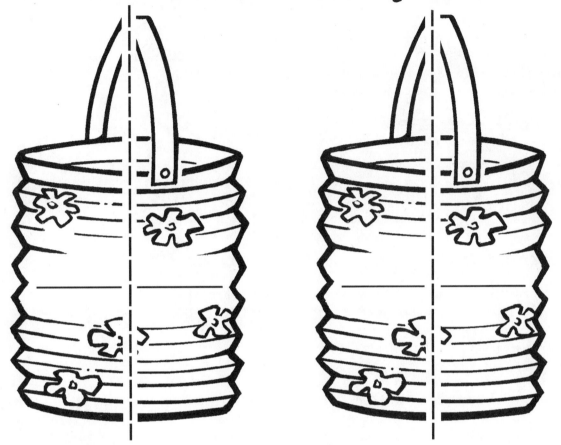

Answer Key

new + clothes

lion + dance

loud + firecrackers

paper + lantern

good-luck + signs

visit + relatives

mandarin + oranges

dragon + parade

clean + house

lucky + money

long + noodles

good + fortune

New Year + cake

lunar + moon

15 + days

① Make your firecrackers...

Ⓐ Cut a sheet of red paper into 16 pieces.

Ⓑ Roll each of the 16 pieces into a tube and glue.

Ⓒ Glue the tubes together into sets of four.

Ⓓ Set aside.

PAPER Firecrackers

② Make a tassel for your string of firecrackers...

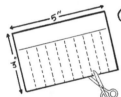

Ⓐ Cut out a 3×5" piece of yellow paper.

Ⓒ Roll the fringed paper and glue to make a tassel.

Ⓓ Set aside.

Ⓑ Cut the paper into thin strips — but don't cut all the way through!

③ Make the firecracker strip...

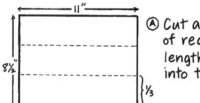

Ⓐ Cut a sheet of red paper lengthwise into thirds.

Ⓑ Fold lengthwise.

Ⓒ Use glue or staples to attach the tassel and a loop of string for hanging.

Ⓓ Fold over and glue the edges closed.

④ Assemble your firecrackers!

Ⓐ Spread glue evenly on one side of your strip.

Ⓑ Attach your sets of firecrackers.

RESTAURANT

Theme Decorations

Decorate to look like a restaurant.

Game and Dramatic Play Areas

You will need these materials for the game area:

- Basic equipment
- Restaurant board game, card games, sorting game, and matching game
- Learning center skill games (Section Five)
- Restaurant vocabulary cards (game cards or index cards with underlined words from game cards written on them)
- A sign that says: "We read menus and signs in a restaurant."
- A poster or sign with student directions: "1. Read the menu and restaurant vocabulary cards to a partner. 2. Play a reading game with a partner."

- Restaurant chart: List the children's names under "Host or Hostess," "Diners," "Wait Persons," "Chefs" daily, and write the day of the week and the role that each child will play in the restaurant.

You will need these materials for the dramatic play area (to create a restaurant scene):

- Table and chairs for two (or more) children
- Tablecloth or place mats, napkins, centerpiece
- Plastic dinnerware
- Cookware and cookbooks (for the chefs)
- Cardboard box (the size of a toy stove)
- Cardboard box (to store other restaurant equipment)
- Serving tray
- Menus (see illustration on page 249)
- Aprons
- White paper bag for chef's hat (roll open edges twice to make a cuff)
- Pencils and notepads (for taking orders)
- Toy telephone (for takeout orders)
- Calculator or toy cash register and play money
- Posters: "Help Wanted," "No Smoking," and "Shoes and Shirts Required"
- Posters with "Today's Specials" or a whiteboard and markers so children can create specials

Post the names of children who will be in the dramatic play area. All others will play reading games.

Theme Setup

1. Set the table with tablecloth, centerpiece, napkins, and dinnerware.
2. Using thick markers, draw burners and an oven door on the cardboard box. Put the chef's hat and cookware on the stove.
3. Store restaurant equipment (menus, aprons, and so on) in the other box.
4. Display restaurant signs.
5. Post the list for role-play and student directions.

Bulletin Boards

See the illustrations on page 241.

Whole-Group Activities

- Learn new vocabulary: *entree, chef, dessert,* and so on.
- Role-play ordering a meal in a restaurant.
- Role-play ordering food at a drive-in window.
- Role-play ordering takeout food over the telephone.
- Discuss meaning of signs such as "Help Wanted," "No Smoking," "Shirt and Shoes Required," "No Pets," and so on.
- Display signs: "No Smoking," "Men's Rest Room," "Women's Rest Room," and so on. Decide where each sign should be displayed.
- Learn the proper way to set a table.
- Visit the school lunchroom while lunch is being prepared.
- Have a chef talk to the class.
- Visit a restaurant and order lunch.
- Collect advertisement cards from supermarket delis. Use them to list foods, list abbreviations, or plan a picnic, or simply arrange them in ABC order.
- Create a doughnut shop. Then list and display words that describe doughnuts.
- Decorate the calendar on page 248.

Doughnut Recipe*

Small deep fryer and oil

Canned biscuits

Paper towels

Strainer

Canned frosting and powdered sugar

1. Heat oil in deep fryer.
2. Poke a finger through each biscuit to make the donut hole.
3. Fry each biscuit until brown, ten to fifteen seconds.
4. Drain on paper towels.
5. Choose frosting or powdered sugar for topping.

Note: Doughnut recipe courtesy of Ardyth Ann Stanley.

Content Area Activities

- Study the food groups.
- Eat popular foods from other countries.
- Compare the school lunchroom with a local restaurant. How are they alike or different?
- Provide math story problems, such as this: If a hamburger costs 80 cents and cheese costs 10 cents, how much does a cheeseburger cost?
- Learn about different types of restaurants, such as fast food, ethnic, and cafeteria-style.
- Gather information about the children's favorite restaurants and graph the results.
- Have children bring in empty food boxes and cans. Use paper bags to sort foods into categories

Word Play Center Activities

- Play skill games that reinforce skills being taught at the Teacher Center.
- Play the restaurant board game, card games, sorting game, and matching game.
- Read restaurant vocabulary cards made by the teacher.

Thematic Books

Emergent and Early Readers

Buono, Anthony. (1997). *A Race Against Junk Food (Adventures in Good Nutrition).* This story introduces the Snak (Super nutritionally active kids) Posse Kids—veggie-people who get children excited about living healthy.

Carle, Eric. (1970). *Pancakes, Pancakes.* Jack makes his breakfast pancake from scratch, including cutting and grinding wheat for flour.

Carle, Eric. (1986). *My Very First Book of Food.* A favorite author writes an easy-to-read book about food.

de Paola, Tomie. (1978). *Pancakes for Breakfast.* This wordless picture book is about a little old lady who tries to make pancakes for her breakfast.

Dooley, Norah. (1992). *Everybody Cooks Rice.* Illustrated by Peter J. Thornton. A child, sent to find a brother at dinnertime, finds a variety of cultures and the many different ways that rice is prepared.

Dooley, Norah. (1995). *Everybody Bakes Bread*. Illustrated by Peter J. Thornton. An errand introduces Carrie to different kinds of bread: chapatis, challah, and papusaa. Recipes are included.

Dooley, Norah. (2000). *Everybody Cooks Soup*. Illustrated by Peter J. Thornton. While shoveling snow to earn Christmas money, Carrie has an idea for the right gift for her mom. Soup recipes are included.

Dooley, Norah. (2002). *Everybody Brings Noodles*. Illustrated by Peter J. Thornton. The block party was Carrie's idea and she is excited about two things—the talent show and the wonderful noodle dishes from many countries that her neighbors are bringing.

Ehlert, Lois. (1990). *Growing Vegetable Soup*. The author presents the gardening cycle and an easy recipe for vegetable soup.

Ehlert, Lois. (1996). *Eating the Alphabet*. The book teaches upper- and lowercase letters while introducing fruits and vegetables from around the world.

Fleming, Denise. (1998). *Lunch*. A hungry mouse eats a big lunch made up of colorful foods.

Gross, Ruth Belov. (1990). *What's on My Plate?* Illustrated by Isadore Seltzer. The author tells where some of our common foods originate.

Leedy, Loreen. (1996). *The Edible Pyramid: Good Eating Every Day*. Animals learn about healthy eating at the Edible Pyramid, a restaurant where foods are grouped in a food guide and customers learn how many servings they need each day.

Modesitt, Jeanne. (1988). *Vegetable Soup*. Illustrated by Robin Spowart. Two rabbits are reluctant to sample anything they haven't eaten before.

Morris, Ann. (1993). *Bread, Bread, Bread*. The author explains the different kinds of bread enjoyed all over the world.

Oxenbury, Helen. (1983). *Eating Out*. A boy's first trip to a restaurant is less than successful.

Sendak, Maurice. (1962). *Chicken Soup with Rice*. In short poems, a boy describes monthly activities to accompany chicken soup with rice.

Developing and Fluent Readers

Berenstain, Stan and Jan. (1985). *The Berenstain Bears and Too Much Junk Food*. Mama Bear tries to convince her family that they eat too much junk food.

English, Karen. (1998). *Just Right Stew*. Illustrated by Anna Rich. Victoria observes as Big Mama seasons her favorite food just right, but doesn't tell her mother and aunts the secret ingredient.

French, Vivian. (1998). *Oliver's Fruit Salad*. Illustrated by Alison Bartlett. Oliver helps Grandpa pick fresh fruit but refuses to eat any until Mom prepares something very special in a big glass bowl.

French, Vivian. (1998). *Oliver's Vegetables.* Illustrated by Alison Bartlett. While visiting his grandfather, Oliver learns to eat vegetables other than potatoes.

Howe, James. (1991). *Hot Fudge.* A family tests their dog's willpower when they leave him alone with a pan of fudge.

Krensky, Stephen. (1992). *The Pizza Book.* Illustrated by Bob Alley. The author tells about the origins of pizza and gives directions for preparing one.

Lasker, Joe. (1977). *Lentil Soup.* A woman cooks seven different lentil soups on seven different days. Then she finds her mother-in-law's secret ingredient.

Lin, Grace. (2001). *Dim Sum for Everyone.* A child describes the various little dishes of dim sum that she and her family enjoy on a visit to a restaurant in Chinatown.

Machotka, Hana. (1992). *Pasta Factory.* A school group takes a tour of the Tutta Pasta factory in New York City.

Rattigan, Jama Kim. (1998). *Dumpling Soup.* Illustrated by Lillian Hsu-Flanders. An Asian-American girl tries to make dumplings for her family's New Year's celebration.

Rockwell, Lizzy. (1999). *Good Enough to Eat: A Kid's Guide to Food and Nutrition.* The author describes categories of nutrients needed for good health, tells how they work in the body, and lists which foods provide each.

Sears, William, M.D., and Sears, Martha, R.N. (1999). *Eat Healthy, Feel Great.* Illustrated by Renee Andriani. The authors explain how eating healthy foods can be fun for the whole family.

Sharmat, Mitchell. (1985). *Gregory, the Terrible Eater.* A goat won't eat the usual goat diet—shoes and tin cans—but prefers fruits, vegetables, eggs, and orange juice.

Restaurant Bulletin Boards

Eat from Each Food Group Every Day — You'll Grow Up the Healthy Way!

FRUITS AND VEGETABLES

MILK

CHEESE

DAIRY PRODUCTS

BREAD AND CEREAL

SPAGHF

OAT MEAL

MEAT AND POULTRY

HAVE KIDS CUT OUT MAGAZINE PICTURES OF FOOD TO PUT IN EACH FOOD GROUP

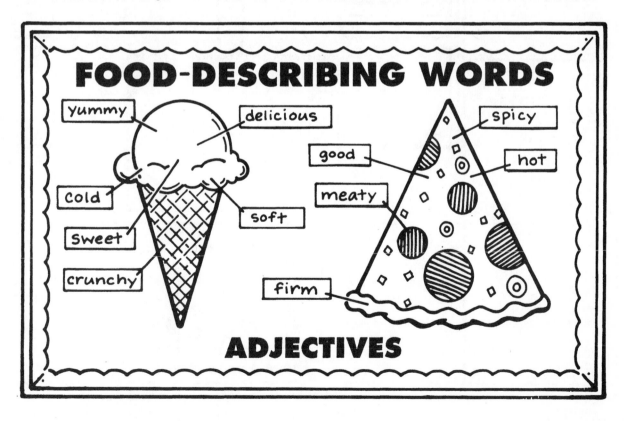

FOOD-DESCRIBING WORDS

yummy

delicious

spicy

good

hot

cold

meaty

sweet

soft

crunchy

firm

ADJECTIVES

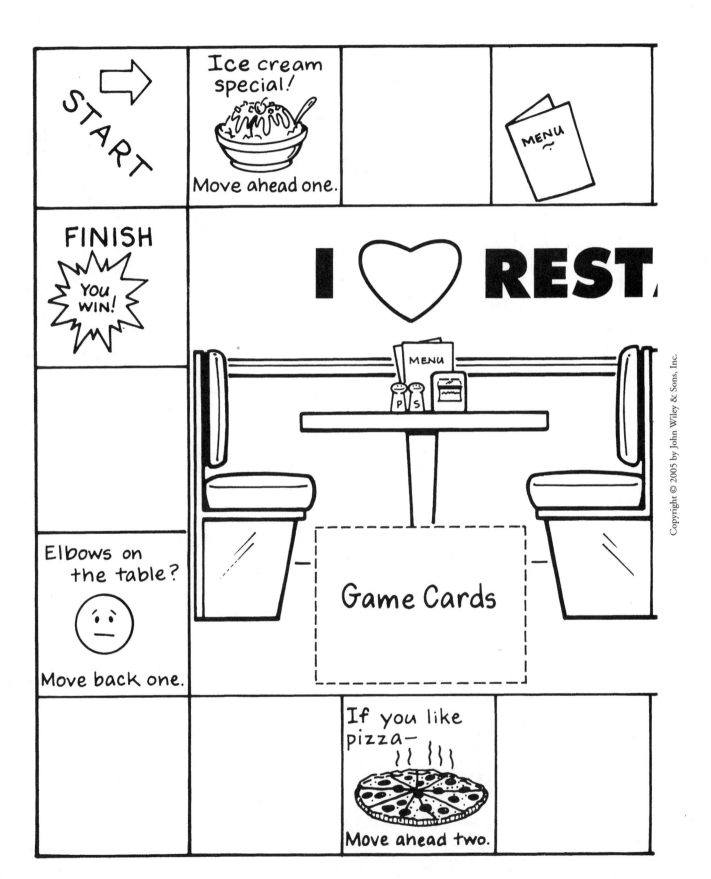

START

Ice cream special!
Move ahead one.

MENU

FINISH
YOU WIN!

I ♥ REST

MENU
P S

Elbows on the table?
Move back one.

Game Cards

If you like pizza—
Move ahead two.

A hamburger tastes good.

Corn is healthy.

Spaghetti has sauce.

Look at the chocolate cake.

Bologna is good.

Broccoli is healthy.

Eat the hot fudge sundae.

Peanut butter is good.

I eat french fries.

Eat vanilla pudding.

I like grilled cheese.

Green beans taste good.

Eat pumpkin pie.

A yummy hot dog is good.

Peas are green.

Lemonade can be sour.	Tossed salad is crunchy.	Ice cream is cold.
Soft drinks are bubbly.	I eat meat loaf.	I ate the potato salad.
Tea is hot.	Fish sticks are tasty.	Order the salad bar.
I like apple juice.	I love chicken nuggets.	I like lettuce and tomato.
Drink your milk.	Pizza is yummy.	Eat the cole slaw.

Restaurant Sorting Game

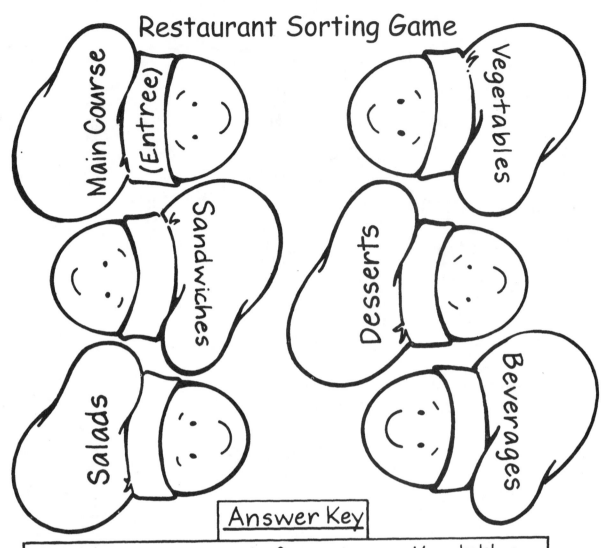

Main Course (Entree)

Vegetables

Sandwiches

Desserts

Salads

Beverages

Answer Key

Salads
salad bar
tossed salad
cole slaw
potato salad
lettuce and tomato

Sandwiches
hamburger
hot dog
grilled cheese
peanut butter
bologna

Main Course
fish sticks
pizza
meat loaf
spaghetti
chicken nuggets

Desserts
ice cream
pumpkin pie
vanilla pudding
hot fudge sundae
chocolate cake

Vegetables
peas
corn
green beans
french fries
broccoli

Beverages
milk
apple juice
tea
soft drinks
lemonade

Restaurant Matching Game

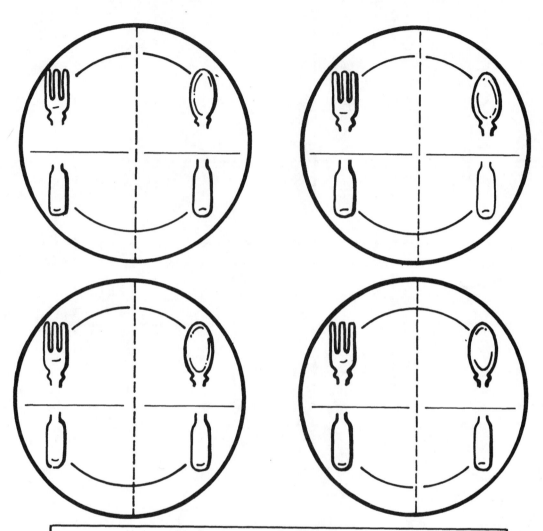

Answer Key

apple + juice
soft + drinks
chicken + nuggets
fish + sticks
meat + loaf
salad + bar
cole + slaw
ice + cream

pumpkin + pie
vanilla + pudding
hot fudge + sundae
green + beans
french + fries
hot + dog
peanut + butter
grilled + cheese

SUNDAY	MONDAY	TUESDAY	WEDNESDAY	THURSDAY	FRIDAY	SATURDAY

WE   LOVE   RESTAURANTS

~ MENU ~

Vegetables

corn
peas
green beans
french fries
broccoli

Salads

tossed salad
cole slaw
lettuce and tomato
potato salad
salad bar

MainCourse(Entree)

pizza
meat loaf
fish sticks
spaghetti
chicken nuggets

Desserts

ice cream
pumpkin pie
vanilla pudding
chocolate cake
hot fudge sundae

Beverages

milk
apple juice
soft drinks
lemonade
tea

Sandwiches

hamburger
hot dog
grilled cheese
peanut butter
bologna

ROMAN HOLIDAY

Why Latin for primary readers? What are the benefits? In her book *Classical Latin Enrichment* (2003, p. 7), Joan Jecko explains:

1. Latin has been called the mother tongue of Western civilization. Our culture is saturated with Latin influences, and even a brief exposure leads to greater understanding of Western literature, grammar, and spelling. Approximately 70 percent of all English words stem from Latin. Many prefixes and suffixes originated in Latin, which means a background in the language increases English vocabulary.

2. The study of Latin can raise verbal scores on standardized tests. Students who learn Latin vocabulary recognize Latin roots and their meaning for many English words used on these tests. Latin vocabulary forms the basis for science, law, and mathematics. It left a mark on early church music, foreign languages, religion, and many other arts and sciences.

3. Latin is the root of the Romance languages: French, Italian, Portuguese, Romanian, and Spanish. Being familiar with Latin makes learning these languages faster and easier.

4. Latin is a phonetic language like English, and the alphabet is similar. Research has shown that learning a second language helps students read and write English.

5. Latin has two pronunciations: classical and ecclesiastical. Classical Latin was probably used during the period of the Roman Empire. Ecclesiastical developed with the Roman Church. The differences between the two forms are slight. Ecclesiastical Latin is closer to English in some of its pronunciation and is the form used [in this theme].

Unlike modern languages, Latin does not have any absolute correct pronunciation. No one alive today knows the correct pronunciation; hence, from this point of view, it is a dead language. Scholars have reasonable guesses of how Latin was pronounced. Letters are usually pronounced as in English, except for these:

a as in *father*

e as in *Ted*; long *e* as in *gate*

i as in *bit*; long *i* as in *knee*

o as in *often*; long *o* as in *dope*

ae as in *bye*

au as in *how*

ei as in *hey*

v as in *wine*

c and *g* always hard, as in *car* and *game*

j as in *yes*

Theme Decorations

Decorate to look like ancient Rome.

Game and Dramatic Play Areas

You will need these materials for the game area:

- Basic equipment
- Roman Holiday board game, card game, sorting game, and matching game
- Learning center skill games (Section Five)

- Roman Holiday vocabulary cards (game cards or index cards with underlined words from game cards written on them)
- A sign that says: "We celebrate Roman Holiday."
- A poster or sign with student directions: "1. Read the Roman Holiday vocabulary cards to a partner. 2. Play a reading game with a partner."

You will need these materials for the dramatic play area:

- *Roman tunics:* a white pillowcase with holes cut for arms and head or a white adult T-shirt with the neck and sleeves cut away, tied around the waist with string or raffia
- *Roman togas:* a twin bed sheet or material that's forty-eight by thirty-six inches, folded lengthwise and worn wrapped around the tunic and draped over one shoulder (fastened with safety pins)
- *Roman sandals:* any type of children's sandals will work
- *Laurels* can be made from silk ivy, which is fastened in a circle to fit around a child's head
- *Tabula (tablets):* Children work with clay or playdough until it is soft enough to cover the bottom of a small box. They write on it with a stylus.
- *Stilus (stylus):* Provide orange sticks or sculpting sticks to use as styluses. Children can use the tabula and stylus to write their names and the Latin words they are learning or they can draw pictures of Latin words they know and practice saying the Latin names for the drawings.
- *Paper scrolls:* Provide scrolls (rolled paper) with newly learned Latin words.

Theme Setup

1. Create the Roman tunics, laurels, and togas. Place them and the children's sandals into a box.
2. Children can help make the tabulas. Place the finished ones, with the styluses, into a separate box.
3. Place the scrolls on a nearby table or shelf.
4. Provide floor cushions for seating.

Bulletin Boards

Use the body-parts bulletin board on page 258 to learn these anatomical terms in Latin. Then play a game using gingerbread men. As the teacher calls out the body part, the children nibble that part of the gingerbread man.

head: *caput*

hand: *manus*

foot: *pes*

arm: *bracchium*

leg: *crus*

fingers or toes: *digiti*

feet: *pes*

ear: *auris*

nose: *nasus*

mouth: *os*

eye: *oculus*

With the Roman numeral bulletin board on page 258, children learn the Roman numerals for one through ten.

Arabic Numeral	English Word	Latin Word	Roman Numeral
1	one	*unus*	I
2	two	*duo*	II
3	three	*tres*	III
4	four	*quattuor*	IV
5	five	*quinque*	V
6	six	*sex* (rhymes with *takes*)	VI
7	seven	*septum*	VII
8	eight	*octo*	VIII
9	nine	*novem*	IX
10	ten	*decem*	X

Card Game

Roman Holiday features one card game—photocopy both pages. Children match the card with the Latin word to the card with the English card.

Whole-Group Activities

- Learn new Latin vocabulary—days of the week, body parts, and so on.
- Fill out the calendar (kalendarium) on page 259.
- Read the book *Hand, Hand, Fingers, Thumb* by Al Perkins (1969). Learn the body parts in Latin. Play "Simon Says" using the Latin words for body parts.
- Label classroom objects with their Latin names. Choose from these: chair: *cathedra;* table: *mensa;* tablet: *tabula;* paper: *charta;* ruler: *regula;* book: *liber;* stylus: *stilus;* scroll: *volumen;* door: *janua.*
- Children learn the Latin names for days of the week. Point out the similarities with the names of the sun, moon, and planets: Sunday: *dies Solis* (sun); Monday: *dies Lunae* (moon); Tuesday: *dies Martis* (Mars); Wednesday: *dies Mercurii* (Mercury); Thursday: *dies Jovis* (Jupiter); Friday: *dies Veneris* (Venus); Saturday: *dies Saturni* (Saturn).

Roman Pudding with Spicy Wafers Recipe

Romans were fond of custards and puddings. They used cinnamon, ginger, and other spices that are familiar to us.

> Instant vanilla pudding—enough for each child to have a small serving
>
> Milk
>
> Hand mixer (manual, not electric, for small children) and a large mixing bowl
>
> Small cups
>
> Ginger snaps or vanilla wafers

1. Make pudding with milk, according to package directions.
2. Serve in small cups with ginger snaps or vanilla wafers.

Content Area Activities

- Using the Roman numeral bulletin board, learn to count to ten in Latin.
- Learn the Latin words for colors. Read *A Bad Case of Stripes* by David Shannon (2004), or any book about colors, and introduce the following words—red: *rubber;* green: *prasinus;* yellow: *flavus;* blue: *caeruleus;* black: *ater;* white: *albus;* pink: *rosacius;* brown: *fuscus.* Then play this

game: Create teams of children and give each a square of colored paper. Call out the colors in Latin. The child holding that color must run and put the correct square in a box. Continue the game until each child has had a turn.

Word Play Center Activities

- Play skill games that reinforce skills being taught at the Teacher Center.

- Play the Roman Holiday board game, card game, sorting game, and matching game.

- Read Roman Holiday vocabulary cards made by the teacher.

For Further Study

The following activities are provided for further study of Latin vocabulary.

Family Members and Common Greetings

mother	*mater*
father	*pater*
girl	*puella*
boy	*puer*
hello	*salve*
good-bye	*vale*
please	*quaeso* (k-wise-o)
pretty good	*satis bene*
thank you	*tibi multas gratias*
you're welcome	*nihil est*

Using puppets of a mother, father, girl, and boy, introduce the family words. Demonstrate a conversation between the puppets using the Latin words. Hold up Mother and say something like "Salve puella (or puer)." Children return the greeting by saying "Salve mater!"

Animals

pig	*porcus*
crocodile	*crocodilus*
horse	*equus*
cat	*feles*
chicken	*pullus*
dog	*canis*
cow	*vacca*

Children create an animal picture dictionary—on each page they draw a picture of one of the animals (named in the preceding list) and label it with both the English and Latin names.

Making a Volcano

First, read aloud *Pompeii Buried* by Edith Kunhardt (1987). Then, build a volcano.

1. Protect the work area using newspapers or other covering—this can get messy!

2. Pour half a cup of baking soda into a half-liter plastic bottle along with sand or soil. (If you cut a larger opening in the bottle, it will make it easier to get the soda, sand, and soil inside.)

3. Using a large half-circle of construction paper (in the shape of a cone) wrap the paper around the bottle. The mountain should look like a rounded pyramid. Fasten the construction paper with glue or tape.

4. Squirt drops of different food colors into the baking-soda mixture. Then pour small amounts of vinegar slowly into the bottle. The chemical reaction between the baking soda and vinegar causes gas bubbles that push the liquid from the bottle. Colored foam will continue to flow as long as you keep adding vinegar.

Teacher Resource Books

Carlson, Laurie. (1998). *Classical Kids: An Activity Guide to Life in Ancient Greece and Rome.* The book describes life in ancient Greece and Rome and notes the contributions of those cultures to modern civilization; includes activities such as making a star gazer, chiseling a clay tablet, and weaving Roman sandals.

Hart, Avery, and Mantell, Paul. (1999). *Ancient Greece: 40 Hands-On Activities to Experience This Wondrous Age.* This activity book introduces people, places, events, myths, culture, and philosophy of ancient Greece.

Morwood, James. (Editor). (2001). *The Pocket Oxford Latin Dictionary.* This dictionary is suitable for the beginner in Latin.

Robbins, Elaine S. (1995). *Discovering Languages: Latin.* Illustrated by Kathryn R. Ashworth. This curriculum book is designed to teach Latin numbers, days of the week, body parts, animals, colors, and cognates. It covers many aspects of the Roman culture—education, food, toys, games, grammar, and much more.

Thematic Books

These books are for fluent readers, so use them as read-alouds.

Aesop. (1972). *Aesop's Fables Coloring Book.* This is a coloring book with a short Aesop tale and a picture that goes along with each story.

Aesop. (1994). *The Aesop for Children.* Illustrated by Milo Winter. The book features 126 fables by Aesop.

Arnold, Eric. (1997). *Volcanoes! Mountains of Fire.* Students learn what it is like to witness the eruption of a volcano.

Kunhardt, Edith. (1987). *Pompeii: Buried Alive!* A simple retelling of the day Mt. Vesuvius erupted and the people in the ancient city of Pompeii died.

Little, Emily. (1988). *Trojan Horse. How the Greeks Won the War.* The story explains how the Greeks used a wooden horse to win the Trojan War.

Roman Holiday Bulletin Boards

LET'S EAT A ROMAN GINGERBREAD MAN!

CAPUT — NASUS
OCULUS — AURIS
BRACCHIUM — OS
MANUS
PES — CRUS

ARABIC	ENGLISH	LATIN	ROMAN
1	one	unus	I
2	two	duo	II
3	three	tres	III
4	four	quattuor	IV
5	five	quinque	V
6	six	sex	VI
7	seven	septum	VII
8	eight	octo	VIII
9	nine	novem	IX
10	ten	decem	X

KALENDARIUM

SOLIS	LUNAE	MARTIS	MERCURII	JOVIS	VENERIS	SATURNI

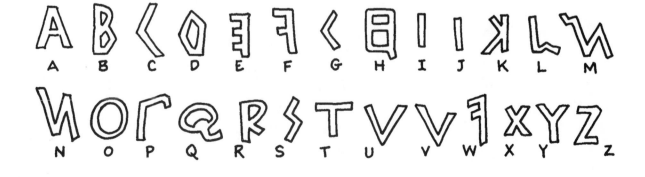

WAKE UP! START HERE

Get ready for school...

THE ROMAN WAY!

Put your tunic on first.

Your <u>crus</u> will show — and so will the other one!

Hold your toga in place with your left <u>manus</u> and flip the toga over your left shoulder with your right <u>manus</u>.

Put your toga around your back and over your left <u>bracchium</u>.

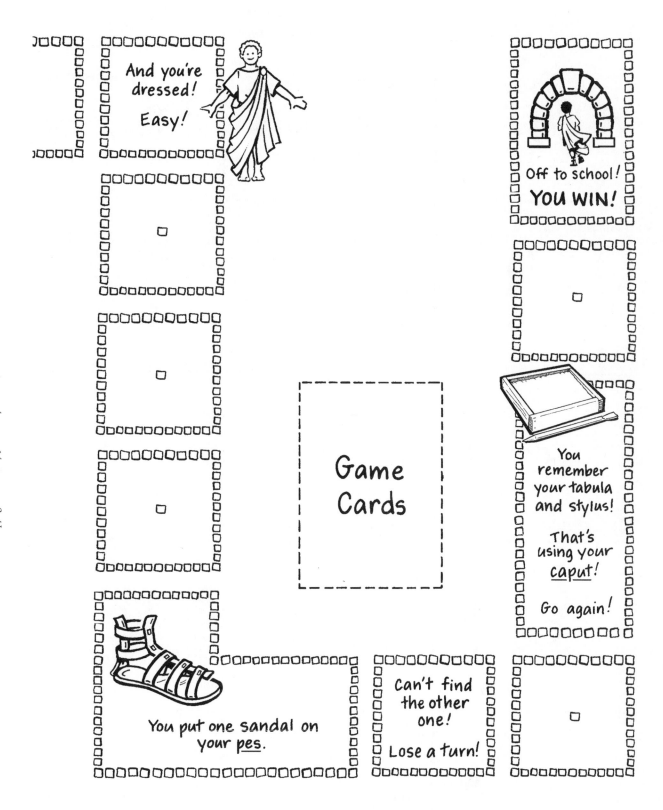

And you're dressed! Easy!

Off to school!
YOU WIN!

Game Cards

You remember your tabula and stylus!

That's using your caput!

Go again!

You put one sandal on your pes.

Can't find the other one!
Lose a turn!

1	2	3	4	5
one	two	three	four	five
6	7	8	9	10
six	seven	eight	nine	ten
hand	head	arm	leg	foot

I	II	III	IV	V
unus	duo	tres	quattuor	quinque
VI	VII	VIII	IX	X
sex	septum	octo	novem	decem
manus	caput	bracchium	crus	pes

Roman Holiday Sorting Game

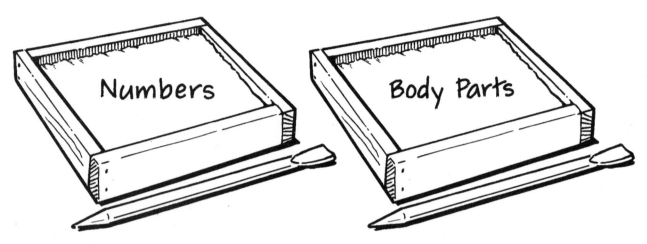

Numbers

one	unus
two	duo
three	tres
four	quattuor
five	quinque
six	sex
seven	septum
eight	octo
nine	novem
ten	decem

Body Parts

head	caput
arm	bracchium
leg	crus
hand	manus
foot	pes

Answer Key

Roman Holiday Matching Game

Answer Key

head + caput

hand + manus

foot + pes

arm + bracchium

leg + crus

1 one + I unus

2 two + II duo

3 three + III tres

4 four + IV quattuor

5 five + V quinque

6 six + VI sex

7 seven + VII septum

8 eight + VIII octo

9 nine + IX novem

10 ten + X decem

VALENTINE'S DAY AND DENTAL HEALTH MONTH

Valentine's Day and Dental Health Month are celebrated in February. You may wish to use these in addition to Black History Month or instead of that theme.

Theme Decorations

Decorate to look like a post office.

Game and Dramatic Play Areas

You will need these materials for the game area:

- Basic equipment
- Valentine board game, card games, sorting game, and matching game
- Learning center skill games (Section Five)
- Valentine vocabulary cards (game cards or index cards with underlined words from game cards written on them)

- Dental health posters, purchased or made by the children.
- A sign that says: "It's fun to get post office messages."
- Poster or sign with student directions: "1. Read the February vocabulary cards to a partner. 2. Play a reading game."

You will need these materials for the dramatic play area (to create a post office):

- Postal employee hats and mailbags
- Postal scale
- Envelopes, pencils, and stickers to use for stamps
- A mailbox

Post names of children who will be in the dramatic play area. All others will play reading games.

Making the Mailbox

- A cardboard box, about eighteen inches square
- Pink and red construction paper
- Lace doilies
- Tape and glue
- Scissors

1. Cut the flaps from the top of the box. Turn the box over.
2. Cut a slit in what is now the top.
3. Cover the cardboard by taping pink, red, or both colors of construction paper to the box. Decorate it with hearts. Show children how to make a heart by folding a square of paper and drawing half a heart shape. Remind them to draw the heart "out" from the fold. Distribute squares of construction paper and lace doilies. Have the children make and decorate hearts of any size they wish. When the hearts are finished, have children glue their hearts to the box.

Theme Setup

1. Set the mailbox on a table or shelf in the dramatic play area.
2. Hang postal employees' clothing nearby.
3. Keep postal scale, envelopes, pencils, and stickers (for stamps) in a box.

4. Post dental health posters on the wall near the mailbox. Arrange student seating nearby.

5. Post student directions.

Bulletin Boards

See the illustrations on page 272.

Whole-Group Activities

- Learn new vocabulary: *valentine, post office, toothbrush, dental care, flossing, brushing,* and so on.
- Create a valentine mailbox.
- Visit a post office.
- Choose pen pals from another classroom. Exchange valentine messages.
- Create a valentine song and write it on the song chart.
- Invite a dentist to speak to the class.
- Create a class song about dental care to add to the song chart.
- Bake cherry pies.
- Complete the valentine calendar on page 273.

Cherry Pie Recipe

Frozen tart shells (one per child)

Canned cherry pie filling (enough to fill tart shells)

Toaster oven

Whipped topping

1. Have each child fill one tart shell with cherry pie filling.
2. Bake in a toaster oven. Follow baking directions on the tart-shell package.
3. Cool, garnish with whipped topping, and serve.

Content Area Activities

- Celebrate Presidents' Day.
- Brainstorm and develop two lists—one with foods that promote good teeth and one with foods that are harmful to teeth.
- Estimate the number of (wrapped) valentine candies in a package, count them, and eat them.

Word Play Center Activities

- Play skill games that reinforce skills being taught at the Teacher Center.
- Play the February board game, card games, sorting game, and matching game.
- Read February vocabulary cards made by the teacher.

Thematic Books

Emergent and Early Readers

Berenstain, Stan and Jan. (1992). *The Berenstains' Funny Valentine.* Sister Bear hopes for more attention from one boy and less from another as Valentine's Day approaches.

Berenstain, Stan and Jan. (1998). *The Berenstains' Comic Valentine.* Brother Bear wonders who is sending him secret valentines, and finds out when he meets the goalie of the opposing hockey team.

Bond, Felicia. (2001). *The Day It Rained Hearts.* Cornelia Augusta makes creative use of a most unusual downpour.

Bridwell, Norman. (1997). *Clifford's First Valentine's Day.* A small red puppy gets into trouble when he gets covered with valentine paste, falls into a post office chute, and gets covered with mail.

Bunting, Eve. (1985). *The Valentine Bears.* Mr. and Mrs. Bear hibernate during the winter, so they have never celebrated St. Valentine's Day.

Cohen, Miriam. (1978). *Bee My Valentine!* First-grade children prepare for their St. Valentine's Day party.

Daly, Catherine. (2000). *Love Is All You Need.* This story celebrates the many meanings of love and the power of friendship.

Foxx, Kylie. (2002). *Bear's Valentine's Day.* Join Ojo, Tutter, Treelo, Pip, and Pop as they create a surprise for Bear. Pull-tabs on the last page reveal a special valentine!

Lee, Quinlan B., and Johnson, Jay. (2003). *Special Delivery*. This is a delightful Care Bears valentine story.

Minarik, Else Holmelund. (2002). *Maurice Sendak's Little Bear: Little Bear's Valentine*. Illustrated by Heather Green. Little Bear looks forward to giving his mother a valentine and to figuring out what secret person sent him one.

Roberts, Bethany. (2001). *Valentine Mice*. Illustrated by Doug Cushman. This is an easy-to-read book about mice delivering valentines.

St. Pierre, Stephanie. (1997). *Elmo's Valentine*. Elmo can't decide who should receive his valentine.

Tanner, Suzy-Jane. (1996). *The Great Valentine's Day Surprise*. Each valentine that the postman delivers contains a clue about who sent the card. Children guess and lift interactive flaps that reveal secret admirers.

Wells, Rosemary. (2003). *Max's Valentine*. Ruby uses all the candy to make her valentine cards, but Grandma makes sure Max gets a very special treat.

Developing and Fluent Readers

Blos, Joan W. (1999). *One Very Best Valentine's Day*. Illustrated by Emily Arnold McCully. Newbery medalist Blos and Caldecott medalist McCully designed this story about a child's creative use of her broken bracelet.

Bourgeois, Paulette. (1999). *Franklin's Valentines*. When Franklin lost all of his valentines and didn't have any for his friends, they still wanted to give him their cards and letters. He learned a good lesson: friends like you for who you are and not for what you can give them.

Carter, David. (1994). *Love Bugs*. A pop-up book that looks like a box of valentine chocolates with its heart shape.

De Groat, Diane. (1997). *Roses Are Pink, Your Feet Really Stink*. Gilbert writes two not-so-nice valentines, which turn into a classroom controversy. But on Valentine's Day, there's always time for a change of heart.

Devlin, Wende and Harry. (1992). *Cranberry Valentine*. Maggie, her grandmother, and the sewing circle send Mr. Whiskers secret valentines.

Duffey, Betsy. (2000). *Cody's Secret Admirer*. Illustrated by Ellen Thompson. Cody tries to find out the identity of the secret admirer who sent him a valentine.

Giff, Patricia Reilly. (1985). *The Valentine Star*. Emilie's class is busy making valentine cards but she is worried about her fight with Sherri, who tells her, "You'll be sorry."

Gregory, Valiska. (2000). *A Valentine for Norman Noggs*. Illustrated by Marsha Winborn. The heart of the valentine maker is far more important than the valentine.

Kneen, Maggie. (2004). *The Very Special Valentine*. Illustrated by Christine Tagg. Bunny Gray looks for the perfect Valentine's Day gift for Rosie.

Levy, Elizabeth. (1992). *The Case of the Tattletale Heart.* Illustrated by Ellen Eagle. A young detective and her magician partner solve a Valentine's Day mystery.

Stevenson, James. (1998). *A Village Full of Valentines.* Here are seven valentine stories about a community of animals that celebrates Valentine's Day.

Wing, Natasha. (2000). *The Night Before Valentine's Day.* Illustrated by Heidi Petach. Like "The Night Before Christmas," these rhymes tell of Valentine's Day fun.

February Bulletin Boards

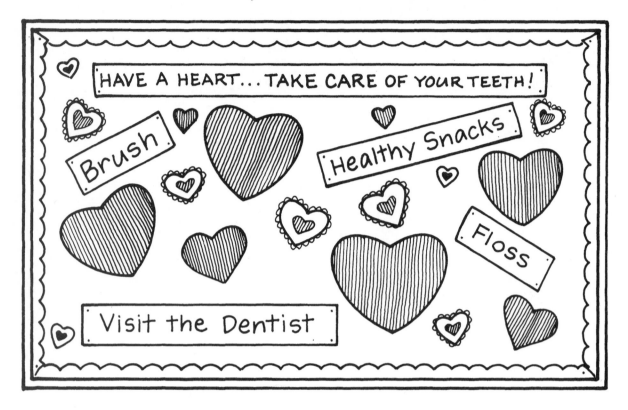

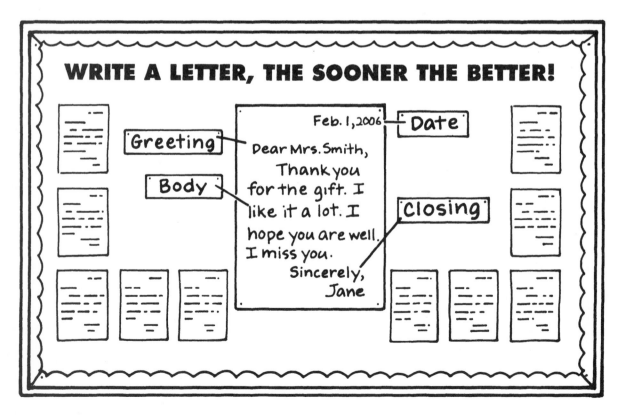

FEBRUARY

SUNDAY	MONDAY	TUESDAY	WEDNESDAY	THURSDAY	FRIDAY	SATURDAY

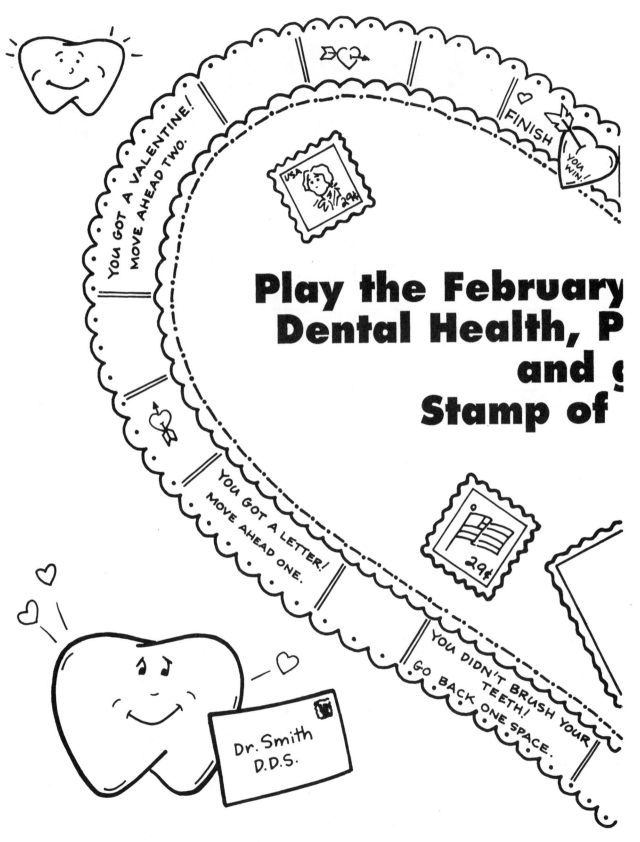

Play the February
Dental Health, P
and
Stamp of

START

NO CAVITIES!
ROLL AGAIN!

DENTAL HEALTH

Valentine's Day,
ost Office Game
get a
Approval!

GAME
CARDS

FORGOT TO MAIL
YOUR VALENTINE!
LOSE ONE TURN.

Look at the mailbox.	See the letter.	The envelope is white.	The heart is a symbol.	A red rose is a symbol of love.
Valentine's Day is on February 14th.	See the Valentine card.	Put the zip code on my letter.	Cupid is an angel.	We show love on Valentine's Day.
Look at the box of chocolate candy.	Cupid shoots a bow and arrow.	The package was delivered.	Put a stamp on the letter.	Do you know your address?

Mr. Joe Smith
5 Red Street
Miami, FL 33149

Make sure to floss.

The dentist's office is busy.

Fight tooth decay.

The mail carrier is friendly.

Metal braces straighten teeth.

Junk food is unhealthy.

The postcard is small.

Dear Sue,
How are you? I am fine.
Love, Jim

Toothpaste should be used.

Everyone likes kisses and hugs.

S.W.A.K.

Put the return address on the letter.

C. Smith
5 Red St.
Miami, FL 32508

Healthy snacks are important.

Mouthwash is useful.

The delivery truck is here.

U.S. MAIL

Brushing teeth is important.

A cavity hurts.

February Sorting Game

Valentine's Day

POST OFFICE

Dental Health

Answer Key

Valentine's Day	Post Office	Dental Health
heart	mail carrier	healthy snacks
Cupid	envelope	floss
love	letter	toothpaste
chocolate candy	package	brushing teeth
bow and arrow	stamp	metal braces
February 14th	address	dentist's office
red rose	zip code	cavity
valentine card	return address	mouthwash
kisses and hugs	delivery truck	junk food
	post card	tooth decay
	mail box	

February Matching Game

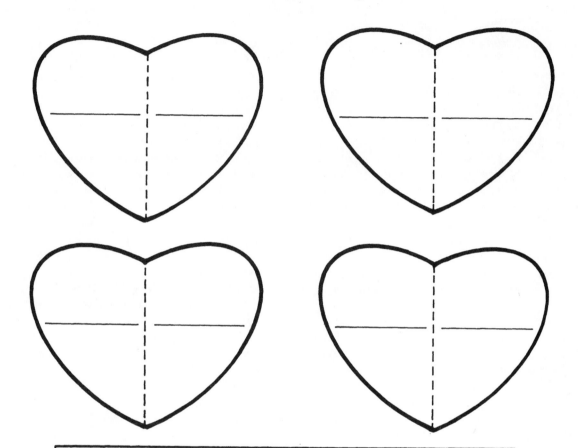

Answer Key

mail + carrier
zip + code
return + address
chocolate + candy
bow + arrow
February + 14th
red + rose
valentine + card
kisses + hugs
delivery + truck

post + card
mail + box
healthy + snacks
tooth + decay
tooth + paste
brushing + teeth
mouth + wash
dentist's + office
metal + braces

5 LEARNING CENTER SKILL GAMES

In this section, you will find directions for assembling forty hands-on reproducible games that may be used with any theme, as well as answer keys and game cards. There are eight board games, seven card games, six sorting games, seven memory-style matching games, and twelve puzzle-style matching games.

This section contains two parts. Part One explains how to assemble board games, card games, sorting games, and matching games. Part Two includes the reproducible game cards (fifteen cards per page) for board games, card games, sorting games, and memory-style matching games; reproducible game cards (ten per page) for puzzle-style matching games; reproducible answer keys; and blank pages for writing your own cards.

PART ONE: ASSEMBLING SKILL GAMES

Assembling Board Games

1. Choose any of the following skills for which to make board games:

    Abbreviations

    Antonyms

    Compound words

    Contractions

    Figurative language

    Homophones

    Syllables

    Synonyms

2. Photocopy and decorate the game board for any theme.

3. Glue the two game-board halves inside a file folder and trim protruding edges. Write the name of the game on the front of the folder (for example, "Antonyms").

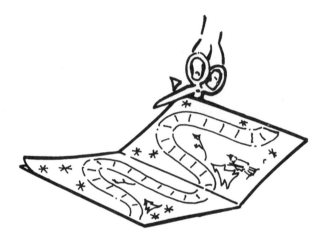

4. Copy the game board directions and glue them on the back of the folder. Write the object of the game on the line provided. The object of the game appears on the answer key page.

5. Copy the skill game cards (fifteen cards per page) onto card stock. To add words, copy blank cards (found on page 368) and write your own. If you wish, set the copy machine to enlarge the size of the cards. Then laminate the sheets and cut them apart on the lines to form cards.

6. Copy the answer key and glue it onto a piece of tagboard. Add your extra words to the key.

7. Attach a small brown envelope to the back of the folder to hold game cards and the answer key. Laminate the game board, and with a sharp instrument, slit the film at the envelope's opening.

BOARD GAME DIRECTIONS

1. Two or three players may play this game. You will need a game board, game cards, an answer key, one die, and a marker for each player.

Object of the game: _____

2. Each player picks a marker and places it on START.
3. Players roll the die. The player with the highest number goes first. Play clockwise.
4. Each player rolls the die, draws a card, and gives an answer.
5. If the answer is correct, the player moves ahead the number shown on the die. If the card is read incorrectly, the player does not move.
6. The player puts the card at the bottom of the pile.
7. The first player to reach FINISH wins!

   Note: If players do not agree on an answer, they check the answer key.

Assembling Card Games

1. The object of the card game is to match pairs of words. Choose any of the following skills to make card games:

   Abbreviations

   Antonyms

   Compound words

   Contractions

   Figurative language

   Homophones

   Synonyms

2. Use both pages of game cards (fifteen cards to a page) to make a card game. Make one copy of each page on card stock. If you wish, set the copy machine to enlarge the size of the cards. To add word pairs, copy the blank cards on page 368 and write your own on them. Then laminate the sheets and cut them apart on the lines to form cards.

3. Use a small box (such as a stationery box), a small brown envelope, or a self-sealing plastic bag to store the cards. Decorate the top of the box or the front of the envelope or plastic bag.

4. Copy the card game directions and glue them inside the box top or on the back of the envelope, or glue them on tag board and place inside the plastic bag.

5. Copy the answer key and glue it onto tagboard. Add your extra words to the key.

CARD GAME DIRECTIONS

1. Two players may play. Players will need game cards and an answer key.

Object of the game: _____

2. Deal five cards to each player. Stack the rest of the cards facedown.
3. Player One draws one card from the stack. The player then discards one unwanted card face up beside the stack.
4. The other player draws one card—from the stack or from the top of the discard pile—and discards one unwanted card.
5. When players get a match, they put the pair down on the table.
6. The first player to lay down all of his or her cards wins!

   Note: If players do not agree on an answer, they check the answer key.

Assembling Sorting Games

1. Choose any of the following skills to make sorting games:

    Consonant blends (four games)

    Consonant digraphs

    Syllables

2. Copy skill-game cards (fifteen cards to a page) on card stock. To add words, copy the blank cards on page 368 and write your own. If you wish, set the copy machine to enlarge the size of the cards. Laminate the sheets and cut them apart on the lines to form cards.

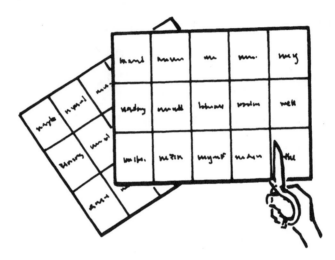

3. Write the names of the sorting categories (one syllable, two syllables, three syllables) on index cards. Categories appear on the answer key page. (See object of the game.)

4. Use cylinder-shaped containers. Attach the index cards to the top edge of the containers with clothespins or jumbo paper clips.

5. Use a small brown envelope or self-sealing plastic bag to store the cards.

6. Glue the game directions on the back of the envelope or glue onto tagboard and place inside the plastic bag.

7. Copy the answer key and glue it onto tagboard. Place the key inside the envelope or plastic bag.

SORTING GAME DIRECTIONS

1. One or two players play this game. You will need game cards, containers, clothespins, index cards, and an answer key.

Object of the game: _____

2. Look at the game cards. Decide which category each card matches. Put the card in that container.

3. When you have sorted all the cards, get out the answer key and check your work.

4. Read the cards aloud.

Assembling Matching Games

1. Choose any of the following skills to make matching games:

   Abbreviations

   Antonyms

   Compound words

   Consonant blends

   Consonant digraphs

   Contractions

   Figurative language

   Homophones

   Syllables

   Synonyms

2. For the memory-style game, copy skill-game cards (fifteen cards to a page) onto card stock. For the puzzle-style game, copy skill-game cards (ten to a page) onto card stock. To add words, copy the blank cards on pages 368 and 369 and write your own. Laminate the sheets if desired, and cut them apart on the lines to form cards. If you wish, set the copy machine to enlarge the size of the cards, then laminate the sheets and cut them apart on the lines to form cards. *Note:* Thirty cards are too many for one memory-style game. Make several games by using four to six card pairs per game.

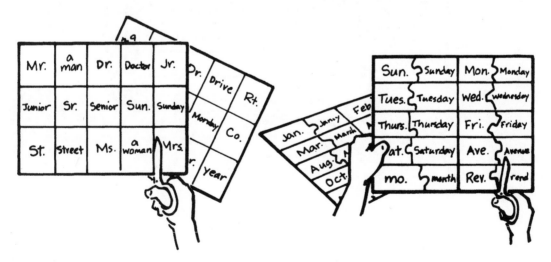

3. Decorate a stationery box, envelope, or self-sealing plastic bag for storing the cards.

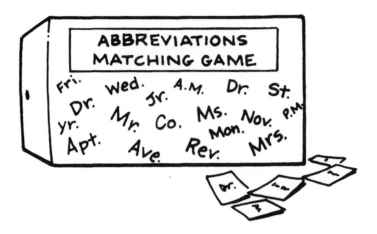

4. Copy the game directions and answer key and glue them onto the box or envelope, or laminate them and put them inside the plastic bag. If you have added extra words, be sure to include them on the answer key.

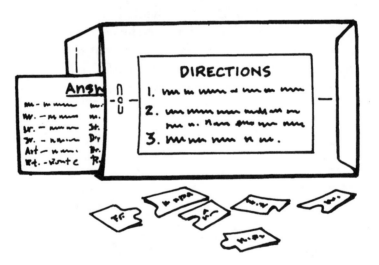

MEMORY-STYLE MATCHING GAME DIRECTIONS

1. Two or three players may play. Players will need game cards and an answer key.

Object of the game: _____

2. Place cards facedown in a pattern (three rows of four).
3. Player One turns over two cards. If the cards show a matching pair, the player may keep the pair. If the cards do not match, the player turns the cards facedown again.
4. Play continues until all pairs are matched.
5. Players count their cards. The player with the most cards wins!

PUZZLE-STYLE MATCHING GAME DIRECTIONS

1. One or two players may play. Players will need puzzle-matching cards and an answer key.

2. Turn the cards face up so that the words show.

3. Try to find the pairs of words that match.

PART TWO: GAME CARDS AND ANSWER KEYS

Abbreviations

- Board game: *Object:* If you draw an abbreviation, name the word. If you draw a word, spell its abbreviation.
- Card game: *Object:* Lay down pairs of words and their abbreviations (Dr. + Doctor).
- Matching game (memory- or puzzle-style): *Object:* Match words with their abbreviations (Sunday + Sun.)

Answer Key

Mr.—a man

Ms.—a woman

Mrs.—a married woman

Dr.—Doctor

Jr.—Junior

Sr.—Senior

Rev.—Reverend

Sun.—Sunday

Mon.—Monday

Tue.—Tuesday

Wed.—Wednesday

Thur.—Thursday

Fri.—Friday

Sat.—Saturday

Ave.—Avenue

Blvd.—Boulevard

Dr.—Drive

St.—Street

Rt.—Route

Apt.—Apartment

Mrs.	Junior	Sun.
a woman	Jr.	Reverend
Ms.	Doctor	Rev.
a man	Dr.	Senior
Mr.	a married woman	Sr.

Tuesday	Fri.	Avenue
Tue.	Thursday	Ave.
Monday	Thur.	Saturday
Mon.	Wednesday	Sat.
Sunday	Wed.	Friday

St.	Drive	Dr.	Boulevard	Blvd.
Apartment	Apt.	Route	Rt.	Street

Mr.	a man	Ms.	a woman
Mrs.	a married woman	Dr.	Doctor
Jr.	Junior	Sr.	Senior
Rev.	Reverend	Sun.	Sunday
Mon.	Monday	Tue.	Tuesday

Wed. **Wednesday**	**Thur.** **Thursday**
Fri. **Friday**	**Sat.** **Saturday**
Ave. **Avenue**	**Blvd.** **Boulevard**
Dr. **Drive**	**St.** **Street**
Rt. **Route**	**Apt.** **Apartment**

Antonyms

- Board game: *Object:* Name an antonym for the word you draw.
- Card game: *Object:* Lay down pairs of antonyms (hot + cold).
- Matching game (memory- or puzzle-style): *Object:* Match pairs of antonyms.

Answer Key

young—old

noisy—quiet

good—bad

useful—useless

on—off

full—empty

thin—fat or thick

warm—cool

weak—strong

buy—sell

well—sick

smile—frown

light—dark

mother—father

first—last

dull—sharp

float—sink

play—work

new—old

bad—good

good	quiet	noisy	old	young
off	on	useless	useful	bad
warm	fat or thick	thin	empty	full

sell	light	last
buy	frown	first
strong	smile	father
weak	sick	mother
cool	well	dark

play	sink	float	sharp	dull
good	bad	old	new	work

young	old	noisy	quiet
good	bad	useful	useless
on	off	full	empty
thin	fat or thick	warm	cool
weak	strong	buy	sell

well	sick	smile	frown
light	dark	mother	father
first	last	dull	sharp
float	sink	play	work
new	old	bad	good

Compound Words

- Board game: *Object:* Name a compound word made from the word you draw.
- Card game: *Object:* Lay down pairs of words that make compound words (some + thing).
- Matching game (memory- or puzzle-style): *Object:* Match pairs of words that make compound words.

Answer Key

airplane

baseball

bookcase

catfish

cowboy

forgive

grandfather

grandmother

housework

into

milkman

notebook

outside

playground

raincoat

something

sunshine

today

walkway

yourself

book	boy	grand
ball	cow	father
base	fish	grand
plane	cat	give
air	case	for

to	in	work	house	mother
out	book	note	man	milk
coat	rain	ground	play	side

to	self	
shine	your	
sun	way	
thing	walk	
some	day	

air) plane

base | ball

book | case

cat) fish

cow (boy

for | give

grand) father

grand | mother

house | work

in | to

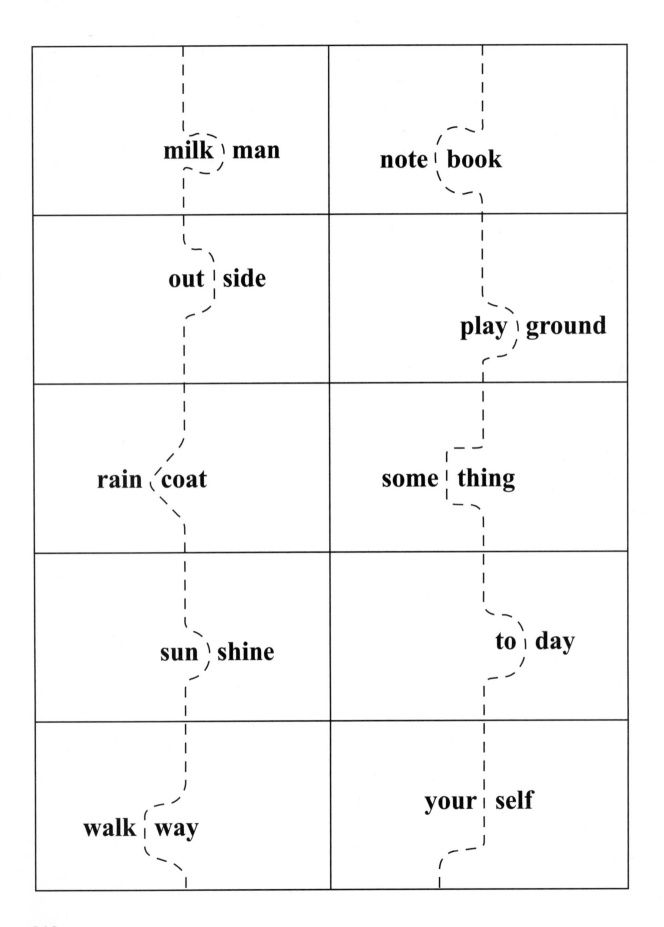

milk) man

note (book

out | side

play) ground

rain (coat

some | thing

sun) shine

to) day

walk | way

your | self

Consonant Blends

- Sorting game: *Object:* Sort words by blend (*bl* = black, blue, blouse; *cl* = clock, climb, class; and so on).
- Matching game (puzzle style): *Object:* Match word parts to make a word (*bl* + ack).

Answer Key

l blends: bl, cl, fl, gl, pl, sl

bl	black, blue, blouse, blow, blend
cl	clock, climb, clean, clap, close
fl	floor, flag, fly, flat, flash
gl	glance, glad, glow, glide, glee
pl	play, plate, plow, please, place
sl	sly, slide, sled, slow, slap

r blends: br, cr, dr, fr, gr, pr, tr

br	break, brown, bread, broken, breeze
cr	cream, cracker, crown, cry
dr	dress, dry, drink, drop
fr	frog, friend, from, front
gr	gray, green, grow, gravy
pr	proud, prize, pretty, present
tr	track, train, truck, try, trip

s blends: sc, sk, sm, sn, sp, st, sw

sc	scare, scale, score, school
sk	skate, skip, skunk, skin
sm	smell, smile, small, smoke
sn	snake, snail, snow, sneeze
sp	spell, speak, spot, speed, spade
st	stop, step, steal, still, store
sw	swing, sweat, sweet, swim

Three-letter blends: scr, spr, thr, str, spl, shr

scr	scrap, scrape, screen, scratch
spr	spring, sprout, spray, spread
thr	throw, through, three, thread
str	straw, strike, strong, stress, string
spl	splash, split, splatter, splurge
shr	shrub, shred, shrimp, shrew, shrink

qu   quick, quiet, queen, quite

blend	blow	blouse	blue	black
close	clap	clean	climb	clock
flash	flat	fly	flag	floor

glee	glide	glow	glad	glance
place	please	plow	plate	play
slap	slow	sled	slide	sly

bl ack

bl ue

bl ouse

bl ow

bl end

cl ock

cl imb

cl ean

cl ap

cl ose

fl) oor

fl ag

fl y

fl at

fl ash

gl ance

gl ad

gl ow

gl ide

gl ee

pl | ay

pl | ate

pl | ow

pl | ease

pl | ace

sl | y

sl | ide

sl | ed

sl | ow

sl | ap

breeze	dress	friend
broken	cry	frog
bread	crown	drop
brown	cracker	drink
break	cream	dry

grow	present	trip
green	pretty	try
gray	prize	truck
front	proud	train
from	gravy	track

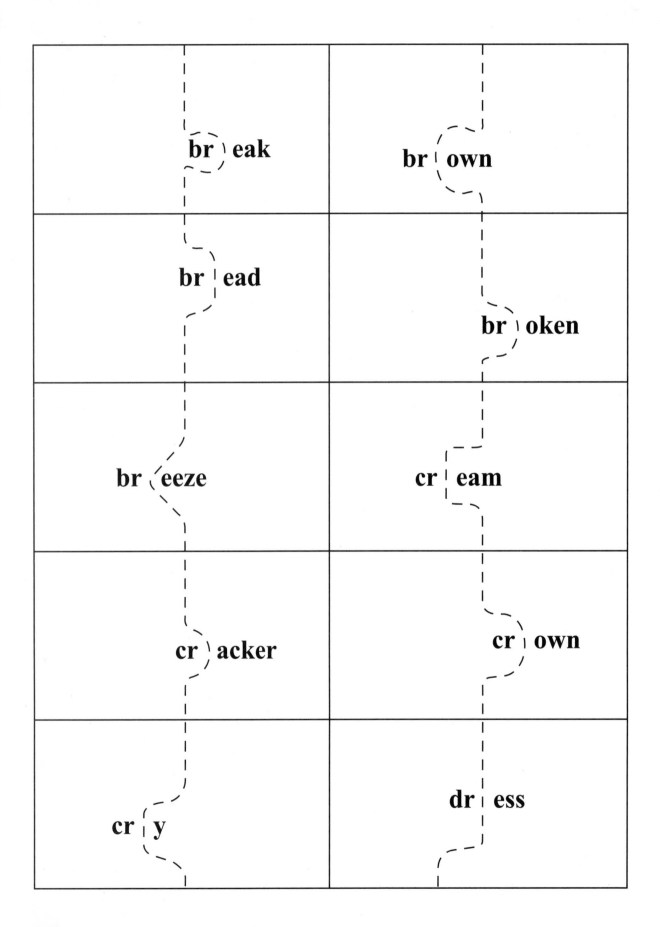

br eak

br own

br ead

br oken

br eeze

cr eam

cr acker

cr own

cr y

dr ess

dr y

dr ink

dr op

fr og

fr iend

fr om

fr ont

gr ay

gr een

gr ow

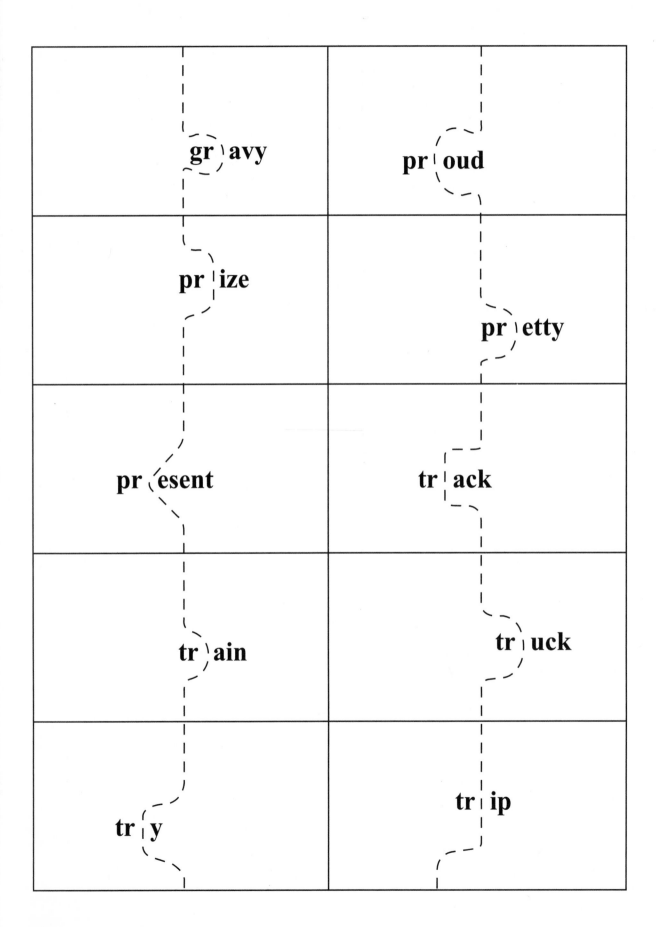

gr|avy

pr|oud

pr|ize

pr|etty

pr|esent

tr|ack

tr|ain

tr|uck

tr|y

tr|ip

skate	school	score	scale	scare
smile	smell	skin	skunk	skip
snow	snail	snake	smoke	small

speed	still	swim
spot	steal	sweet
speak	step	sweat
spell	stop	swing
sneeze	spade	store

sc | are

sc | ale

sc | ore

sch | ool

sk | ate

sk | ip

sk | unk

sk | in

sm | ell

sm | ile

sm all

sm oke

sn ake

sn ail

sn ow

sn eeze

sp ell

sp eak

sp ot

sp eed

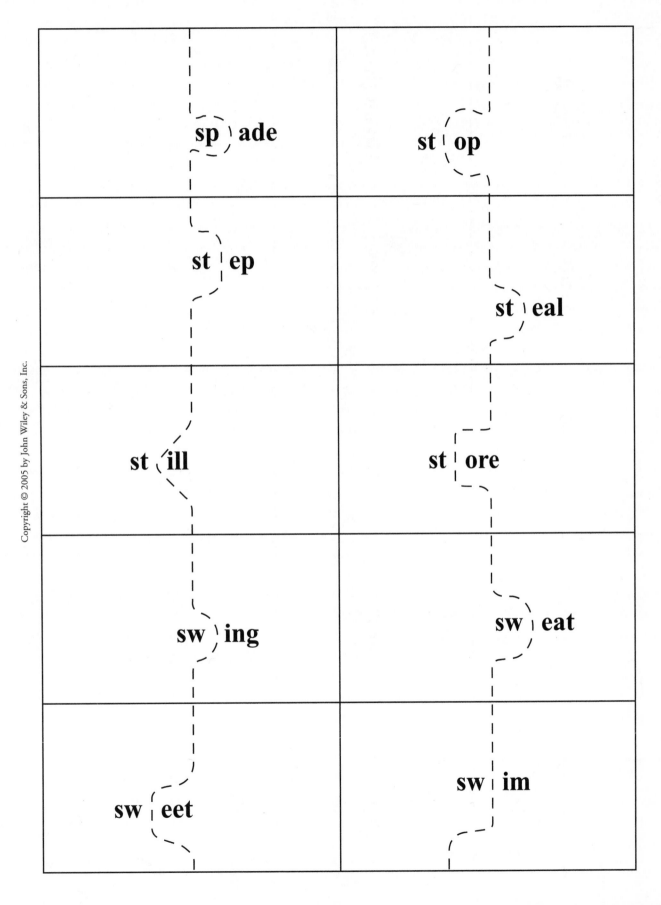

sp) ade

st | op

st | ep

st) eal

st (ill

st | ore

sw) ing

sw | eat

sw | eet

sw | im

spring	through	strong
scratch	throw	strike
screen	spread	straw
scrape	spray	thread
scrap	sprout	three

splatter	shrew	quite
split	shrimp	queen
splash	shred	quiet
string	shrub	quick
stress	splurge	shrink

scr ap

scr ape

scr een

scr atch

spr ing

spr out

spr ay

spr ead

thr ow

thr ough

thr ee

thr ead

str aw

str ike

str ong

str ess

str ing

spl ash

spl it

spl atter

spl urge

shr ub

shr ed

shr imp

shr ew

shr ink

qu ick

qu iet

qu een

qu ite

Consonant Digraphs

- Sorting game: *Object:* Sort words by digraph (*ch* = children, chair, rich; *sh* = shire, shoe, fish; and so on).
- Matching game (puzzle-style): *Object:* Match word parts to make a word (*sh* + ell).

Answer Key

ch	*th*
children	thumb
chicken	Thursday
chair	thirty
chimney	thank
catch	with
rich	math
hatch	month
sh	mouth
shirt	both
shell	*wh*
shoe	whistle
short	when
fish	wheel
dish	whale
splash	where
wish	why

catch	chimney	chair	chicken	children
shoe	shell	shirt	hatch	rich
wish	splash	dish	fish	short

with	thank	thirty	Thursday	thumb
whistle	both	mouth	month	math
why	where	whale	wheel	when

ch ildren	ch icken
ch air	ch imney
cat ch	ri ch
hat ch	sh irt
sh ell	sh oe

sh ort	fi sh
di sh	spla sh
wi sh	th umb
Th ursday	th irty
th ank	wi th

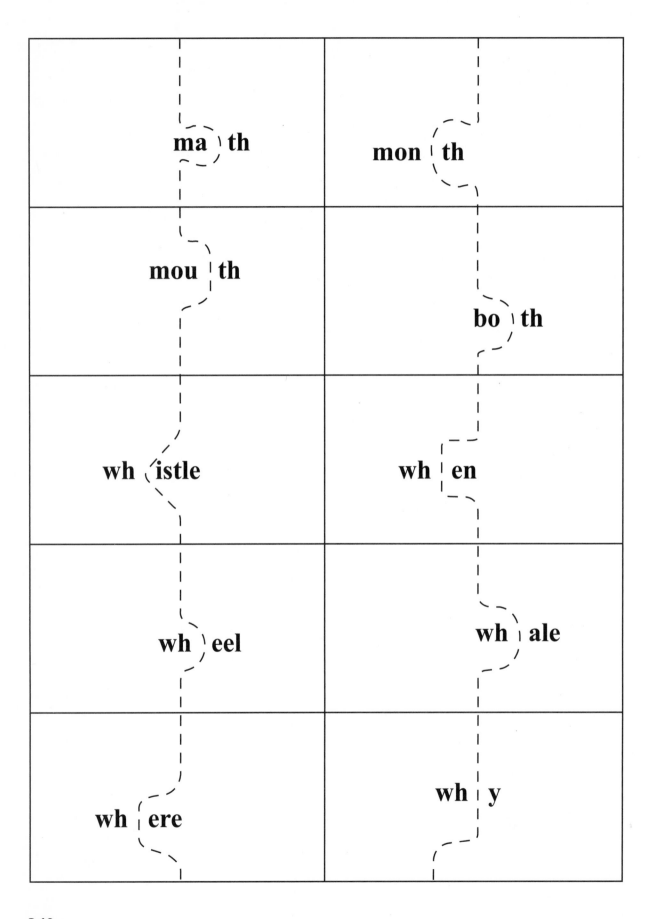

ma th

mon th

mou th

bo th

wh istle

wh en

wh eel

wh ale

wh ere

wh y

Contractions

- Board game: *Object:* If you draw a contraction, name two words that make it. If you draw two words, name the contraction.
- Card game: *Object:* Lay down pairs of words and contractions (can not + can't).
- Matching game (memory- or puzzle-style): *Object:* Match words with their contractions (is not + isn't).

Answer Key

cannot—can't

do not—don't

are not—aren't

will not—won't

have not—haven't

is not—isn't

has not—hasn't

would not—wouldn't

did not—didn't

had not—hadn't

I will—I'll

it is—it's

that is—that's

he is—he's

let us—let's

was not—wasn't

he will—he'll

here is—here's

there is—there's

you are—you're

are not	haven't	would not
don't	have not	hasn't
do not	won't	has not
can't	will not	isn't
can not	aren't	is not

hadn't	that is	let's
had not	it's	let us
didn't	it is	he's
did not	I'll	he is
wouldn't	I will	that's

here is	you're	
he'll	you are	
he will	there's	
wasn't	there is	
was not	here's	

cannot can't	do not don't
are not aren't	will not won't
have not haven't	is not isn't
has not hasn't	would not wouldn't
did not didn't	had not hadn't

I will **I'll**	**it is** **it's**
that is **that's**	**he is** **he's**
let us **let's**	**was not** **wasn't**
he will **he'll**	**here is** **here's**
there is **there's**	**you are** **you're**

Figurative Language

- Board game: *Object:* Draw a figure of speech and name its meaning.
- Card game: *Object:* Lay down pairs—figures of speech and their meanings (tickled pink + happy).
- Matching game (memory- or puzzle-style): *Object:* Match figures of speech with their meanings.

Answer Key

skin of my teeth—barely

shake a leg—hurry up

put your best foot forward—use good manners

in a pickle—in trouble

piece of cake—easy

apple of my eye—my favorite person

feeling blue—depressed

tickled pink—happy

green with envy—jealous

raining cats and dogs—a downpour

frog in my throat—hoarse

spring chicken—young person

eats like a bird—light or picky eater

fish out of water—feeling out of place

smell a rat—suspect something

my lips are sealed—I won't tell

off the top of my head—without thinking about it

head in the clouds—daydreaming

foot in my mouth—said the wrong thing

stiff upper lip—be brave

put your best foot forward	easy	tickled pink
hurry up	piece of cake	depressed
shake a leg	in trouble	feeling blue
barely	in a pickle	my favorite person
skin of my teeth	use good manners	apple of my eye

a downpour	raining cats and dogs	jealous
eats like a bird	young person	spring chicken
suspect something	smell a rat	feeling out of place

green with envy	happy
hoarse	frog in my throat
fish out of water	light or picky eater

head in the clouds	be brave	
without thinking about it	stiff upper lip	
off the top of my head	said the wrong thing	
I won't tell	foot in my mouth	
my lips are sealed	daydreaming	

skin of my teeth	barely
shake a leg	hurry up
put your best foot forward	use good manners
in a pickle	in trouble
piece of cake	easy
apple of my eye	my favorite person
feeling blue	depressed
tickled pink	happy
green with envy	jealous
raining cats and dogs	a downpour

frog in my throat / hoarse	spring chicken / young person
eats like a bird / light or picky eater	fish out of water / feeling out of place
smell a rat / suspect something	my lips are sealed / I won't tell
off the top of my head / without thinking about it	head in the clouds / day dreaming
foot in my mouth / said the wrong thing	stiff upper lip / be brave

Homophones

- Board game: *Object:* Name the meaning of the homophone you draw.
- Card game: *Object:* Lay down pairs of homophones (pear + pair).
- Matching game (memory- or puzzle-style): *Object:* Match pairs of homophones.

Answer Key

hair—hare

tail—tale

hay—hey

tea—tee

heal—heel

to—two—too

hear—here

tow—toe

heard—herd

their—there—they're

hi—high

told—tolled

hoarse—horse

hole—whole

cell—sell

ring—wring

cent—sent

root—route

chili—chilly

sail—sale

hay	heel	here
tale	heal	hear
tail	tee	too
hare	tea	two
hair	hey	to

their	told	whole
herd	high	hole
heard	hi	horse
toe	they're	hoarse
tow	there	tolled

cent	chilly	
wring	chili	
ring	route	
sell	root	sale
cell	sent	sail

hair hare	tail tale
hay hey	tea tee
heal heel	to two
hear here	tow toe
heard herd	their there

hi	high	told	tolled
hoarse	horse	hole	whole
cell	sell	ring	wring
cent	sent	root	route
chili	chilly	sail	sale

Syllables

- Board game: *Object:* Name the number of syllables in the word you draw.
- Sorting game: *Object:* Sort words by number of syllables (one syllable = is, far, less; two syllables = almost, someone, without; and so on).

Answer Key

One syllable	*Two syllables*	*Three syllables*
boy	almost	fishermen
her	someone	imagine
pet	sunshine	beautiful
shape	without	together
moon	picture	elephant
door	around	Saturday
smell	shoelace	bicycle
mouth	farmer	hummingbird
fast	princess	understand
send	follow	
black		

moon	shape	pet
send	fast	mouth
without	sunshine	someone

her	boy	
smell	door	
almost	black	

princess	together	understand
farmer	beautiful	hummingbird
shoelace	imagine	bicycle
around	fisherman	Saturday
picture	follow	elephant

Synonyms

- Board game: *Object:* Name a synonym for the word you draw.
- Card game: *Object:* Lay down pairs of synonyms (pretty + beautiful).
- Matching game (memory- or puzzle-style): *Object:* Match pairs of synonyms.

Answer Key

big—large

near—close

fast—quick

fix—repair

ship—boat

crawl—creep

gift—present

easy—simple

pretty—cute

forest—woods

quiet—still

happy—jolly

neat—tidy

harm—hurt

join—connect

allow—permit

unfasten—loosen

nearest—closest

brave—fearless

blend—mix

fast	boat	easy
close	ship	present
near	repair	gift
large	fix	creep
big	quick	crawl

woods	forest	cute	pretty	simple
neat	jolly	happy	still	quiet
connect	join	hurt	harm	tidy

nearest	mix	
loosen	blend	
unfasten	fearless	
permit	brave	
allow	closest	

big	large	near	close
fast	quick	fix	repair
ship	boat	crawl	creep
gift	present	easy	simple
pretty	cute	forest	woods

quiet	still	happy	jolly
neat	tidy	harm	hurt
join	connect	allow	permit
unfasten	loosen	nearest	closest
brave	fearless	blend	mix

Appendix: Correlation with Standards

The following learning center activities help prepare students for the standards noted after each listed skill.

READING

Standard 1: The student uses the reading process effectively.

Teacher Center. *Instruction:* Read-aloud sessions, big books, shared books, predictable books, songs and chants, choral reading, poetry, storytelling, book talks, LEA, rhyming, beginning sounds, ending sounds, counting phonemes, clapping syllables, segmenting, blending, substituting phonemes, word families, matching sounds, blending onsets/rimes, alliteration, individual/small group instruction, guided reading, reciprocal teaching, short lessons, individual conferences, children's presentations, new activity instruction, games, pocket chart, flannel board. *Activities:* Joan's Choices, classroom labels, pocket chart activity, story extensions, KWL, name games, fill in the blank, author study.

Library Center. *Materials:* Excellent literature, fiction, folk/fairy tales, biographies, trade books, big books, joke books, cartoon books, poetry, predictable books, alphabet books, song books, student-written books, factual books, catalogues, telephone books, cookbooks, kids' magazines, newspapers, atlases, maps, globes, environmental print, poetry, dictated charts, thematic books, rebuses, materials for special-needs students, flannel board, puppets, labels, LEA charts. *Activities:* Books I Have Read, book talk, projector stories.

Listening Center. *Materials:* Books, songs, student writing, big books, charts, LEA stories, all with matching audiocassettes or CDs. *Activities:* 1-2-3 listening, record and listen, compare/contrast, character study.

Computer Center. *Story and book software:* Internet Public Library Youth Division stories and books, Living Books, *Cat in the Hat, How the Leopard Got*

His Spots, Stories & More, Antelope Publishers' CD-ROM books, WiggleWorks books. *Skill software:* Reader Rabbit, Dr. Seuss Kindergarten, Dr. Seuss Preschool. *Word processing:* Kidspiration 2, PixWriter. *Software for special-needs students:* UKanDu Interactive Reading Series, UKanDu Little Books, UKanDu Switches, Too!, Write:Outloud, Keyboarding for Individual Achievement, Words Their Way.

Art Center. *Book/poetry illustrations: The Cherry Tree* by Daisaku Ikeda, *Caps for Sale* by Esphyr Slobodkina, *Five Little Pumpkins Sitting on a Gate.* *Story extensions: Brown Bear, Bear, What Do You See?* by Bill Martin Jr., *Have You Seen My Cat?* by Eric Carle, *Smarty Pants* by Joy Cowley. *Alphabet art:* Cookie-dough letters, playdough letters, felt letters, clay letters, finger-paint letters. *Seasonal art:* Farm-animal book, seasonal patterns, fall leaf creatures, fall trees.

Writing Center. *Activities:* Word Wall, Word Wall Word Bank, Word Wall Buddies, alphabet books, class-storybook, mailbox, seasonal mailbags, classroom mail, class diary, story extensions/big books, read-alouds, signs of winter, candy-heart writing.

Word Play Center. *Game area:* Thematic/seasonal vocabulary; board, card, sorting, and matching games. *Skill games:* Abbreviations, antonyms, compound words, consonant blends, consonant digraphs, contractions, figurative language, homophones, initial and ending sounds, syllables, synonyms.

Standard 2: The student constructs meaning from a wide range of texts.

Teacher Center. *Instruction:* Read-aloud sessions, big books, shared-book experiences, predictable books, songs and chants, choral reading, poetry, storytelling, book talks, LEA, individual/small group instruction, guided reading, reciprocal teaching, short lessons, individual conferences, children's presentations, new activity instruction, games, pocket chart, flannel board. *Activities:* Joan's Choices, classroom labels, pocket chart activity, story extensions, KWL, name games, fill in the blank, author study.

Library Center. *Materials:* Excellent literature, fiction, folk/fairy tales, biographies, trade books, big books, joke/cartoon books, poetry; predictable, alphabet, wordless, song, student-written, factual, thematic, and telephone books; cookbooks, catalogues, kids' magazines, newspapers, atlases, maps, globes, environmental print, dictated charts, rebuses, materials for special-needs students, flannel board, puppets, labels, LEA charts. *Activities:* Books I Have Read, book talk, overhead projector stories.

Listening Center. *Materials:* Books, songs, student writing, big books, charts, LEA stories, all with matching audiocassettes or CDs. *Activities:* 1-2-3 listening, record and listen, compare/contrast, character study.

Computer Center. *Story and book software:* Internet Public Library Youth Division stories and books, Living Books, *Cat in the Hat, How the Leopard Got His Spots,* Stories & More, Antelope Publishers' CD-ROM books, WiggleWorks books. *Skills software:* Reader Rabbit, Dr. Seuss Kindergarten, Dr. Seuss Preschool. *Word processing:* Kidspiration 2, PixWriter. *Software for special-needs students:* UKanDu Interactive Reading Series, UKanDu Little Books, UKanDu Switches, Too!, Write:Outloud, Keyboarding for Individual Achievement, Words Their Way.

Art Center. *Book/poetry illustrations: The Cherry Tree* by Daisaku Ikeda, *Caps for Sale* by Esphyr Slobodkina, *Five Little Pumpkins Sitting on a Gate. Story extensions: Brown Bear, Brown Bear, What Do You See?* by Bill Martin, Jr., *Have You Seen My Cat?* by Eric Carle, *Smarty Pants* by Joy Cowley. *Seasonal art:* Farm-animal book, self-portraits, fall leaf creatures, fall trees, classroom giant.

Writing Center. *Activities:* Process writing, writing workshop, journal writing, class storybook, mailbox, seasonal mailbags, classroom mail, class diary, story extensions/big books, read-alouds, signs of winter, candy-heart writing.

Word Play Center. *Game area:* Thematic/seasonal vocabulary; board, card, sorting, and matching games.

WRITING

Standard 1: The student uses writing processes effectively.

Teacher Center. *Instruction:* LEA, group dictation, one-on-one dictation, individual/small group instruction, short lessons, individual conferences, Author's Chair, new activity instruction, games. *Activities:* Classroom labels, pocket chart activity, story extensions.

Library Center. Books I Have Read.

Writing Center. *Activities:* Word Wall, process writing, writing workshop, journal writing, morning sign-in, Word Wall Word Bank (sentence building), alphabet books, class storybook, seasonal mailbags, classroom mail, class diary, story extensions, elf/leprechaun book, signs of winter, candy-heart writing.

Listening Center. *Activities:* Children record books they have written, 1-2-3 listening.

Computer Center. *Word processing software:* Kidspiration 2, PixWriter, Creative Writer. *Keyboarding software:* Type to Learn Jr., UltraKey, Garfield's Typing Pal. *Art:* Disney Magic Artist Deluxe. *Software for special-needs students:* UKanDu Interactive Reading Series, UKanDu Little Books, UKanDu Switches, Too!, Write:Outloud, Keyboarding for Individual Achievement, Words Their Way. *Thematic activities:* Back-to-school stories, greeting cards, totem-pole stories, posters, Spanish writing, Lunar New Year messages, Latin writing, valentines.

Art Center. *Activities:* Book/poetry illustrations, story extensions, alphabet art.

Standard 2: The student writes to communicate ideas and information effectively.

Teacher Center. *Instruction:* LEA, individual/small group instruction, short lessons, individual conferences, Author's Chair, new activity instruction, games. *Activities:* Classroom, pocket chart activity, story extensions.

Library Center. Books I Have Read.

Writing Center. *Writing:* Word Wall. *Activities:* Process writing, writing workshop, journal writing, morning sign-in, Word Wall Word Bank (sentence building), alphabet books, class storybook, seasonal mailbags, classroom mail, class diary, story extensions, elf/leprechaun book, signs of winter, candy-heart writing, thematic activities.

Listening Center. Children record books they have written.

Computer Center. *Word processing software:* Kidspiration 2, PixWriter, Creative Writer. *Keyboarding software:* Type to Learn Jr., UltraKey, Garfield's Typing Pal. *Art:* Disney Magic Artist Deluxe. *Software for special-needs students:* UKanDu Interactive Reading Series, UKanDu Little Books, UKanDu Switches, Too!, Write:Outloud, Keyboarding for Individual Achievement, Words Their Way. *Thematic activities:* Back-to-school stories, greeting cards, totem-pole stories, posters, Spanish writing, Lunar New Year messages, Latin writing, valentines.

Art Center. *Activities:* Book/poetry illustrations, extensions, alphabet art, farm-animal book, self-portraits, fall leaf creatures, fall trees, quill writing, winter celebrations, Santa's workshop, thematic activities.

LISTENING, VIEWING, AND SPEAKING

Standard 1: The student uses listening strategies effectively.

Teacher Center. *Instruction:* Read-aloud sessions, big books, shared-book experiences, predictable books, songs and chants, choral reading, poetry, storytelling, book talks, LEA, individual/small group instruction, guided reading, reciprocal teaching, short lessons, individual conferences, children's presentations, new activity instruction, games, flannel board. *Activities:* Joan's Choices, flannel board activities, classroom labels, story extensions, KWL, name games, fill in the blank, author study.

Library Center. *Activities:* Book talk, overhead projector activity. *Thematic activities:* Reading aloud, partner reading, share a book at home, sharing with friends, book talk, book discussion, big book with a buddy, story chart with a buddy, partners read bulletin boards.

Writing Center. *Activities:* Writing conference, Author's Chair, writing workshop, journal sharing, Word Wall Word Bank activities, Word Wall buddies, class storybook, class diary.

Listening Center. *Materials:* Books, songs, student writing, big books, charts, LEA stories, all with matching audiocassettes or CDs. *Activities:* 1-2-3 listening, record and listen, compare/contrast, character study.

Computer Center. *Story and book software:* Internet Public Library Youth Division Stories and Books, Living Books, *Cat in the Hat, How the Leopard Got His Spots,* Stories & More, Antelope Publishers' CD-ROM books, WiggleWorks books. *Software for special-needs students:* UKanDu Interactive Reading Series, UKanDu Little Books, UKanDu Switches, Too!, Words Their Way.

Art Center. *Activities: Caps for Sale, Five Little Pumpkins Sitting on a Fence,* fall leaf creatures, story extensions.

Word Play Center. *Dramatic play area:* Listening/viewing/speaking are the main activities. *Game area:* Listening/viewing/speaking required for all games, including thematic and seasonal vocabulary.

Standard 2: The student uses viewing strategies effectively.

Teacher Center. *Instruction:* Individual/small group instruction, children's presentations, new activity instruction, flannel board.

Library Center. *Materials:* Alphabet books, wordless books, catalogues, environmental print, materials for special-needs students, flannel board, puppets.

Writing Center. Mailbox, seasonal mailbags.

Listening Center. Video stories.

Computer Center. *Art:* Disney Magic Artist Deluxe.

Art Center. *Activities:* Seasonal sewing, Self-portraits, thumbprint art, Thanksgiving home-school connection, tinsmith art, Native American clothing, classroom giant.

Word Play Center. *Dramatic play area:* Listening/viewing/speaking are the main activities. *Game area:* Listening/viewing/speaking required for all games, including thematic and seasonal vocabulary.

Standard 3: The student uses speaking strategies effectively.

Teacher Center. *Instruction:* Book talks, LEA, guided reading, reciprocal teaching, individual conferences, children's presentations, flannel board. *Activities:* Pocket-chart activity, story extensions, KWL, name games.

Library Center. *Materials:* Flannel board, puppets. *Activities:* Book talk, overhead projector stories.

Writing Center. *Activities:* Writing conference, Author's Chair, writing workshop, journal sharing, Word Wall Word Bank activities, Word Wall buddies, class storybook, class diary.

Listening Center. *Thematic activities:* Record messages, record books.

Art Center. *Activities:* Leaf people (story extension), self-portraits, fall leaf creatures, classroom giant.

Word Play Center. *Dramatic play area:* Listening/viewing/speaking are the main activities. *Game area:* Listening/viewing/speaking required for all games, including thematic and seasonal vocabulary.

LANGUAGE

Standard 1: The student understands the nature of language.

Teacher Center. *Instruction:* Songs and chants, choral reading, poetry, LEA, rhyming, word families, alliteration, children's presentations, new activity instruction.

Library Center. *Materials:* Poetry, flannel board, puppets. *Activities:* Book talk.

Computer Center. *Story and book software: Cat in the Hat,* Dr. Seuss Kindergarten, Dr. Seuss Preschool.

Art Center. *Poetry illustrations:* Example: *Five Little Pumpkins Sitting on a Gate. Story extensions:* Example: *Brown Bear, Brown Bear, What Do You See?* by Bill Martin Jr.

Writing Center. *Activities:* Poetry writing.

Word Play Center. *Skill games:* Figurative language.

Standard 2: The student understands the power of language.

Teacher Center. *Instruction:* Book talks, songs and chants, LEA, individual/small group instruction, individual conferences, children's presentations, flannel board, rhyming, alliteration.

Library Center. *Materials:* Songbooks, catalogues, telephone books, newspapers, atlases, maps, globes, environmental print, poetry.

Listening Center. *Materials:* Poetry and songs/matching audio, CDs.

Computer Center. *Story and book software: Cat in the Hat. Skills software:* Dr. Seuss Kindergarten, Dr. Seuss Preschool.

Art Center. *Book/poetry illustrations: The Cherry Tree* by Daisaku Ikeda, *Caps for Sale* by Esphyr Slobodkina, *Five Little Pumpkins Sitting on a Gate. Story extensions: Brown Bear, Brown Bear, What Do You See?* by Bill Martin Jr. *Seasonal art:* Farm-animal book, seasonal patterns, fall leaf creatures, fall trees.

Writing Center. *Activities:* Process writing, writing workshop, journal writing, class storybook, classroom mail, class diary, story extensions/big books, read-alouds, candy-heart writing.

Word Play Center. *Skill games:* Figurative language, synonyms and antonyms.

LITERATURE

Standard 1: The student understands the common features of a variety of literary forms.

Standard 2: The student responds critically to fiction, nonfiction, poetry, and drama.

Teacher Center. *Instruction:* Read-aloud sessions, big books, shared books, predictable books, poetry, storytelling, book talks, LEA, individual/small group instruction, guided reading, reciprocal teaching, short lessons, individual conferences, children's presentations, new activity instruction, flannel board. *Activities:* Joan's Choices, classroom labels, story extensions, KWL, author study.

Library Center. *Materials:* Excellent literature, fiction, folk/fairy tales, biographies, trade books, big books, poetry, predictable books, student-written books, factual books, poetry, thematic books, rebuses, materials for special-needs students, flannel board, puppets, LEA charts. *Activities:* Books I Have Read, book talk, projector stories.

Listening Center. *Materials:* Fiction, nonfiction, fables, legends, fairy tales, poetry, LEA stories, all with matching audiocassettes or CDs. *Activities:* 1-2-3 listening, compare/contrast.

Computer Center. *Story and book software:* Internet Public Library Youth Division stories and books, Living Books, *Cat in the Hat, How the Leopard Got His Spots,* Stories & More, Antelope Publishers' CD-ROM books, WiggleWorks Books. *Word processing:* Kidspiration 2, PixWriter.

Art Center. *Book/poetry illustrations: The Cherry Tree* by Daisaku Ikeda, *Caps for Sale* by Esphyr Slobodkina, *Five Little Pumpkins Sitting on a Gate. Story extensions: Brown Bear, Brown Bear, What Do You See?* by Bill Martin Jr., *Have You Seen My Cat?* by Eric Carle, *Smarty Pants* by Joy Cowley.

Writing Center. *Activities:* Process writing, writing workshop, journal writing, class storybook, mailbox, seasonal mailbags, story extensions/big books, read-alouds.

Additional Resources

Allen, Roach Van. (1976). *Language Experiences in Communication*. Boston: Houghton Mifflin.

Allen, Roach Van, and Allen, Claryce. (1982). *Language Experience Activities*. Boston: Houghton Mifflin.

Bergeron, Betty S., and Bradbury-Wolff, Melody. (2003). *Teaching Reading Strategies in the Primary Grades*. New York: Scholastic Professional Books.

Burns, M. Susan, Griffin, Peg, and Snow, Catherine E. (Editors). (1999). *Starting Out Right: A Guide to Promoting Children's Reading Success*. Washington, D.C.: National Academy Press.

Calkins, Lucy McCormick. (1994). *The Art of Teaching Writing*. Portsmouth, N.H.: Heinemann Educational Books.

Clay, Marie. (1975). *What Did I Write? Beginning Reading and Writing Behavior*. Auckland, New Zealand: Heinemann Educational Books.

Cullinan, Bernice E. (Editor). (1987). *Children's Literature in the Reading Program*. Newark, Del.: International Reading Association.

Hall, Mary Anne. (1981). *Teaching Reading as a Language Experience*. Columbus, Ohio: Merrill.

Heald-Taylor, Gail. (2001). *The Beginning Reading Handbook: Strategies for Success*. Portsmouth, N.H.: Heinemann Educational Books.

Holdaway, Don. (1979). *The Foundations of Literacy*. Sydney, Australia: Ashton Scholastic.

International Reading Association (IRA). (1998). *Phonemic Awareness and the Teaching of Reading* (Brochure). Newark, Del.: International Reading Association.

Jecko, Joan. (2003). *Classical Latin Enrichment*. Tampa: Florida Council of Independent Schools.

Miller, Wilma H. (2000). *Strategies for Developing Emergent Literacy*. New York: McGraw-Hill Higher Education.

Owocki, Gretchen. (2001). *Make Way for Literacy! Teaching the Way Young Children Learn*. Portsmouth, N.H.: Heinemann Educational Books.

Robinson, Violet B., Ross, Gretchen, and Neal, Harriet C. (2000). *Emergent Literacy in Kindergarten*. San Mateo: California Kindergarten Association.

Schickendanz, Judith A. (1999). *Much More Than the ABC's: The Early Stages of Reading and Writing*. Washington, D.C.: National Association for the Education of Young Children.

Schwartz, Judith I. (1988). *Encouraging Early Literacy: An Integrated Approach to Reading and Writing.* Portsmouth, N.H.: Heinemann Educational Books.

Smith, Frank. (1982). *Understanding Reading.* New York: Holt, Rinehart and Winston.

Soderman, Anne K., Gregory, Kara M., and O'Neill, Louise T. (1999). *Scaffolding Emergent Literacy: A Child-Centered Approach for Preschool Through Grade 5.* Needham Heights, Mass.: Allyn & Bacon.

Sullivan, Joanna. (2004). *The Children's Literature Lover's Book of Lists.* San Francisco: Jossey-Bass.

Taberski, Sharon. (2000). *On Solid Ground: Strategies for Teaching Reading K–3.* Portsmouth, N.H.: Heinemann Educational Books.

Trelease, Jim. (2003). *Read-Aloud Handbook.* Magnolia, Me.: Peter Smith.

Whitehead, Marian. (1999). *Supporting Language and Literacy Development in the Early Years.* Philadelphia: Open University Press.